# The Psychology
of Self-
Determination

# The Psychology of Self-Determination

**Edward L. Deci**
University of Rochester

**LexingtonBooks**
D.C. Heath and Company
Lexington, Massachusetts
Toronto

**Library of Congress Cataloging in Publication Data**

Deci, Edward L
  The psychology of self-determination.

  1. Autonomy (Psychology) I. Title.
BF575.A88D42          155.2          80-8373
ISBN 0-699-04045-2

Second printing, February 1982

Published simultaneously in Canada

Printed in the United States of America

International Standard Book Number: 0-669-04045-2

Library of Congress Catalog Card Number: 80-8373

# Contents

List of Figures and Tables     vii

Preface and Acknowledgments     ix

**Part I**     *Freedom and Boundedness in Human Behavior*     1

**Chapter 1**     **The Nature of Self-Determination**     3

Self-Determination, Will, and Free Will     3
Mentalism and Behaviorism     7
The Person-Environment Interaction     13
The Determinants of Behavior     16

**Chapter 2**     **Will and the Motivation to Will**     19

Theories of Will     19
Will and Self-Determination Defined     26
Intrinsic Motivation     30
Cognitive Evaluation Theory     35
Motivational Subsystems     40

**Chapter 3**     **An Organismic Theory of Motivation**     47

Self-Determined Behavior     49
Automatized and Automatic Behaviors     56
Motivational Subsystems     65
Cognitive Evaluation Theory     69

**Chapter 4**     **Emotional Processes in the Organismic Theory**     73

Cognitive Mediation in Emotions     76
Perturbation?     81
Repression     84
Emotion Defined     85
Motivation, Emotion, and Behavior     89
Emotions and the Motivational Subsystems     96
Other Theories of Emotion and Motivation     98

**Part II**     *Self-Determination and Organismic Well-Being*     103

**Chapter 5**     **The Loss of Self-Determination and Well-Being**     105

Empirical Evidence     105
Self-Determination or Control?     112

251701

Inner Control                                      114
Reactance                                          115
Freedom: Reality, Perception, Deception            117
Motivational Subsystems                            119
Biased Perceptions of Self-Determination           120
Individual Differences in Self-Determination       121
Causality Orientations as Personality Types        124

**Chapter 6**     **Development and Self-Determination**    131

Stages of Personality Development                  132
Development of Personality Orientations            142
Adult Development                                  150
Innate Differences                                 151

**Chapter 7**     **The Dynamics of Ill-Being**             153

Cognitive Evaluation Theory                        154
Causality Orientations and Well-Being              157
The Organismic Framework                           167

**Chapter 8**     **The Restoration of Well-Being**         177

Causality Orientations and the Environment         177
Toward Self-Determination                          179
Therapy and the Organismic Framework               183
Therapeutic Approaches                             190

*Part III*        *Overview and Integration*                205

**Chapter 9**     **Summary and Comment**                   207

Types of Behavior                                  207
Motivation and Will                                208
Motivational Subsystems                            209
Personality Orientations                           210
Environments and Cognitive Evaluation Theory       211
The Person and the Environment                     212
The Current Framework and Others                   214
Values in Society and Psychology                   217

**References**                                     219

**Author Index**                                   233

**Subject Index**                                  237

**About the Author**                               241

# List of Figures
# and Tables

**Figures**

| | | |
|---|---|---|
| **3-1** | A TOTE Unit | 50 |
| **3-2** | Basic Structure of an Organismic Theory of Self-Determined Behavior | 55 |
| **3-3** | Automatized and Automatic Behavior | 64 |
| **3-4** | Relationships among the Motivational Subsystems and Types of Behavior | 68 |
| **3-5** | Organismic Theory of Motivation | 70 |
| **4-1** | The Role of Emotion in Self-Determined Behavior | 92 |
| **7-1** | The Self-Determination and Competence Components of the Motivational Subsystems and Causality Orientations | 156 |
| **7-2** | Relationships among Informational Inputs, Motivational Subsystems, and Types of Behavior | 166 |
| **7-3** | Self-Determined and Automatic Behavior | 168 |

**Tables**

| | | |
|---|---|---|
| **5-1** | Relationships among Locus-of-Control, Locus-of-Causality, and Helplessness Concepts | 124 |
| **5-2** | Causality Orientations | 129 |
| **9-1** | Concepts in the Organismic Framework | 215 |

# Preface and
# Acknowledgments

My previous book, *Intrinsic Motivation*, published in 1975, presented some early empirical studies on intrinsic motivation and began to integrate these into a theoretical framework. The empirical research has continued, and a comprehensive review of it appears in Deci and Ryan (1980). The present book, which is largely theoretical, builds on the earlier work while moving into new realms. Taken together, the works remind me of a set of Japanese stepping stones; each piece is a separate unit, yet the sequential arrangement forms the beginning of a larger system.

*The Psychology of Self-Determination* outlines a macrotheory of behavior that focuses on the interplay of freedom and boundedness in human responding. The theory recognizes people's capacity for self-determination, but it also recognizes and elaborates the limitations on that freedom. The book presents a motivational theory that explores both adaptive and maladaptive behaviors and considers the relationship among motivation, emotion, self-determination, ill-being, and well-being. I consider behavioral, cognitive, affective, psychoanalytic, and humanistic theories. Each has made an important contribution, though I am critical of each, for my aim is to move toward synthetic theorizing that allows the contributions of each approach to complement one another.

I have attempted to make my assumptions clear and to present a framework that is internally consistent and, where research evidence is available, externally valid. Some parts of the book are quite specific and supported by data; other parts are rather vague and speculative. This was necessary given my aim of presenting a broad theoretical framework that could encompass existing research findings and fill in the gaps where none existed. My hope is that the speculations and hypotheses will stimulate empirical exploration that will verify some aspects of the system and suggest modifications to others.

Many people have helped me on this project; I am grateful to all of them. Richard M. Ryan, Charles A. Lowe, and Allan J. Schwartz made the most significant contributions. Some of the ideas in the book were developed in collaboration with Rich Ryan. Our discussions have been exciting and helpful; often he understood what I was saying before I did. Skip Lowe made extensive and insightful comments on the entire first draft. Dialogues with Allan Schwartz when I was first beginning the manuscript helped me figure out where I was headed. Chris Argyris, Roger Sperry, and Salvatore Maddi also made important suggestions. I used the manuscript in a graduate seminar during the fall of 1979, and many of the students in that class made usefully pointed criticisms. Betsy Whitehead did a masterful job of editing and typing the manuscript (many times).

I do not have to thank anyone for perservering through the ordeal of my writing this book, for it was not an ordeal. Writing it has been a great joy for me, and the people who are closest to me know that I am more agreeable when I am working on a project like this than when I am not.

I wrote this book during the summer and fall of 1978, while living on Monhegan Island in Maine, and during the winter of 1979, while living on the Island of Oahu in Hawaii. I was on sabbatical from the University of Rochester and was supported in part by a research grant from the National Institute of Mental Health (MH 28600). I am extremely grateful both to the University and to NIMH for providing me the opportunity to do this work.

On Monhegan there is a small rock ledge overlooking the harbor. The ledge is about 20 feet above the high-tide line and provides a marvelous view of the ducks that bob on the waves, the cormorants that dive into the water, the gulls that soar overhead, the fish that arc in the distance, and the ever-changing sea and sky. I wrote five chapters of this book while sitting on that ledge; and during preceeding years I had done much of the preliminary reading, writing, and thinking while sitting there. It was an ideal place to work for it facilitated the internal quiet that allows me to work well.

Many people have enriched my experience on Monhegan: my parents, Chuck and Jean Deci; my D-bury family, Ken Cohen, Amanda Morrice, Louise Morrice, Allan Schwartz, and Louise Sheinman; my friends, Rich Ryan and Alan Weisenfeld; my island compatriates, Jim Balano, Hannah Woods, Joe Walsh, Jackie Boegel and Billy Boynton, Debbie Bates and Dougie Boynton, Alice Becker and Barry Berg, Phyllis and Jamie Wyeth, Anne and Ed Hubert; and many others. To all these people I dedicate this book with affection and appreciation. And especially to two who have touched me deeply: Charlotte Selver, the mother of American sensory awareness. Charlotte introduced me to Monhegan and since that time has been an important teacher and a dear friend. And Zero Mostel, the late actor and painter. Shortly before Zero died, I told him that one day I would dedicate a book to him; now I have done so within the context of the island that he so loved.

# Part I
# Freedom and Boundedness in Human Behavior

# 1 The Nature of Self-Determination

Few human concerns are more universally central than that of self-determination. The earliest European immigrants to America are said to have come for the opportunity to be self-determining; the phrase "control yourself" seems to enjoy almost as common a usage as "good morning"; and every parent knows the tribulations of having a child pass through those terrible twos in which self-determination is an ever-present issue.

## Self-Determination, Will, and Free Will

For centuries philosophers have pondered the matters of self-determination and will. Volumes have been written on the topic, with much of the discussion focused on the debate of free will versus determininism. Psychologists, on the other hand, have paid relatively little attention to concepts like freedom and self-determination. This discrepancy is not surprising when one recognizes the different concerns of the two groups. As Harré and Secord (1972) have noted, philosophers are concerned largely with the logical or conceptual properties of words, whereas psychologists are concerned largely with empirical generalizations. As empiricists, psychologists adopted a scientific orientation, which was patterned largely after Newtonian physics and has tended to view people mechanistically. Empirical generalizations were judged on their parsimony and were to be as simplistic as possible. Within the framework of mechanism and parsimony, notions such as self-determination were said to have no place.

In recent years, there has been some movement away from the mechanistic metatheory. Internal, mental events (both conscious and nonconscious) have been shown to be useful in explaining behavior, and numerous phenomena have been investigated that are relevant to the larger issue of the interplay of freedom and boundedness in human behavior. These developments have set the stage for an extended discussion of self-determination.

This book argues that self-determination has utility both as a means of integrating empirical findings and as a basis for understanding therapeutic interventions. The book presents a macrotheory of human motivation that highlights the interplay of self-determined and nonself-determined behaviors. This first chapter discusses the metatheoretical basis of the

3

theory; then I move on to the theoretical framework and its ramifications. Some elements of the framework have substantial empirical support; others are quite speculative. The speculative elements, which I hope will constitute an agenda for future research, have been derived logically to tie together the empirically grounded conclusions.

## The Law and Order of Behavior

In dealing with the idea of self-determination, we are really raising the question, To what extent can people decide their own behaviors? Part of the reason that self-determination has been held in such disfavor is that this question is similar to the question of whether people are free and has led to a confusion between self-determination and free will. This alignment of concepts, however, is inappropriate. The concept of self-determination stands independent of the notion of free will and has considerable potential as an integrating concept. Let us first consider the question of free will so as to dispose of the confusion (and the free-will concept) straightaway.

At the level of free will versus determininism, the freedom question asks whether a person's behavior is fully determined by some set of (perhaps unspecified) forces or can be freely chosen by the person. The early existential, free-will position, held by Sartre (1957), among others, posited that existence precedes essence. People come into existence as empty organisms and take on their essence through their totally free choices. The implication of this point of view is that behavior is not lawful and ordered. In other words, when people accept the free-will assumption, they accept that behavior cannot be understood or predicted. It is, however, precisely the order and lawfulness of behavior with which psychologists are concerned. Thus we must reject this free-will position; otherwise it makes little sense for us to continue our psychological inquiries into why people do what they do.

The idea of self-determination has been confused so often with the idea of free will that many people mistakenly infer that self-determination means the nonlawfulness of behavior. Within the simplistic-mechanistic conception of people that has been so characteristic of twentieth-century psychology, this confusion between self-determination and free will is quite understandable. All constructs that did not operate on straightforward physical (observable) principles were relegated to the spiritual, psychic, or occult. Self-determination is not a physicalistic concept, so it was relegated. Recently we have begun to understand how mentalistic principles can work in ordered ways that can be tested. The rigid adherence to a mechanistic conception of people has been extremely useful in bringing about a greater understanding of the human being. However, it is now time for psychology to move beyond the mechanistic to a more organismic conception of the human being, still recognizing that the human organism operates in an understandable fashion. In doing this we can utilize what has been learned from the mechanistic approach in a way that does greater justice to the dignity of the human being and has greater utility for practitioners working with clients.

## Self-Determination: The Capacity for Choice

It is quite plausible to postulate that people can be self-determining through ordered processes, that people have will, which operates in understandable ways. Such a postulate would be meaningful if we were to view will as the capacity of human beings to make choices about how to behave based on the information, both internal and external, that is available to them. In other words, people would be assumed to be flexible and able, at will, to change their behaviors as the information available to them changes. As Sperry (1976, p. 15) noted, will does not mean freedom from causation; rather it means having "the kind of control which allows one to determine one's own actions according to one's wishes, one's own judgment, perspective, cognitive aims, emotional desires, and other mental inclinations." Using this conceptualization there need be no inconsistency between the rejection of free will and the acceptance of will as a meaningful concept for psychology (meaningful in the sense of providing an opportunity for developing a consistent and predictive system for explaining behavior).

People have considerable capacity for self-determination, and the operation of will—that capacity to choose behaviors based on inner desires and perceptions—is the basis of self-determination. However, this capacity is not unbounded. Tomkins (1969, p. 103) summarized it well when he stated, "Man is neither as free as he feels nor as bound as he fears." It is important to recognize that even if people used their capacity for self-determination to its fullest, it would be limited by a range of physicalistic and physiological forces. Furthermore, the ways in which they exercise their self-determination is in part a function of sociohistorical factors. Still, within those boundaries, the possibilities for self-determined responding are fascinating.

People have substantial latitude to determine their own existence, yet this latitude exists within the context of various confines. It is fascinating to realize that most people fail to utilize the full extent of their capacity for self-determination. For quite understandable reasons, they often lose some of their self-determination and can be said to become governed by various mechanistic principles. At such times they may feel as if they lack and cannot get control over themselves. This book will deal with some of the processes through which people lose their sense of self-determination. It will also consider the results of those losses and the possibilities for their restoration.

*Self-Determination and Behavioral Options*

Often when the idea of freedom is considered, it is addressed in terms of the number of behavioral options that are available. A person with four behavioral options is said to be freer than one with only two options. I do not intend for self-determination to be understood in that way. Self-determination is a psychological construct referring to people's flexibility and capacity both to choose from among the behavioral options (regardless of the number of options) and to accommodate to the situations in which only one option is available. Conversely one can be said to be nonself-determining if one behaves automatically by not considering the various behavioral options when they do exist or by not accommodating and responding flexibly when only one behavioral option exists.

To illustrate, consider a sailor who is steering a ship. He has many options for which course to follow. If his sailing has become so habitual that he always follows the same route, even though many others are available, and especially if he follows the same route habitually even when he learns that another route would be better for achieving his aims, he would not be self-determining; his behavior is automatic and inflexible. There is no choice. If a storm came up that was so rough that the course of the ship was determined and did not respond to his attempts to steer it, his options for where to take the ship would be limited to one, but he could still be self-determining. He could remain calm and respond flexibly to the storm, in which case he would be said to be self-determining, or he could become upset and inflexible in dealing with the storm, responding automatically without utilizing the information available to him, in which case he would be said to be nonself-determining. In sum, people are nonself-determining when their behavior becomes habitual and inflexible (always steering along the same course even when it is not the best course, in this example) or when their behavior is controlled by emotional processes that preclude choice and the flexible use of information (becoming upset and ineffective in dealing with the storm).

Often people lose self-determination without even realizing it. For example, the repeated experience of doing a behavior to get a reward can undermine one's self-determination of that behavior. One no longer chooses whether to do the behavior; one does it automatically when the reward is present and refrains automatically when the reward is absent.

Although people can lose self-determination without being aware of it, the restoration of self-determination requires awareness and deliberateness.

While one can choose to regain self-determination, the process is not just a simple matter of deciding and then doing it. Whereas one can decide to raise an arm and then do it (assuming one is not paralyzed or hypnotized), one cannot typically, in the same fashion, decide and then undo an acquired, automatic response. The undoing is typically a tedious process. Much of what happens in therapy involves learning to undo automatic responding.

## Mentalism and Behaviorism

The framework for the interplay of self-determined and automatic behavior is based on the assumption that mental events, both conscious and nonconscious, are useful and necessary explanatory concepts.

### The Use of Mentalism

Behaviorists (Watson 1913; Skinner 1953) have long asserted that mentalistic concepts have no place in the explanation of behavior. Skinner (1974, p. 14) stated, "Mentalistic concepts allay curiosity and bring inquiry to a stop." He did not deny the existence of internal states such as feelings, motives, and desires; he simply asserted that there is no need to use these concepts in the causal analyses of behavior. Skinner asserted that since mental events are not observable, they should not be used as causal concepts. He called for a physicalistic perspective, and asked, "How can a mental event cause or be caused by a physical one?" (p. 10). Finally, he suggested that even if the progression of events in a behavior goes from physical (stimulus) to mental (cognition, affect, and so forth) to physical (response), there is no sense in looking at the mental when the physical-physical (stimulus-response) analysis allows equally satisfactory prediction and control of behavior.

The methodological behaviorists (Watson 1913) took the most clear-cut stance on mental events. They stated quite simply that since mental events are not observable, there can be no consensus through observation, and therefore they should be ruled out of consideration. The concomitant point—that since internal states are knowable only through postbehavioral attributions or through introspection, they are not useful for predictive purposes and not necessary for control purposes—is often made as a justification for a physicalistic stimulus-response approach to the study of human behavior.

There is considerable merit to the point that a science of human behavior must deal with variables that are measurable and verifiable; however, variables need not be directly observable to be measured. Procedures of self-report and calculated inference based on careful experimental manipulation of independent variables are widely and satisfactorily used to measure and study nonobservable variables. Such procedures may yield less precision and require more skillful design and interpretation, but in return they provide greater explanatory power and richness of theory.

To conclude that because variables are not directly observable they are not useful in a causal analysis of behavior is a logical fallacy. To be useful for a scientific account of behavior, variables must be measurable or inferable, yet their observability says nothing about their importance in a causal sequence. Skinner (1974) has stated that mental events can be useful to the person in predicting his or her own behavior, but at the same time he held that they are not useful for scientific prediction. If they have predictive utility for the person, they can have equal utility for the scientist. The challenge for the scientist is to devise ways of measuring them.

In response to the query of how physical and mental events can cause each other, one need give up only the most simple of physicalistic conceptions in order to imagine a functional relationship that would transform one type of event (or class of events) into the other. If one defines causality in the simplest of physical relationships, such that only physical principles are admissible, by definition one must discard mentalistic conceptions. But there is no compelling reason to do so. Even if we had no ideas about the possible processes of transformation, to assume that there is none is, in Skinner's words, to allay curiosity and impede meaningful inquiry.

**Conscious Determinants**. Sperry (1965, 1969) has outlined a mind-brain theory that provides one answer to the question of how physical and physiological events could cause mental events and how mental events, in turn, could cause physiological and hence physical events. He discussed consciousness, a class of mental events, and outlined its relationship to physiological events. By demonstrating how consciousness can affect physiology and therefore behavior, he was countering the assertion that mental activity (of which consciousness is a subset) should not be given a role in the determination of behavior. Sperry said that although most scientists who explore cerebral functioning would resist the idea that the causal sequence of behavior could be influenced by consciousness, his own physiological studies of split-brain functioning have suggested that a person's phenomenological or conscious experience does interact causally with brain functioning. He stated, "Consciousness is conceived to have a directive role in determining the flow of cerebral excitation" (1969, p. 533).

Sperry defined conscious awareness as "a dynamic emergent property of cerebral excitation" (p. 533). By dynamic emergent properties, he meant configurational occurrences in which the pattern of excitation is more than the summation of the individual neural firings. He was utilizing a conception of consciousness that is analogous to the Gestalt principle of perception in which elements such as dots, blocks, or lines are not perceived as a collection of elements but rather are formed into a whole, assimilated into an existing cognitive structure. Thus consciousness is the gestalt created by a set of neural firings.

Sperry then asserted that the emergent properties have causal influence on further neural excitation. Thus consciousness (or mental activity) is said to cause physiological activity. Sperry's view takes full cognizance of physiological principles, yet he conceived of the operation of causally determinative mental events that are based in (and hence controlled by) physiological activity but are different from and more than the physiological occurrences. Sperry added that although there is this mutual interdependence such that neurophysiology controls mental events and mental events control neurophysiology, the conscious phenomena of mental events are higher in command. Consciousness is at the apex of a hierarchical structure that causes cerebral activity.

Giving the mental activity of consciousness a causal role in behavior involves a chain of events in which external, physical events cause neural excitation, the emergent properties of which are consciousness. Consciousness, being at the apex of the physiological-mental interplay, in turn causes physiological activity that produces external, physical events, namely behavior.

It makes good sense within an evolutionary perspective to give consciousness a role in the determination of behavior. Believing that no prominent organismic characteristic will endure through time if it does not have important survival value to the organism or species leads to the conclusion that an epiphenomenon or excess-baggage view of consciousness is wholly untenable. Self-determination theory holds that consciousness operates to cause behavior within the context of physiological activity in such a way as not to violate the organization of the central nervous system. Sperry's formulation provides a transformation function that can map physicalistic activity into mental and vice versa.

The third of Skinner's points suggested that even if mental events mediate between physicalistic inputs and outputs, there is no need to attend to them since a focus on the physical-physical relationship allows the same predictability and control. I address this point in two ways. First, I note that whether a stimulus-response (S-R) approach is as useful for predicting and controlling behavior as an approach that focuses on internal states of the organism is an empirical question and that there is evidence to indicate that the S-R approach is not as useful. Second, I argue that predictability and control of behavior do not assure understanding.

A strict S-R approach looks only at stimuli and responses in an attempt to predict responses from objective stimuli and to control responses with the presentation of eliciting stimuli. Whether an S-R analysis or an analysis that focuses on internal events has greater predictability has been frequently debated and is ultimately an empirical question. Frequently cited data by Breland and Breland (1961) show that certain behaviors in animals defy operant conditioning. It is necessary to consider the organism, the O between the S and R, in order to understand these breakdowns in the conditioning principles. Garcia and Koelling (1966) discovered that, in an avoidance-conditioning paradigm, behaviors produced by noxious events occurred only in certain sensory modalities. For example, electric shock could produce avoidance responding for audiovisual stimuli but not for gustatory stimuli, whereas toxins could produce avoidance responding in gustatory but not audiovisual stimuli. The evidence seems clear, even with subhuman species, that organismic variables are necessary for an understanding of behavior. Clearly with humans, given their capacity for conscious awareness, the need is even greater for consideration of organismic variables.

People often attach unique meanings to stimuli, and responses follow from these meanings rather than from the objective properties of the stimuli. This does not deny that some behaviors proceed automatically and predictably from an objective interpretation of a stimulus event; it simply asserts that there are also behaviors that are understandable only when attention is paid to the processes of "meaning making" or psychological interpretation that intercedes between physical inputs and physical outputs. An analysis that utilizes internal events as mediating variables will have greater predictive power, for it can include all of the observable variables that an S-R analysis examines, and in addition it attends to the psychological interpretations of stimuli that are the direct antecedents of behavioral responses.

Empirical evidence, in response to Skinner's third point, confirms that a focus on the physical-physical (S-R) relationship does not allow adequate prediction and control. But even if an S-R approach did allow adequate prediction and control, it would not ensure an understanding of human behavior.

**Prediction, Control, and Understanding.** In the science of psychology, prediction and control are generally accepted as the criteria for understanding phenomena. They are certainly important factors in the understanding of behavior. To predict an event with an accuracy that consistently defies chance suggests some level of understanding of the phenomenon; and to fail to predict with better than chance level accuracy suggests nonunderstanding. Similarly the ability to control one variable through the manipulation of another yields some degree of understanding, and the inability to control one variable with another suggests nonunderstanding. However, I assert that prediction and control do not guarantee understanding. Hence even if an S-R approach led to greater prediction and control, it would not provide full understanding. A description of internal, mental events is necessary for an understanding of human behavior.

Consider the example of an old man who lives in an apartment on the main street of a small town and who hates to see people walk under ladders on Main Street. The man never leaves the window of his apartment during daylight. To punish the world for doing what he hates, he rigs up a set of small bombs and detonates one each time he sees someone walk under a ladder on Main Street. A careful observer might note the relationship of "walking under ladders on Main Street during the day" and "the explosion of a small bomb." The predictability would be perfect. Further, as an eager scientist, the observer might find that he or she can control the bombs by controlling people's "walking under ladders on Main Street in the daytime." There is perfect prediction and reliable control. But is there a full understanding of the phenomenon when the eager scientist says, "Walking under ladders on Main Street in the daytime causes bombs to explode"?

There is certainly utility in knowing the sequential relationship between the events for one who wishes to terminate further bombings. Yet the understanding of the phenomenon is superficial at best. If one wants predictability and control, one gets it in this example; if one wants understanding, one does not get it without considering the old man. From a pragmatic perspective, predictability and control are often enough, but for understanding, they are not. An understanding would require an explication of the old man's involvement. In an analogous way, an understanding of the relationship between stimuli and responses in the study of behavior requires an explication of intervening mental events.

*Conscious and Nonconscious Processes*

In asserting that mental events are necessary for the explanation of behavior, I have focused primarily on conscious events, but the use of nonconscious events is similarly important. One of the main contributions of psychoanalytic theory (Freud 1924, 1969) has been its emphasis on the importance of nonconscious processes in human functioning. While neo-Freudian theorists such as Horney (1939) and Erikson (1950) have modified psychoanalytic theory, the emphasis on the unconscious has remained a cornerstone in the theory. In spite of Freud's impact on psychiatry and psychotherapy, his work has been virtually ignored by experimental psychologists. Only recently has a body of research begun to accumulate that points to the importance of nonconscious processes as determinants of behavior (Shervin and Dickman 1980).

One such line of research involves subliminal perception (Dixon 1971). Here a stimulus is presented to subjects for a period so brief that the stimulus cannot be consciously perceived, regardless of how much attention is directed to the stimulus field. Nevertheless such stimuli affect people's conscious processes and behavior. For example, Bach and Klein (1957) found that when subjects looked at a neutral face while the word *angry* was subliminally presented, they tended to judge the face as being angry, whereas when they saw the same face paired with the subliminal word *happy*, they tended to judge the face as being happy.

Nisbett and Wilson (1977) have reviewed evidence from a variety of social-psychological experiments that suggest that subjects may respond to a stimulus without awareness of the stimulus and that they may be aware of a stimulus but be unaware that it has affected their behavior. Hilgard's (1973, 1977) experimental work on hypnosis has also helped to highlight the importance of nonconscious processes. He reported experiments in which subjects who were hypnotized held their hands in very cold water. Nonhypnotized subjects had reported considerable pain from the ice water, yet hypnotized subjects reported that they felt no pain.

Often in hypnosis experiments, subjects are induced to engage in a procedure called automatic writing. Subjects write, yet they have no conscious awareness of what they are writing. Presumably they are communicating from a different sphere of mental activity, which is segmented from conscious awareness. When Hilgard had his subjects engage in automatic writing, the written words reported pain comparable to that of the nonhypnotized subjects. In accounting for these phenomena, Hilgard suggested that hypnosis creates barriers in consciousness between the part that experiences pain and the part that we say is consciously aware. Further, the part that experiences the pain is barricaded from the normal communication channels but is accessible through the automatic writing procedures.

Hilgard suggested that there are many control systems in human cognitive functioning, that these systems are somewhat hierarchical in their arrangement, and that one of the systems serves the role of executive. This executive system, which, Hilgard added, is subject to a variety of internal and external constraints, is similar to what I am calling the will or the capacity of the human organism to choose behaviors. For our purposes, the important part of Hilgard's work is a point also made by Shallice (1978): the existence of subordinate control systems that work out of conscious awareness to motivate behavior. Nonconscious as well as conscious mental events are important determinants of behavior.

## Freedom or Illusion

Many writers (such as Immergluck 1964; Skinner 1971) have asserted that freedom, or the capacity for self-determination, is merely an illusion. They have held that people's belief in mental events as causal antecedents of behavior is mistaken and that people are not free to decide how to be. Immergluck suggested that people, being trapped by the illusion of freedom, look in the wrong places for an understanding of themselves and others.

In response to this reasoning, Lefcourt (1973) pointed out that although freedom may be an illusion or a conceptual fabrication, control is similarly an illusion. The important question is not whether one is free or controlled but whether the belief in (illusion of) freedom versus the belief in (or illusion of) control has empirical consequences. Lefcourt reported a variety of experimental and anecdotal findings suggesting that the illusion of freedom leads to greater motivation, learning, and well-being. The important point is that people's beliefs about themselves lead them to feel and behave in ways that are commensurate with the beliefs. Thus, Lefcourt (1973, p. 425) concluded, it is important to maintain the illusion of freedom, for "to submit to however wise a master planner is to surrender an illusion that may be the bedrock on which life flourishes."

## The Person-Environment Interaction

Internal, person variables are necessary for an understanding of behavior and volitional states are lawful antecedents of some behaviors. However, environmental events are also functionally related to behaviors. The person-environment interaction, rather than the person or the environment, is the appropriate focus for exploration. The person and environment are like a figure and ground in interaction. One can discuss the environment as figure, but this necessitates a person as ground; for example, an environmental event will not reinforce if the person does not have an operative need. And similarly one can discuss the person as figure, but this necessitates the environment as ground; for example, people can behave in an attempt to satisfy a need, but the behavior will be affected by the presence or absence of the environmental means for satisfying the need.

Different schools of psychology tend to focus on one type of factor, failing to take the other adequately into account. This single focus provides some predictability and control, since a description of reinforcement assumes an organism that needs the reinforcing agent, and a description of personal dynamics assumes an environment within which the dynamics are played out. In either case the ground tends to be assumed rather than explicated, so much of the variance in behavior becomes random since the interplay of person and environment is not dealt with. To illustrate this point, consider an everyday example.

One day, while playing in his yard, an eight-year-old boy named Georgie noticed his neighbor's paper in the bushes; the paper deliverer had

had poor aim that day. Being a well-socialized boy, Georgie took the paper to the front door and rang the door bell. The woman, delighted by his behavior and the receipt of her paper, praised him lavishly and gave him a candy bar. The next day Georgie, spotting the paper at the base of the porch where it belonged, took it to the door and rang the bell. How might one explain his behavior on that second day?

In the history of psychology, there have been two primary ways of approaching the question. One way has focused on the environment, placing the causal elements of Georgie's behavior in the candy, praise, and newspaper, while the other has focused on the person, placing the causal elements in his drives, desires, and other internal processes. This difference in focus has been a point of much debate in psychology, one with wide-ranging implications.

A common-sense explanation of the behavior involves Georgie's doing it for the rewards: "He did it to get the candy and praise" or "He wanted the candy and praise." Implicit in each statement is an interaction between person and environment. The person elements are "to get" and "wanted," each of which derives out of some inner process of the person. Georgie wants, desires, needs, or likes; there is an active motivational process implied by the explanations. Also apparent in the explanations are the environmental elements of candy and praise. These are the rewards, the reinforcers, the gratifiers, which exert force on Georgie, however complicated the interaction may be.

In spite of the wisdom in this naive explanation, psychologists tend to favor just half the picture when they give more scientific accounts. Thus, for example, a behavioral explanation (Skinner 1971) typically would place the causality for the act in the environmental contingencies and reinforcements. Georgie would be said to have engaged in the behavior because of the presence of the paper today and because of having received the rewards or reinforcements yesterday. The curious thing about this account is that nothing was said about Georgie; from this perspective, it could as easily have been any other person, a llama (who likes candy and could carry a paper), or a robot that delivered the paper to the woman.

By contrast, and equally inappropriately, a dynamic account (see Maslow 1970; Freud 1969) shifts the causality to the person's internal states and processes, emphasizing either conscious desires and decisions (the humanistic tradition; Maslow 1970) or unconscious forces (the psychoanalytic tradition' Freud 1969). Thus Georgie's behavior might be said to be based in his needs for affection and food (humanistic) or in his unconscious desires for oral gratification from his mother (psychoanalytic). Either of these accounts would be fuller and more sophisticated than my characterizations of them, yet the focus would be on the person, and one would be left with the feeling of an incomplete picture. What about the environment? Why is Goergie taking that paper to that woman instead of washing his grandmother's car to get affection and food from her or sucking a lollipop to get oral gratification?

To summarize, either an environmental approach or a person approach is able to explain considerable variance in behavior, for the two parts of the interaction are like two sides of a coin. Yet a fuller account of behavior necessitates attending to the person, the environment, and their interactive effects. Both the person approach and the environment approach have their advantages and disadvantages. Whereas an environmental focus emphasizes the power of environmental contingencies and bases explanations on observable (thus easily manipulable) events, it fails to give credit to people's unique interpretation of stimuli and does not provide an account of the behaviors that makes sense only when one considers people's experience of themselves. On the other hand, a person approach emphasizes people's capacity to control themselves (humanistic) and goes deep into the strong, internal forces of the person (psychoanalytic), yet it tends not to recognize the impact of the environment nor does it formulate theory in testable ways.

A person who is to be self-determining, like the scientist who wishes to understand self-determined behavior, will need to recognize the impact of nonconscious and environmental forces, as well as the strength of his or her capacity for choosing behaviors and managing those person and environmental forces. That way the person can use the various forces to advantage and can realize what forces may need to be contained or countered. For example, if one wished to stop smoking, it might be sensible to surround oneself with people who do not smoke and who will reinforce (by reward or praise perhaps) not smoking. Similarly it might be useful to find other means (such as candy) to satisfy one's need for oral gratification. Each year, millions of people break their New Year's resolutions such as stopping smoking because they fail to take account of the compelling forces in themselves and in the environment.

On the other hand, while it may be easier to give up smoking when one is surrounded by supportive nonsmokers and when one uses candy for oral gratification, it is possible to give up smoking when one is surrounded by smokers (even smokers who punish one for trying to give it up) and when one does not add means for oral gratification. It is one's will, one's capacity to make choices and to mobilize energy in support of these choices, that allows one to **counteract forces from the environment and from drives.**

The interplay of the organism and the environment is important for a workable conception of self-determination. It emphasizes that one's decisions can be causal elements in behavior, but it also recognizes that the environment and nonconscious motivational forces will control behavior when one is not consciously attending to these various internal and external stimuli.

**The Determinants of Behavior**

The human organism operates in an environment in such a way that the environment impinges on the organism and the organism acts on the environment. Humans are not passive agents of the environment; they are active agents within the context of the environment. Still, the environment exerts forces on the individual, and these forces vary in potence. Some forces determine the behavior of the person; others have impact only as inputs to volitional responding; and others have no impact; they are ignored or discarded from consideration. The organism operates within a physiological, psychological, and environmental context, which may exert varying degrees of influence on behavior. Within this context of environmental and person forces is an executive, termed the *will*, that constitutes the human capacity for self-determination. The will may or may not be operative in relation to a particular behavior or behavioral sequence. To the extent that the will is operative, we say the person is being self-determining. Let us categorize three types of responding in relation to self-determination.

In the first type, there is no self-determination; behavior is fully determined by physical or physiological principles, vis-à-vis the environment. For example, if a man is standing interestedly gazing at a flower and someone comes up behind him and forcefully hits him in a certain way, the man will fall down; there is no decision and no possibility of doing other than falling down. Similarly at times one's bladder may be so bloated that urination is determined; a personal decision cannot counteract the operative physical and physiological forces. Reflexes such as the knee jerk are in this category of nonself-determined behavior. From a psychological perspective this context-determined behavior is the least interesting and will not be addressed in this book.

The second category of responding involves the type of behavior that was initially in the realm of volitional responding but has become controlled by some mechanized or automated process. This category will be refined to consider two types of automated behavior, termed *automatized behavior* and *automatic behavior*. The behavioral tradition has focused attention on this type of responding, though that tradition has considered all behavior to be of this type.

It is often said that these automated behaviors are stimulus bound, suggesting that they are initiated and controlled by stimuli. I, at times, refer to them as being controlled by the environment. Yet it is important once again to emphasize the person-environment interaction. It is useful heuristically to say that they are controlled by the environment, but the environment would not have its impact if the organism were not, at that time, disposed toward responding to that stimulus, if the structures of the person did not mesh with the stimulus event. Here again is the figure-ground interplay of the person and environment; behavior that is said to be controlled by the environment is behavior that involves structures of the person that bypass the will.

An interesting aspect of automated responding is that it can be reclaimed by the will. The process of doing so may not be easy, though it is possible. The reclaiming of this responding by the will may involve reprogramming the behavior and delegating it once again to the realm of automatized behavior under the control of a different program, or it may involve keeping it within the realm of chosen responding. The processes of psychotherapy and of the so-called growth movement are specifically concerned with the reclamation of automatized and automatic responding.

Automatized and automatic behaviors can be distinguished operationally from each other on the basis of the ease with which they can be reprogrammed or brought into the realm of self-determination. Automatized behaviors are more easily reprogrammed than automatic behaviors. In terms of psychological dynamics, I suggest that automatic behaviors are ones that have been acquired to satisfy nonconscious motives, and it is the fact of the behavior being associated with these nonconscious motives rather than merely being governed by nonconscious programs or structures that makes them so resistant to change.

Automatized and automatic responding can be either adaptive or maladaptive, though automatized behavior, being flexible, tends not to be maladaptive for long. Even behavior that is maladaptive was adaptive in the particular situation in which it was acquired. If the environment is uncertain or if it specifically thwarts one's attempts at need satisfaction, one acquires certain behaviors, which are the best one can do given one's interpretation of that situation. Behaviors become maladaptive because they persist when they are inappropriate for the situation; it is their inflexibility in an ever-changing environment that makes them maladaptive.

The third category of behavior is self-determined or volitional behavior. This involves the operation of the will, that human capacity for deciding how to behave. Thus we can say that self-determined behavior is determined by decisions based on information from the environment and the person as it is perceived and interpreted by the person. These decisions are made in the service of human needs. Self-determined behavior is the archetype of motivated behavior.

Of the three classes of human behavior that vary along the self-determination continuum, this book provides an explication of the latter two types of behavior, automated, and self-determined. The extent of self-determination is a reflection of the extent to which the will is operative.

# 2 Will and the Motivation to Will

The psychology of self-determination is an explication of those behaviors that are chosen or willed. The operation of will does not vitiate the concept of determinism in psychology; instead it locates the determination for some behaviors in conscious choice processes.

## Theories of Will

The first psychologist to discuss will in detail was William James, who in the second volume of *The Principles of Psychology* (1890) outlined a theory of will. It is, he asserted, a state of mind with which everyone is so familiar that a formal definition could hardly elucidate it. For him, to will is to desire an outcome that the person believes is attainable. It is a state of mind or an image that precedes voluntary behavior. The behavior follows the image, and if the person's beliefs about being able to achieve the outcome were accurate, the outcome would be achieved.

In willing, an outcome is imagined and what follows are movements of the organism that bring about (or at least aim to bring about) the outcome. These movements, according to James, occur automatically when the results of the movements are brought to mind. Thus, one thinks of having a word on paper and the necessary movements occur to put it there. These movements will occur only if a trace of them exists in memory, for no movement can occur as a voluntary behavior without being in memory. According to James, most new behaviors are reflexive or expressive. Once they have occurred, they are available for willed-behavior sequences. This seems to imply that behavioral possibilities are transmitted genetically and that the organism is predisposed to utilize behavioral possibilities through the type of responding that does not require volition. The primary example of such responding, in James's theory, is emotion. For example, when frightened, one's heart rate and breathing change, one is inclined to run, one may cover one's face, and so on. James defined emotion as the awareness of these reactions. Having once occurred as reactions (reflexes or emotions), the behaviors are available in one's behavioral repertoire for willful responding.

A second possibility for the initial occurrence of a movement utilizes the human capacity for conceptualizing. One can cognize a behavior by

19

observing it in others, and through doing so the mind is provided with the ideas that are required for voluntary responding. This process was called remote effects. Finally, a behavior can be caused initially by an external force—for example, a baby may be stood up by his or her mother—and provide the memory with traces of movement. Memory traces of movements need not be in cognitive awareness; learning of behaviors is partially a kinesthetic rather than cognitive process.

James emphasized that in voluntary behavior, an image of the outcome of the movements rather than a decision to perform the movements may be all that is needed. One need not decide to make the movements that are involved in scratching one's ear; one simply thinks of scratching one's ear and the movements occur. On the other hand, James added, a decision is required when there is some opposition to the movement; for example, one might have to decide quite deliberately to walk into a very cold ocean for a swim. The extent of the actual deciding or fiat, according to James, depends on the strength of opposing or conflicting notions. The thought, "I'm cold already," would oppose the image of going in swimming and therefore would necessitate greater fiat to bring about the outcome of swimming in the cold ocean.

The existence of conflict would require more will, though to some extent the amount of conscious attention and deciding which is required is simply a matter of familiarity with the behavior. As a behavior is repeated, it becomes more automatized and requires less conscious attention. Whereas, even in the absence of opposing notions, one must decide to do and attend to doing unfamiliar behaviors, familiar ones seem simply to occur as one imagines the outcome because the behavior patterns have been programmed.

Each mental imaging of a behavioral outcome initiates movement toward the outcome. When this movement is neutralized by opposing images, movement fails to occur unless a decision is made to overcome the opposing force. The essence of willing, then, is the achievement of a mental image that has greater strength than any opposing force. The directive function of the will, according to James, involves keeping one's attention directed toward a certain image or images, which, because of the opposition of, say, powerful drives, one may find difficult to do. Hence, the essence of James's theory of will is the directing of one's attention to an idea and the deciding to overcome the resistance to the execution of that idea.

James's theory of will bears some similarity to recent cognitive theories of motivation (see Deci 1975, chapter 4). James stated that will is a desire, a particular state of mind. Although "state of mind" is not used in psychology today, it is essentially a cognition, so will is similar to what cognitive theorists call a motive. A motive (see Kagan 1972) is a cognitive representation of some desired future state. James theorized that behavior follows automatically from the desire or image unless it is blocked by some opposing force. Here is an important difference between James's theory and the cognitive approach to motivation. The latter would maintain that a motive precedes decision making about what behaviors to engage in to achieve the desired satisfaction. In the cognitive approach, decision making is a central element.

Cognitive theories hypothesize that these decisions are based on people's expectations about the outcomes that are likely to follow from each of the behavioral alternatives. These outcomes take on psychological value in accord with their potential for satisfying people's needs. James did not speak directly about the relationship between will and needs. Nonetheless I derived from what he did say that desire (will) is based in needs. If my derivation is correct, then there is additional similarity between a cognitive approach to motivation and James's theory of will: both would consider thoughts to be antecedents of voluntary behavior and both would consider this voluntary behavior to be in the service of human needs. The most critical difference between the two approaches lies in whether decision making need be an aspect of the process. In James's theory, behavior follows automatically from an image, so the voluntariness of will occurs primarily in bringing the image to mind and keeping the mind on track. In cognitive theories of motivation, the voluntariness of will occurs when people choose and execute behaviors (see Atkinson 1974; Vroom 1964).

Shortly after James's theory was presented, the emphasis in psychology became strongly behavioristic, and most theorizing about internal, cognitive, and effective determinants of behavior was abandoned. It was several decades before the next coherent, psychologicl theory of volition and will was presented.

*Quasi-need Theory*

In his writings on will, Lewin (1951) seemed to have two primary agendas: to show that an international theory of behavior works better than a behavioristic, associationist theory and to outline the consequences of the act of intending. He characterized two types of willful behavior: controlled actions, in which someone resolves to behave in a highly controlled way in the face of a difficult, emotion-eliciting event, and intentional actions, which are generally less forceful and in which one resolves to accomplish a certain kind of, perhaps vague, outcome such as communicating with a friend. It is this second category of willful responding to which Lewin directed his attention. Lewin further mentioned, though did not elaborate, that there are volitional behaviors that are neither intentional nor controlled.

According to Lewin, there are three phases to an intentional action: a struggle between motives, a decision or intention that ends the struggle, and the consummatory action itself. Lewin considered the second phase to be the central element in the psychology of will. It is also the central element in cognitive theories of motivation, which developed in large measure from Lewin's work.

The first phase is a motivational process in which one or more of a person's needs vie for the upper hand so the person's behavior will be directed toward the satisfaction of that need. This conflict among needs may be short and relatively uncharged or somewhat longer and more tense. The second phase, the intention, is the core of willful behavior and determines which need will energize the person's behavior. This creation of an intention is in essence a decision among needs. In situations where there is only one prominent need and hence there is no struggle, no intention is required. Willfull behavior, as Lewin conceived it, occurs only in the presence of conflicting forces and is therefore similar to that class of events that in James's theory requires a fiat or decision to overcome an opposing force. Thus James included a wider range of behaviors under the rubric of willful than did Lewin.

Once an intention is made, said Lewin, a tension remains until the intention is satisfied through a consummatory action. Although Lewin did not speak of gestalts, he was saying that an intention creates an incomplete gestalt and a consummatory action completes the gestalt and dissipates the tension. Lewin acknowledged that there are drive-actions, ones that follow directly from strong natural needs in a nonvoluntary fashion. However, his experiments indicated that when needs are in conflict and the conflict is resolved by an intention, there are a variety of consequences.

Lewin's experiments showed that when an intention was made and the consummatory action completed, the presentation of the stimulus (or, as Lewin called it, the occasion) did not initiate the behavior. Further, substitute behaviors, which served to satisfy the same intention but which were behaviorally quite dissimilar to the planned behaviors led to completion of the gestalt and rendered the occasion impotent. A decision to head to the store for a roast may cease to be meaningful if a friend shows up with fresh fish that will work satisfactorily for dinner. Finally, once an intention has been made and the appropriate eliciting occasion (stimulus) is not present, the person will seek out an occasion so as to complete the behavior. One would look for a store to buy a roast if none presented itself.

Experiments by Lewin's colleagues, Zeigarnik (1927) and Rickers-Ovsiankina (1928), have shown that incompleted activities are more likely to be resumed and that people remember interrupted activities better than they do completed activities. One would predict from drive theories that completed, and therefore reinforced, activities would be more likely to be resumed or remembered; hence the Zeigarnik and Rickers-Ovsiankina results tend to disconfirm drive theories. It is further curious to note that incompleted activities will be resumed or remembered even in the absence of a relevant stimulus. The press for consummation of an intention appears to operate as an internal state of affairs that may be prompted by stimulus occasions but which can also lead one to search for occasions or behave in the absence of occasions.

Having found associationist theories inadequate, Lewin proposed a quasi-need theory of intentional behavior. He posited that the act of intending sets up an inner tension that bears remarkable similarity to natural needs (drives). This tension remains over a long period of time until the spirit of the intention is realized. It returns one to interrupted activities and motivates one to find appropriate situations to engage in the consummatory action.

Lewin emphasized that the energy for intentional behavior comes from the underlying natural need, even though the intention sets up a quasi-need. The quasi-need derives its motivational potential from the need, which won the struggle in the motivational phase of the action sequence. Thus the strength of the quasi-need (and therefore the intensity toward resumption of an unfinished activity and the probability of carrying out an intention in the face of obstacles) depends, according to Lewin, not on the intensity of the act of intending but rather on the intensity of the natural needs upon which the intention rests. Lewin then stated that an intention that is not based on a natural need (such as a drive) will surely fail.

Anecdotal evidence suggests that this assertion is incorrect, for one repeatedly sees instances in which people who intensely will an event are able to overcome obstacles to achieve the event, whereas people who will the event with less determination fall by the wayside before attainment. An example might be giving up smoking. The natural needs for giving up smoking are certainly important and would seem to be relatively constant across people when age and health are held constant. Yet people may use intense determination and overcome the habit, whereas in previous, less concerted attempts they were not able to stop.

The point is not to say that strong determination is the best way to achieve an outcome; indeed events are more likely to come to fruition when the less intense act of willing rests on a strong natural need than when an intense act of willing rests on a weak natural need. Nonetheless the point remains that the intensity with which one wills, as well as the strength of natural needs, is a factor that can and often does influence behavior.

Lewin was a bit inconsistent on this point. Although he asserted strongly that the strength of quasi-needs derives from natural needs, he also mentioned that an intention could be based on a "general goal of will." Although he did not discuss this concept, a general goal of will was said to be a kind of long-term guiding plan, such as to become a physician. How such a goal gets its motivating properties was unspecified, though as conceived there appears to be some discrepancy in his reasoning. Nonetheless the essence of Lewin's theory was that an intention sets up a quasi-need, which derives its energy from the underlying natural need, and this quasi-need presses for satisfaction until a consummatory action is completed.

## Will and Morality

Piaget (1967) has also discussed will. He asserted that will is a regulator of energy that comes into existence in middle childhood (seven to twelve years) in connection with what he called autonomous moral feelings. At that stage of development, children are moving from a morality based on authority to a morality based on mutuality among people. Will, he suggested, emerges as an equilibrated version of affective regulation, which operates in the presence of conflicts between internal tendencies. When a conflict exists between, say, a drive and a moral principle, the will comes into play to help the moral principle win. Its function is to bolster the strength of the moral side of the conflict. For example, suppose someone experiences a strong urge to beat a child but also has a moral belief against such behavior. If the moral belief is faltering from the force of the intense urge, one's will may be used to push the moral thought to victory over the urge.

In explicating the operation of will, Piaget spoke of inferiority and superiority of tendencies. In an example, he talked of duty being superior and the desire for pleasure being inferior. In this kind of moralizing, I think he clouded the issue of will, narrowing its operation and making it the servant of an arbitrary morality. When we strip the moralizing from his conceptualization, we are left with a conflict among internal forces and a resolution of the conflict with one force achieving centrality. These two elements, when abstracted from contextual specifics, are common to the theories of James, Lewin, and Piaget.

For James, will need not involve a conflict; any desire that is obtainable is said to be willed. However, in the presence of some obstacle or opposing force, one must make a decision, or fiat, to overcome the obstacles. It is this fiat that is more analogous to what Lewin and Piaget referred to as will. Lewin used the phrase "act of intention" to refer to an event that terminates a struggle of internal forces whereas Piaget called it will. For Lewin, the forces are simply different needs rather than an urge and a moral principle. Presumably Lewin would incorporate a moral principle by considering it an instance of what he called "goal of will," those long-term guiding thoughts that he indicated could be energy sources.

Of the three theories, James's is the broadest in that it encompasses all voluntary behavior, whether or not there are conflicting forces. For Lewin, will (or more precisely, an act of intention) is operative only in situations of conflicting needs. Piaget's is the narrowest conception, since he linked will directly to morality, claiming that it emerges in middle childhood and asserting that it is operative only when a weaker though morally superior force opposes a stronger though morally inferior force.

Considering the occurrences within James's theory that require fiat to resolve a conflict, all three theories involve decision making among forces. To be logically consistent with the premise of being voluntary, the decision making would be a cognitive activity involving information processing, though that was not made specific by any of the three writers. As such, their theories seem quite compatible with theories of motivation that are based upon concepts of decision making and information processing.

In the three theories of will, the matter of energy and underlying needs is a point of some confusion. James did not discuss the relationship of will to needs, though I inferred from what he did say that will derives out of underlying needs. When a human organism experiences some need, it imagines an outcome that involves the satisfied need or the means to satisfaction of the need. It is that image which James called will and which, he said, precedes all voluntary behavior. In the event of a counterforce, one must make a decision that overcomes the counterforce and allows the desire to achieve fruition. I am left wondering, however, how the will works when it overcomes a counterforce; where does it get the energy to do so? Consider a situation in which a force is equal to or less than a counterforce. A fiat is necessary for the force to overcome the counterforce, thereby motivating the activity that had been imaged to create the force. The fiat must have some energy at its disposal independent of the force. Either the fiat itself needs to be motivated and therefore have an independent energy source, or it needs to be able to direct energy from some other source. But from where might it siphon energy? Surely not from the counterforce. It seems to me that the only sensible place would be some type of independent energy source.

Lewin asserted that quasi-needs—those tensions that arise from acts of will—are powered by the needs upon which they rest. Yet here too is a problem. If an act of intentionality resolves a struggle between needs and the act of intending has no reserve of energy independent of the needs that are in the struggle, then there is no basis for supposing that an intention could in fact resolve such a conflict of needs. It must either add force to one of the needs in conflict or subtract it from the other.

Piaget also failed to address adequately the relationship among will, need, and energy. His theory, like that of James and Lewin, was based on the relative strength of forces. He did say that will itself is not an energy source but that it directs energy. Yet he did not discuss how it directs or tell from where it gets the energy to direct. Since, for Piaget, will comes into play when morality clashes with needs and since will pushes the moral force to victory over the need, he seems to have implied that morality itself is a source of energy, that will works in opposition to basic needs, and that will supplements the energy of morality with energy from some unspecified source. These conclusions contradict Lewin and James in that Lewin stated specifically and James implied that willed activities must be based in needs of the organism. The three theories are similar, however, in that they all failed to concretize the motivational basis of will.

I propose that the act of willing is motivated by one's intrinsic need for competence and self-determination and therefore has the energy of intrinsic motivation available to it. First, I offer a characterization of will and then discuss its intrinsic motivational basis.

## Will and Self-Determination Defined

*Will is the capacity of the human organism to choose how to satisfy its needs.* This means, first, that people can decide among the behavioral options that are available or that they can create for themselves. As Lewin (1951, p. 136) stated, "The extraordinary liberty which [a human] has to intend . . . actions . . . is amazing." Second, it means that will is capable of managing motives so as to attempt satisfaction of as many as possible while holding the others in abeyance. Will involves flexibility in behavior that follows from people's ability to utilize information, as they interpret it, so as to pursue satisfaction of their own needs within the context of their environments. People are able to choose, and their choosing operates lawfully. The governing law is attempted need satisfaction given one's understanding and interpretation of oneself functioning in the environment.

People's will is not wholly free, of course. There are a variety of boundaries and limitations to one's actions and to one's capacity to disattend to pressing needs. Forces in the person and the environment constitute limitations to one's will, and these limitations, like the will itself, operate in understandable, lawful ways.

*Self-determination is the process of utilizing one's will.* This involves accepting one's boundaries and limitations, recognizing the forces operating on one, utilizing the capacity to choose, and enlisting the support of various forces to satisfy one's needs.

Will, the capacity for conscious choices to determine behavior, is inextricably involved with the intrinsic need for competence and self-determination. The capacity and the need go hand in hand. People need to will; they need to be self-determining and competent, and that requires that they make choices. People would not be satisfied if all their drives were somehow automatically satisfied without their making choices and being creative and competent in carrying out those choices. People need to decide and to act on the environment. Intrinsic motivation, the human need to be competent and self-determining in relation to the environment, energizes people's will. The process of willing is powered by intrinsic motivation and therefore has at its disposal the energy of intrinsic motivation to oppose or supplement the force of drives, to resolve conflicts among needs, and to hold needs in abeyance.

Willing is a necessary aspect of healthy human functioning. Just as not being able to satisfy one's hunger need leads to sickness and eventually to death, evidence is mounting to indicate that not being able to satisfy one's need for self-determination can lead to sickness and eventually to death.

The conceptualization of intrinsic motivation as a basic human need for feeling competent and self-determining provides a framework for the study of self-determination and will, and it provides a means to handle the difficult energy problem that was left unresolved in the earlier theories of will.

Since one aspect of intrinsic motivation is the need to be self-determining, one's intrinsic need will be gratified whenever one behaves willfully. If one is self-determining in the service of the hunger drive, one will experience some intrinsic gratification for having self-determined in addition to the gratification one gets from satisfying one's hunger. That does not mean that hunger is an intrinsic need, nor that eating is intrinsically motivated; it means that the process of being self-determining is intrinsically motivated, and if one is self-determining in relation to eating, one will experience intrinsic rewards while also satisfying the hunger drive. One can achieve many goals either in a relatively free, self-determining fashion or in a relatively bounded, mechanistic fashion. Regardless of the nature of the goal, the self-determining mode of achieving it will yield some intrinsic gratification, whereas the bounded, automatic mode will not.

## Willing and "Willing"

The concept of will has been employed most frequently to account for behavior that seems contraindicated by drive concepts. For example, Lewin (1951, p. 115) stated, *"Only when there is no natural need for an action, or where there is a counter-need, is it necessary to form an intention."* Piaget discussed will as a regulator of energy that allows morality to counteract dives. And James spoke of a fiat to overcome an opposition. In each of these cases, the characterization of will is similar to the common usage of will, willpower, or determination. One wills, as with gritted teeth, to overcome some strong force, whether internal or environmental. One wills abstinance from a tempting dessert; one wills perseverance in a frightful storm. Such behaviors do require a nondrive-based construct like will to be explained adequately. On the other hand, there are many behaviors that are volitional and are in the service of drives. These too would be considered willful, since they involve choice among behavioral options; they are free in the sense of following from decisions that are based on processing of varied pieces of information. The important point is that drive-based behaviors are not always automatic; they do not always follow from S-R associations. They often depend on interpreting the stimulus event, seeking relevant information, and choosing among a variety of behavioral possibilities.

I am suggesting that there are two somewhat different types of willful or volitional behavior. The first is willing in the gritting-one's-teeth sense and involves the enlistment of energy from one's intrinsic need for self-determination to counteract a strong drive such as hunger or a strong environmental force. The second type can be characterized better by the sense of being willing to do something. This is more a willingness or an allowing than a determination and involves being aware of one's needs and guiding the processes of need satisfaction. The common element to these two types of willing is that both involve volition or choice rather than the mechanization or automatization of conditioned or overlearned behaviors.

May (1969a, 1969b) distinguished between intentionality and willpower, the former involving a movement in accord with one's organismic condition and the latter involving a forcing of oneself to act in opposition to one's organismic desires. This distinction is similar to the two types of willing I have suggested. May emphasized that willpower, which was evident in Victorian moralism, involves rationalization and self-deceit. Lewin, similarly, stated that intensive willing involves suppressing or concealing the motives that lost the struggle for control.

The more intensive form of willing, as I have characterized it, often involves either self-deceit or concealment from others, though it need not involve either. People often use their will to hold strong needs in abeyance, and frequently they are quite aware of these needs and may even express them to others. Deceit is not the will's purpose; however, people may use deceit as a way of easing the struggle between opposing needs and as a way of presenting themselves more positively to others.

Often we see people resolve to abstain from something and then proceed to do the very thing from which they vowed abstention. It is likely that these situations involve considerable self-deceit and are precisely the situations that led Lewin to the paradox that if one has no genuine need for an action one must will, yet when one wills without the support of a genuine need, the willing is doomed to failure. If one resolves without recognizing the extent to which one is bounded and without acknowledging the true strength of various internal forces such as drives, then indeed one's resolutions will be for naught. Yet Lewin did not leave room for the successful willing of behavior in opposition to genuine needs by using one's intrinsic motivational energy to counteract the genuine need. To the extent that one is clear rather than deceitful about the strength of the genuine needs that one is opposing, and to the extent that one has access to one's intrinsic motivation rather than being blocked from it, then one can counteract one's genuine needs successfully.

In the less intense form of willing, self-deceit is far less probable. The archetype of this process if following one's interest. One behaves in conjunction with needs, and the function of will is to keep out distractions, to keep one focused. It is a process akin to guiding a moving vessel; no pushing, simply an artful directing, is required. This is not passivity; it is activity of a different sort from the intense determination of countering strong forces.

*Willfulness*

We have seen that will is the combination of a capacity to choose satisfying behaviors and a need to choose satisfying behaviors, that is, to be self-determining. This raises the question of whether will exists in equal amounts for all people. Observation reveals quite clearly that it does not. Some people demonstrate far greater amounts of willfulness than others. They may fast for days, endure considerable pain, or barge into a frightening situation, while others give in to the urges to eat or to avoid pain or fear. Or they may explore an inner fascination, guide the expression of a feeling with oils on a canvas, or prepare a subtly delectable meal, while others ignore the inner experiences and turn out a slapdash painting or meal. I am suggesting that willfulness be conceptualized as an individual difference variable that reflects the extent to which people utilize their will.

White (1959) proposed that people have a "sense of competence," which I would elaborate as a "sense of competence and self-determination." This is precisely what is meant by willfulness. A stronger sense of competence and self-determination represents the basis of greater willfulness; a weaker sense of competence and self-determination underlies lesser willfulness. One's sense of competence and self-determination results from one's history of effective and ineffective interactions with the environment. These interactions influence one's willfulness and in turn have various consequences.

Placing someone on a personality dimension such as willfulness or sense of competence and self-determination is a kind of averaging process. People have a greater sense of competence and self-determination in some domains and a lesser sense in others. And even in the same domain sometimes they are willful and sometimes not. So creating a personality dimension and placing people along it is a simplifying process that serves a purpose of classifying people and explaining variance in behavior, yet it also does a disservice in that it collapses some of a person's rich variability into a single number.

One mistake often made by psychologists and lay people alike is to assume an either/or stance in relation to individual characteristics. A person is thought to be either dominant or submissive, free or constrained, strong or weak, anxious or confident, angry and aggressive or loving and docile. Such a point of view may be useful and accurate in the averaging sense, but it fails to recognize one of the fundamental aspects of human functioning: that these characteristics exist complementarily. Where one exists, the other exists as well. Generally one is more central, yet where one exists as figure the other is ground, where one is in foreground, the other is in background. These characteristics are different parts of the person whose interactions explain much of the behavior that people find puzzling. Utilizing this point of view allows one to understand sets of seemingly inconsistent behaviors—behaviors that seem inconsistent with one's central characteristics. People who display strong will also have a part that is weak-willed. There will be times when they choose to behave in the latter way and times when they fall into behaving that way without choosing to do so.

Recognizing the variability in responding and the interplay of different aspects of the person allows a framework for education and treatment that makes fuller use of one's potentials. For example, people who are rigidly strong-willed might find themselves in interpersonal or intrapsychic difficulty because of that characteristic. Recognizing that the rigidity in this responding may be a way of avoiding one's weak-willed or submissive aspect provides an opportunity for understanding and treating the difficulty. Utilizing an idea such as interacting parts or characteristics of the person sacrifices parsimony and simplicity of prediction for the gain of greater understanding. This trade-off is, of course, the basis of continual debate in the science of psychology. The more superficial one's framework for the study of behavior, the less one is willing to recognize polarities and their interplay.

There is utility in conceptualizing people in terms of their degree of willfulness, their general sense of competence and self-determination, for it explains variance in behavior and allows for empirical research. But it is also important to realize that this involves a focus on a dominant aspect of the person and ignores other interacting aspects.

## Intrinsic Motivation

The distinction between intrinsic and extrinsic motivation is frequently made on the basis of whether there is an externally mediated reward or constraint present in the situation. When people receive a reward such as money, praise, or the avoidance of punishment for doing an activity, they are considered to be extrinsically motivated. If there is no apparent external reward, they are said to be intrinsically motivated. In the latter case, the reward is supposed to be in the activity itself.

This definition is useful as an operational one in the experimental tradition. The key elements are readily observable, verifiable, and quantifiable, and therefore they lend themselves to experimental procedures. Yet it is also a superficial definition bearing little relationship to the human psyche and therefore does little to further our understanding of human motivation. For me, the study of human motivation is the study of human needs and the dynamic processes related to these needs.

Systems for understanding motivation have developed in two quite separate settings: the therapy room and the experimental laboratory. In the realm of therapy, Freud's work has been by far the most influential. As expanded and clarified by Rapaport (1960), Freudian theory represents an approach to motivational phenomena and personality development that has guided clinical work for several decades. Within the same general realm, humanistic theorists (such as Perls 1973) have rejected, expanded, elaborated, and refuted his theory. Still, all this work has had very little impact on the academic area of motivation theory. Instead motivation theory has developed primarily from laboratory experimental studies with rats, monkeys, and more recently, people.

The beginning of the area of motivation theory is largely attributable to the work of Hull (1943) who postulated and refined a drive theory of motivation as an integral part of his learning theory. His theory was behavioristic in that it placed central importance on associative bonds that developed as a result of the reinforcement process of drive reduction. It differed from Watsonian behaviorism in that Hull did postulate about internal processes. It also differed from current organismic theories in that Hull did not consider the thoughts, feelings, or attitudes that make up a person's phenomenology to be causal determinants of behavior. Instead he utilized nonphenomenological concepts such as "effective reaction potential" and "habit strength." These related to the primary drives that have their bases in the non-nervous system tissue deficits, and they related to secondary reinforcement processes that develop out of the primary drives.

The commonality between Freud's psychoanalytic theory of motivation and Hull's reinforcement theory of motivation is that both were drive theories; they asserted that the primary drives and their derivatives were the basis of all motivated behavior. In both of these approaches to the study of motivation, the need for a concept such as intrinsic motivation became apparent. In psychoanalytic psychology, this need emerged from the observation that ego functions related to growth, development, and mastery appeared at times and in ways that did not seem consistent with the idea that the ego is a derivative of the id and results from clashes of the id and the environment. This reasoning led Hartmann (1958) and White (1963) to propose the concept of an idependent ego-energy.

In experimental psychology, the need for this concept emerged from studies of exploratory and manipulative behaviors. Studies indicated that animals seemed to need a certain amount of stimulation to function effectively; that they would endure pain such as crossing an electrified grid to have the opportunity to explore; and that exploration and manipulation could be used as reinforcements to strengthen other responses. The initial reaction to these findings was the positing of a variety of new drives, such as a manipulative drive (Harlow 1953), an exploratory drive (Montgomery 1954), and a sensory drive (Isaac 1962). This, however, seemed quite inadequate as a means of handling the new findings both because the list of drives seemed to be growing rapidly and because these new drives did not conform to the definition of drive (see White 1959). They were not based in tissue deficits that led to consummatory action and produced learning.

Drive theory was also used in other ways to try to account for the newer data. Exploratory and manipulative behaviors were said to reduce anxiety, yet this explanation was inadequate since animals seemed to behave in ways that would, utilizing this approach, be interpreted as increasing rather than decreasing anxiety. Secondary reinforcement was also tried as an explanation, yet this too must be ruled out since, as Berlyne (1966) noted, avid exploration appears so soon after birth that secondary reinforcement could not possibly account for it. Further, in laboratory studies, exploration resisted extinction even when there was no repairing with primary drive reduction.

The inability of drive theory to account for the phenomena of exploration and manipulation has probably been the most important factor in the shift away from drive theory as a focus of motivation theorists and toward intrinsic motivation as an explanatory concept. Other than the attempts to explain intrinsically motivated behaviors with drive-theory concepts, there have been two classes of explanations. The first focuses on the organism's need for an optimal level of physiological or psychological stimulation. Hebb (1955), for example, postulated that organisms need an optimal level of arousal in the physiology of the central nervous system for effective functioning. Thus responses that move the organism toward its optimum are strengthened.

Most of the theorizing about optimal stimulation has dealt with the psychology rather than physiology of the person, suggesting that people need to maintain an optimum of psychological incongruity (see, McClelland et al. 1953; Dember and Earl, 1957; Hunt 1965). In this view, exploratory and manipulative behaviors are seen as being aimed at providing incongruity. In situations of overstimulation, behaviors would be directed toward the reduction of incongruity. This approach therefore has the advantage of being able to explain behavior that serves either to induce or to reduce incongruity.

The second and more widely used conceptualization of intrinsic motivation has evolved out of the work of White (1959). He proposed that people have a need to be effective in their interactions with the environment. This need is a basic motivational propensity that is persistent and energizes such things as exploration, attention, thought, and play. Behaviors motivated by competence or effectance motivation are purposive and directed rather than random or chance occurrences. In a similar vein, deCharms (1968) suggested that people have a basic motivation for experiencing themselves as causal agents in their interactions. He stated that people strive to be the origin of their behavior rather than pawns to the environment and that this desire for personal causation contributes to all motives.

Elaborating on the work of White, Hunt, Berlyne, deCharms, and others, I proposed (Deci 1975) that intrinsically motivated behaviors are based in people's need to be competent and self-determining in relation to their environment. This need, which is based in the central nervous system, is ever-present and motivates ongoing thoughts and behaviors unless it is interrupted by basic drives or emotional responses. The need for competence and self-determination leads people to *seek* out and *conquer* challenges that are optimal for their capacities. These challenges can be viewed as incongruities that exist between a stimulus input and some internal structure of the organism, thereby reconciling the two approaches to conceptualizing intrinsic motivation.

Hunt (1965) suggested that people need to maintain an optimal level of psychological incongruity, but that represents only one part of the ongoing process of instrinsic motivation. People do, indeed, seek out situations of optimal incongruity (or optimal challenge); however, their goal is not to maintain this optimal level. Rather they seek the optimal level as part of the life process of seeking and reducing optimal incongruities. The latter part relates to what Kagan (1972) has called uncertainty reduction and Festinger (1957) has called dissonance reduction. People need to reduce the incongruity (or uncertainty or dissonance) once they have found it. The cyclical process of seeking and conquering challenges that are optimal for one's capacities represents the heart of intrinsically motivated behavior. The need is for being competent and self-determining, and the processes of seeking and conquering the challenges lead to the satisfaction of that need: the feeling of competence and self-determination.

Piaget (1952) proposed that children are intrinsically motivated to encounter situations that are moderately but not completely assimilable. This means that children are attracted to situations that partially match an existing cognitive structure. Some aspects of the situation will be assimilated or made to fit the structure. Other aspects will be accommodated to; people will modify their existing cognitive structure to reflect the situation. This exemplifies the process whereby children seek and then conquer, through accommodation, a moderate challenge. If a situation is overly challenging—if, in other words, it is not at all assimilable—it would be avoided since the child would be unable to assimilate and accommodate to the new material. If the situation is not at all challenging, it would be fully assimilable and therefore not interesting to the child.

Intrinsic motivation is innate to the human organism and develops in rather systematic ways. Hunt (1965) has outlined the epigenesis of intrinsic motivation in infants, pointing out that the seeking of optimal challenges begins to emerge clearly as purposive behavior around the ninth month. Intrinsic motivation begins as a basic undifferentiated need to use one's capacities in an effective and autonomous manner in dealing with the environment. As the child acquires a history of interactions with the environment, the basic need begins to differentiate into specific needs—for achievement, self-actualization, cognizance, and so on (White 1959; Deci 1975).

The differentiation process has two key determinants. First, as Woodworth (1918) suggested, people's "native equipment" or innate capacities are likely to be utilized. Thus, for example, if people's native equipment allows them to be intellectuals, one might expect them to tend toward the development of a need for cognizance. The second element is the socialization process. The behavioral alternatives available to people and the reward contingencies present for them will also influence the way their intrinsic motivation becomes channeled into specific needs. A child raised in a home where several family members derive great pleasure from musical camaraderie and performance is more likely to channel intrinsic motivation toward music than is a child raised with no exposure to music.

McClelland (1961) has reported research indicating that certain child-rearing practices seem to precede people's achievement motivation in a predictable way. Parents who expect and reward independence and achievement behaviors in their children, especially when the mother is warm and affectionate, tend to foster high achievement motivation in their children. These kinds of child-rearing patterns influence the differentiation of the general need for competence and self-determination into the intrinsic need for achievement.

Earlier, I criticized the drive-naming approach to intrinsic motivation, and yet my approach of conceptualizing intrinsic motivation as a need for competence and self-determination is similar to drive-naming in a very superficial sense. The present approach is, however, fundamentally different. First, and perhaps foremost, the criticism of drive-naming is primarily a criticism of drive theory as an explanation of behavior. Specifically it is a criticism of the mechanistic, associationistic characteristics of drive theory and of the focus on the equilibrium-disequilibrium in non-central-nervous-system tissues as the heart of all motivation. Second, the idea of a need for competence and self-determination is a much broader concept than, say, a drive for visual exploration (Butler 1953). The naming of specific, narrowly defined drives has little utility for integration and explanation of wide ranges of behavior. A generalized need for competence and self-determination has enormous potential as an integrative concept that allows for the development of systems of explanation and derivation. Indeed this book and a previous book about intrinsic motivation (Deci 1975) constitute attempts to use that concept in an integrative way. How much behavior can one integrate with the concept of a drive for visual exploration?

## Cognitive Evaluation Theory

In recent years, a considerable amount of research has been carried out to investigate the effects of extrinsic rewards on intrinsic motivation. What, for example, might happen to a child's interest in drawing if the child is given candy for each picture; or what might happen to a person's fascination for math problems once the person has begun to get graded on them?

In a typical experiment, subjects—either children or adults—who were responding to some involving (target) activity, such as puzzles, toys, or art materials, were either rewarded or not rewarded with things like money, awards, or praise for working at the activity. Following this phase of the experiment, subjects were given a period of free-choice responding in which they could work further with the target activity, become involved with some alternative activity, or do nothing. They were alone during this period, were unaware they were being observed, and did not expect to do any more puzzle-solving for the experimenter. It was reasoned that the more time they spent on the target activity when there were no reward contingencies present, the more intrinsically motivated they were for that activity.

Deci (1975) reported that when money or the avoidance of an aversive stimulus was used as reward for the completion of puzzle problems, the rewarded subjects displayed less involvement with puzzles during the free-choice period than did nonrewarded subjects. Thus the extrinsic rewards decreased subjects' intrinsic motivation for the puzzle activity. Lepper, Greene, and Nisbett (1973) found that good-player awards decreased children's intrinsic motivation for working with art materials. Deci and Ryan (1980) have reviewed more than four dozen research articles that have reported similar results along with various limiting conditions.

Previously I outlined a cognitive evaluation theory (Deci 1975) that has successfully integrated the experimental findings on the effects of extrinsic factors on intrinsic motivation. It suggested that there are two processes through which external factors can affect intrinsic motivation. The first involves the development of an instrumentality between the activity and the external reward or constraint such that the activity becomes a means of attaining the reward or complying with the constraint rather than something that is done simply for intrinsic reasons. Following the lead of Heider (1958) and deCharms (1968), I referred to this process as a *change in perceived locus of causality*, since that seems to provide a description of the perceptions and cognitions that accompany the underlying change in motivational processes. Whereas people perceive the locus of causality to be internal when they are intrinsically motivated, they perceive it to be external when extrinsic factors are present and the behavior is instrumental to attaining an external reward or satisfying an external constraint. People feel self-determining when they perceive the locus of causality to be internal and they feel nonself-determining when they perceive the locus of causality to be external.

Most studies on rewards, constraints, and intrinsic motivation have looked at the effects of the presence of rewards or constraints and the absence of choice. Thus the change in locus of causality process typically has been considered only in terms of the shift from internal to external. However, when there is a relative absence of controlling rewards or constraints and a presence of the opportunity for choice, the perceived locus of causality should become more internal, leaving people feeling more self-determining. Zuckerman et al. (1978) reported an experiment in which matched pairs of subjects worked on interesting puzzle activities. One member of each pair selected which three of six puzzles he or she would like to work with, whereas the matched subject was assigned the three puzzles chosen by the first subject. These subjects were run separately so that they did not know about the condition other than their own. We found that those subjects who had had choice—who had had greater opportunity for self-determination—spent significantly more free-choice time involved with the puzzles than did those subjects who had worked on the same puzzles without having had choice. I interpret this as indication that the perceived locus of causality became more internal; they felt more self-determining and were more intrinsically motivated.

Feedback to people about their performance on interesting activities can also affect their intrinsic motivation. Positive information about performance has been shown to increase intrinsic motivation, while negative information about performance has been shown to decrease intrinsic motivation (see Deci and Ryan 1980). According to cognitive evaluation theory, the second process through which intrinsic motivation can be affected involves a person's perceptions of competence vis-à-vis the activity being either enhanced or diminished. When one perceives oneself to be more competent as a result of an interaction with some activity, one's intrinsic motivation for the activity will be increased; when one perceives oneself to be less competent, one's intrinsic motivation will be diminished. Thus positive feedback will bolster intrinsic motivation, and negative feedback will undermine intrinsic motivation through this process of a *change in perceived competence*.

Just as feelings of more or less self-determination accompany the change in perceived locus of causality process, feelings of more or less competence accompany the change in perceived competence process. The cognitive and affective components work together and are tied into the underlying motivational processes.

I have asserted that a change in perceived competence will affect one's intrinsic motivation. For this relationship to be operative, however, one must be self-determining because forced competence will not leave one more intrinsically motivated. One sees oneself as being good at it, but one will not be intrinsically motivated; instead one will do it well to get the reward or satisfy the constraint. Similarly, forced incompetence will not decrease one's intrinsic motivation through the change in perceived competence, for one can readily attribute the incompetence to the external factors and therefore not feel incompetent. Of course, in either case, whether forced to be competent or incompetent, the force may decrease one's intrinsic motivation through the change in perceived locus of causality process, but the competence must be internally determined to affect intrinsic motivation through the change in perceived competence process. Fisher (1978) reported data to support this assertion; she found a correlation between perceived competence and intrinsic motivation only in self-determined conditions.

The point is that the self-determination aspect of intrinsic motivation is more fundamental than the competence aspect. Often self-determination and competence go hand in hand, though that is not always the case. When they are separate, the self-determination component is more critical for intrinsic motivation. A robot can be made competent, but a competent robot is not intrinsically motivated.

To summarize, intrinsic motivation will be undermined when extrinsic factors induce a change in perceived locus of causality from internal to external (with the accompanying decrease in feelings of self-determination) or when negative feedback induces a perception of incompetence (with the accompanying decrease in feelings of competence). Intrinsic motivation will be enhanced when situational factors (such as the absence of constraints and the presence of choice) induce a change in perceived locus of causality from external to internal (with the accompanying increase in feelings of self-determination) or when positive feedback induces the perception of comtence (with the accompanying increase in feelings of competence). For perceived competence to affect intrinsic motivation, it presupposes that the competence or incompetence was self-determined.

By suggesting that the perception of self-determined incompetence will decrease intrinsic motivation, I do not mean to imply that all information of self-determined nonsuccess will decrease intrinsic motivation through the change in perceived competence process. Trial-and-error learning, motivated by curiosity, is perhaps an archetype of intrinsically motivated behavior and necessarily involves some nonsuccess. One learns what does not work as well as what does work. The point is that the effects on intrinsic motivation of information about how one is doing at an activity depends on how the information is interpreted, how it is cognitively evaluated. If the person understands it as indication that the environment will not be responsive, that he or she cannot do the activity or produce the desired effects, it will undermine the person's perception of competence and leave the person less intrinsically motivated. If the information conveys that the goal is attainable and that path B rather than path A will move one toward the goal, then the negative information will not decrease intrinsic motivation. It is interesting to note that the same feedback may be interpreted by some people in one fashion and by others in the opposite fashion. In later chapters, when we consider personality orientations, we shall see why negative feedback may be useful to some people while leaving others helpless and nonresponsive.

I suggested that extrinsic rewards tend to decrease intrinsic motivation through the change in perceived locus of causality process, whereas positive feedback tends to increase intrinsic motivation through enhancing one's perceptions of competence. Actually extrinsic rewards often can convey positive, competence information just as feedback does. The presence or absence of a reward and the size of the reward often are used to provide information to people about their performance at an activity. For example, a monetary bonus implies that a person has been performing effectively. Thus rewards and other extrinsic factors may either decrease or increase intrinsic motivation. To understand how this occurs, one must recognize that every reward—whether money or praise, citations or candy bars—has two essential aspects. One aspect I have called a *controlling aspect* since it is the aspect of rewards that brings one's behavior under the control of the reward. The other aspect to every reward is an *informational aspect*, which conveys information about one's competence. Whether a reward decreases intrinsic motivation by changing the perceived locus of causality from internal to external or increases intrinsic motivation by enhancing one's perceptions of competence will depend upon *the relative salience of the two aspects of the reward*. When the controlling aspect of a reward is more salient, it will decrease one's intrinsic motivation by initiating the change in perceived locus of causality process; when the informational aspect is more salient (and when the information is positive), it will increase one's intrinsic motivation by initiating the change in perceived competence.

Cognitive evaluation theory is stated as a set of three propositions, the first two describing the processes of change in perceived locus of causality and change in perceived competence. The third proposition describes the two aspects of rewards and relates the salience of the two aspects to the two processes.

The relative salience process works more generally than I have previously stated. First, I suggest that there are controlling and informational aspects to many situational factors other than just rewards. Threats, punishments, and communications in general convey both control and information, and the salience of these two aspects of the external factor will determine the impact of that external factor. For example, in asking a question, one can convey competence information to the other person; asking the person may imply respect for him or her. But asking questions can be very controlling. One may ask as a way of manipulating. "Why did you do that?" may be a way of telling someone that he or she should not have done that.

The controlling versus informational aspect of any external event can initiate one or the other process described in cognitive evaluation theory. If the control aspect is salient and conveys self-determination, it will increase intrinsic motivation by shifting the perceived locus of causality from external to internal; if it is salient and conveys nonself-determination, it will decrease intrinsic motivation by shifting the perceived locus of causality from internal to external. On the other hand, if the informational aspect is salient and conveys competence, it will increase intrinsic motivation by enhancing one's perceived competence; if it is salient and conveys incompetence, it will decrease intrinsic motivation by diminishing one's perceived competence.

Three types of factors affect whether the controlling versus informational aspect of external events will be more salient for a person: characteristics of the rewardee, characteristics of the rewarder, and characteristics of the reward situation. First, different people are likely to interpret the same events differently. Deci, Cascio, and Krusell (1975), for example, reported that praise had different effects on males and females. Whereas it enhanced the intrinsic motivation of males (presumably by strengthening their perceived competence), it undermined the intrinsic motivation of females (presumably by inducing a change in perceived locus of causality from internal to external). Apparently socialization practices have tended to make the informational aspect of praise more salient for males and to make the controlling aspect of praise more salient for females. People's orientation toward causality will also affect whether they perceive various rewards as controlling or informational and whether they interpret feedback as conveying useful information or conveying that they are incompetent.

Second, characteristics of the rewarder or communicator will affect whether external events, such as the administration of rewards, are perceived as controlling or informational. For example, imagine one man who uses rewards to get other people to do what he wants them to do, in the way he wants it done, and at the time he wants it done. With this rather authoritarian approach, he will probably use rewards in a way that is perceived by the recipient to be very controlling; these rewards will tend to undermine intrinsic motivation. Then imagine a second man who uses rewards to convey to others that they are doing well at an activity. His attitude is supportive of the other people and facilitative of their doing the activity in their own way. This person will probably use rewards in a way that is perceived by the recipient as informational; these rewards will tend to strengthen intrinsic motivation.

To test this reasoning we (Deci, Nezlek, and Sheinman, in press) did a study in thirty-five public-school classrooms. We measured teachers' attitudes toward the use of rewards—whether they tended to be more controlling or more informational. We also measured the intrinsic motivation and self-esteem of the children in each of the classrooms. We found that the children who had teachers with an informational orientation toward the use of rewards were more intrinsically motivated and had a higher self-esteem than were children who had teachers with a more controlling orientation toward the use of rewards.

Third, aspects of the situation will affect the way external events are perceived and therefore will affect their impact on intrinsic motivation. It is possible, for example, to structure rewards in such a way as to convey positive competence information, in which case they will tend to enhance intrinsic motivation, whereas the same rewards, when administered with no attention to informative feedback, will tend to decrease intrinsic motivation. Enzle and Ross (1978) found that when monetary rewards were structured to convey positive competence information, they increased intrinsic motivation, whereas, when the same rewards were not structured to convey the positive information, they decreased intrinsic motivation.

### Motivational Subsystems

Feelings about self-determination and about competence accompany perceptions of the locus of causality and perceptions of competence. These perceptions and feelings are aspects of underlying motivational processes that organize a complex of interrelated changes in perceptions, feelings, performance (see McGraw 1978), and beliefs about self and others.

The concept of motivational subsystems is a means of explaining how people respond differently to various environments and how, when they are in different environments, there is a complex of consistent internal states that is operative. I am asserting that environmental factors do not cause behavior. Instead the interaction of environmental factors and personality factors invokes a particular motivational subsystem, and behaviors, as well as cognitions, feelings, and beliefs that are consistent with the subsystem, will follow from the operation of the subsystem. Just as environments do not cause behaviors, neither do cognitions. Although the simple statement of cognitive evaluation theory would seem to imply that perceptions cause behaviors and changes in internal states, I am claiming that cognitions or perceptions are an aspect of the underlying motivational subsystems. When a subsystem is invoked by an interaction of environment and personality, the subsystem has characteristic ways of processing information and responding.

A motivational subsystem is a set of affective experiences, beliefs, and attitudes about oneself, the environment, and others, and programs for interacting with one's environment. These internal states and processes and their corresponding behaviors are all organized by motivational processes. There are three motivational subsystems: intrinsic, extrinsic, and amotivational.

The intrinsic motivational subsystem is based in the need for competence and self-determination. It involves behavioral decision making (self-determined behavior), managing motives effectively, an internal perceived locus of causality, feelings of self-determination, and a high degree of perceived competence or self-esteem (Deci et al., in press). The extrinsic motivational subsystem is based in extrinsic motivation. It involves greater responsivity to external than to internal cues, and it involves behaviors for which the rewards are separable from the behaviors and the accompanying feelings. Whereas the rewards for the intrinsic subsystem are the feelings that accompany self-determined, competent behavior, the rewards for the extrinsic subsystem—for example, praise or money—are separable from the behavior and the integrally accompanying feelings. The perceived locus of causality for the extrinsic system is external and when operating extrinsically, people experience themselves as less self-determining than when they are operating intrinsically. Behaviors tend to be controlled by reward contingencies rather than by choices, and people's self-esteem tends to be somewhat lower than when they are intrinsically motivated. The amotivational subsystem is characterized by nonactivity. The accompanying perception is of no relationship between behaviors and rewards or outcomes, so there is no activity; the outcomes are unattainable. Perceived competence, self-determination, and self-esteem would tend to be extremely low. When the amotivational subsystem is operative, people will feel helpless; they will feel incompetent and out of control.

These three motivational subsystems parallel three different beliefs about the nature of causality (Heider 1958; Deci 1975). The intrinsic motivational subsystem involves a belief in the dependence of behavior and outcomes with the causality for behavior being seen as internal. The extrinsic motivational subsystem involves a belief in the dependence of behavior and outcomes with the causality for behavior being seen as external—in the outcomes and contingencies. The amotivational subsystem involves a belief in the independence of behavior and outcomes that implies a futility in behavior. I believe that it is useful to characterize people as having a particular personality orientation depending on which motivational subsystem—internal, external, or amotivational—tends to be predominant in their interactions with their surroundings. The characterization of these three personality orientations will appear in part II of the book.

The postulate of motivational subsystems and the various elements of each are highly speculative. There are, of course, data that suggest internal consistency among behaviors, attitudes, motives, and feelings; for example, the principles of balance (Heider 1958) and consistency (Abelson et al. 1968) have been the basis for much research that has demonstrated the interrelatedness of various internal states and behaviors. Still, the specific hypotheses about the components of the three subsystems deserve direct test.

*Subsystems and Cognitive Evaluation Theory*

In terms of cognitive evaluation theory, I suggest that the process labeled a change in perceived locus of causality is really a change from the intrinsic to extrinsic or the extrinsic to intrinsic subsystems, which is reflected in people's perceptions as a change in locus of causality. In the extrinsic motivational subsystem, people may be highly competent even when they are pawns to external contingencies rather than self-determined. The change in perceived competence process involves a shift from the extrinsic to amotivational or the amotivational to extrinsic subsystems if behavior is nonself-determined, or from the intrinsic to amotivational, or the amotivational to intrinsic when the behavior is self-determined. The intrinsic subsystem includes an internal locus of causality and a high degree of perceived competence. The extrinsic subsystem includes an external locus of causality but can include a moderate to high degree of perceived competence (when someone is a pawn to contingencies, that person may behave very competently to get the desired outcomes). The amotivational subsystem involves an external locus of causality and perceived incompetence.

The concept of motivational subsystems is useful in interpreting an interesting aspect of the results in the Deci et al. (in press) study: the finding that the effects of teacher characteristics on children had come about during the first six weeks of the school year and then remained constant over the remainder of the year. Children, being relatively flexible, tended to respond to the teacher and classroom environment by operating out of the motivational subsystem that was correspondent. With more-controlling teachers, children utilized an extrinsic system, displaying less intrinsic motivation and lower self-esteem. With more-informational teachers, the children utilized an intrinsic subsystem, displaying greater intrinsic motivation and higher self-esteem. The key point is that the adaptation occurred within the first six weeks and remained constant over the next seven months. Utilizing a concept such as trait to account for intrinsic motivation and self-esteem would suggest a slower and continual adaptation, whereas the concept of subsystems, with consistent, existing (though modifiable) programs and interrelationships among various internal variables, is consistent with the relatively rapid adaptation that remains constant over the period that the situation remains constant. This study was done with children, and it is probable that they may be more flexible than all older people, so it is possible with adults that the adaptation may not be so rapid. Still, the observed consistencies among internal variables argues for the use of the subsystem concept.

In psychology there has been much debate about consistency across situations versus situational determination. They hypothesis that motivational subsystems are invoked by an interplay of the situation and the person and the motivational subsystems organize a consistent operation of affective, cognitive, and behavioral aspects of the person provides an answer to the difficult problem of situational specificity. There would be consistency within subsystems and across the various situations for which a subsystem is operative, but there would be inconsistency across the situations that invoke different subsystems.

*Cognition or Motivation*

Recent trends in theorizing (see, for example, Bandura 1977; Mischel 1979) have focused only on cognitive variables as mediators between stimuli and responses. My assertion is that motivational variables are the more fundamental mediators and that cognitive variables are aspects of underlying motivational processes. There are two reasons why it is important to move deeper into the person and study motivational rather than just cognitive variables. First, there is the question of why cognitive variables affect behavior. Why, for example, do efficacy expectations (Bandura 1977) promote effective behavior? My answer is that the person needs to be efficacious (competent and self-determining), and those behaviors that allow the person to feel efficacious will be undertaken. Second, there is evidence from clinical literature of self-deceptions around efficacy and self-determination, and the clinical evidence suggests a closer match between the motivation and behavior than the cognitions and behavior. For example, people who are confident that they can and will stop smoking often do not stop smoking. The motivational elements rather than the cognitions seem to determine the behavior. The point is simple: there is more to the person than cognitions, and if one is willing to consider person variables (rather than just environmental variables), the theorizing needs to include motivational and affective considerations. These may be more difficult to study, yet an ever-expanding research literature on intrinsic motivation (see Deci and Ryan 1980) attests to the possibility of studying these concepts and to the utility of the concepts for integrating divergent research findings. The characterization of motivational subsystems involves much speculation, yet it can provide a framework for empirical exploration that aims at an integration of various person variables with situation variables.

## Intrinsic Motivation and Will

Intrinsic motivation is based in a generalized, innate need to feel competent and self-determining. I use both terms, *competence* and *self-determination*, to emphasize the breadth and nature of intrinsic motivation even though the two concepts are related integrally. Competence emphasizes doing something well; self-determination emphasizes deciding for oneself. Of the two, self-determination is more fundamental and is necessary for intrinsic motivation. If one is forced to do something well, one will not experience intrinsic satisfaction; to the extent that the person feels satisfaction in that situation, it will be of an extrinsic, obedience-approval type. Conversely if one is feeling self-determining in a situation, one is less likely to feel like a failure when one initially does poorly on a task. Self-determination allows one to try out new activities, to explore new spaces, and to experience gratification from the exploration. However, if repeated attempts continue to prove unsuccessful, if one is unable to produce the desired effects after trying hard and being committed to doing well, the nonsuccess will affect one's perception of efficacy and then will have a negative effect on intrinsic motivation. The fullness of intrinsic satisfaction associated with doing well necessitates being self-determining, and the experience of being self-determining allows one to have some failures without their negatively affecting intrinsic motivation.

Intrinsic motivation, the need to be competent and self-determining, energizes the process of willing—that is, the process of utilizing one's capacity to choose what motive satisfaction to pursue and how to behave. The process of choosing provides gratification to one's intrinsic need to be self-determining in addition to whatever other motives (such as a basic drive) may be satisfied by the chosen behaviors. And the process of choosing maintains or strengthens one's intrinsic motivation. This assertion was supported by the Zuckerman et al. (1978) study.

The opportunity to be self-determining (or willful) has intrinsically motivating properties. Furthermore, when people are denied the opportunity to be self-determining they lose motivation, their performance and learning become impaired, they may become ill, and in some cases they may die. Clearly there is a human need to will, to be self-determining, since evidence confirms that willing has motivating properties and that being denied the opportunity to will can cause sickness.

# 3 An Organismic Theory of Motivation

I have classified all behaviors into three broad categories: those that are voluntary or chosen—in other words, self-determined behaviors; those that were initially in the domain of voluntary responding but have become either automatic or automatized; and those that are determined by the structural and physiological properties of the organism as exemplified by reflexes. An adequate theory of motivation must provide an account of the first two categories; those in the third category are generally considered to be outside the realm of motivation theory.

Behavioral theories (Hull 1943; Skinner 1953) have not acknowledged the distinction between the behaviors of the first two categories; instead all nonreflexive behaviors have been said to be conditioned through reinforcement processes. Skinnerian theory generally ignored motivational factors; in experimental studies, for example, motivation was handled simply by depriving animals of the substance, like food or water, that would be used as a reinforcer. In Hullian theory, the motivational variables were given central importance, though the theory ignored intrinsic motivation, and the variables that were considered were nonphenomenological and mechanistic. I contend that a theory of motivation must recognize the intrinsic need for competence and self-determination as a basic, innate motivational propensity and that the role of phenomenological variables such as choice and desire must be recognized as causal factors in behavior so that the important distinction between the first two categories of behavior can be made clearly.

Cognitive theories of motivation (for example, Lewin 1938; Peak 1955; Atkinson 1964; Vroom 1964) have focused on decision making as the core of their theories, and they have outlined specific formulations for the prediction of behavioral choices. Atkinson's and Vroom's theories are referred to as expectancy theories of motivation and have derived out of the earlier work of Lewin (1938) and Tolmon (1932). The central assertion in this approach is that motivation to engage in a behavior is a multiplicative function of two variables: the valence (or psychological value of the outcomes which could follow from the behavior) times the subjective probability or expectancy that the behavior will lead to those outcomes.

A second thrust within the cognitive approach to motivation has studied the way people attribute or infer their own motivations. This approach, which developed out of Heider's (1958) commonsense psychology, suggests that people observe their own behavior and the situation within which it occurs. They process that information, considering variables such as effort, ability, luck, and task difficulty to conclude whether they did an activity because they liked it, were forced to do it, or could get a reward for doing it. The approach asserts that people's subsequent behavior in similar situations will be determined by these self-attributions, so the attributions provide the basis for behavioral predictions (Weiner 1972).

Cognitive theorists agree that there is considerable utility in assuming that people choose what to do by assessing the likely outcomes of their actions. Further, their theories underscore the importance of information as it is perceived and interpreted by the person, thereby emphasizing that behavior should be analyzed in terms of people's interpretation of stimulus events rather than in terms of the objective stimulus events. The cognitive approach maintains that behavior is lawful and predictable; however, the lawfulness must be understood in terms of people's cognitions and motives rather than in terms of external (objective) stimuli, responses, and reinforcements. The guiding law in the expectancy theories is that people will choose to behave in ways that maximize their expected outcomes, as they perceive them.

Cognitive theories represent an important break from behavioral theories in that they emphasize the role of choice in the determination of behavior. However, they tend to have three major shortcomings. First, they tend to give little attention to the nature of human needs that underlie the choice process, focusing instead on the valences of outcomes without exploring the human needs out of which the valences derive. Bandura (1977), for example, specifically criticized attempts to posit underlying needs or motives, suggesting that since they cannot be measured independent of the cognitions or behaviors they produce, they are not useful concepts. Second, cognitive theories fail to give proper consideration to the role of emotions in the motivational process, viewing them instead as interferences to motivational processes. Emotions play a vital role in the motivation of behavior, and some theorists even assert that they are the central motivational construct (Izard 1977). Finally, cognitive theories of motivation overemphasize the role of choice, treating all behaviors as if they were chosen. They fail to acknowledge that some behaviors have become automatic or automatized, thereby short-circuiting the choice process. Like the behavioral theorists, they make no distinction between voluntary and automatized responding; however, whereas the behaviorists see all behavior as conditioned (automated), cognitivists tend to see all behavior as chosen.

The final criticism may be countered by saying that cognitive expectancy theories are "as if" theories rather than actual descriptions of people's psychological processes. In other words, one would say that people do not actually go through a process of assessing such things as valences and subjective probabilities and then decide how to behave based on these calculations; rather these formulations are useful because behavior is determined by some processes that work as if people were making these calculations. If that is so, then the theories may have utility for predictive purposes, yet they are not really furthering our understanding of human behavior because they are not attempting to describe the processes that actually determine human behavior.

This chapter outlines what I call an organismic approach to the study of human motivation. For me, the term *organismic* signifies a number of distinct characteristics. Most importantly, it conveys the sense of an active, living organism as opposed to a passive mechanism or a robot. It does not oppose the idea of determinism; it simply implies that people's thoughts, feelings, and motives constitute unique determinative elements in their behavior. It connotes flexibility in responding, and it explores the interplay between flexibility and boundedness in behavior. It accepts the importance of one's experience and emphasizes that one's phenomenological interpretation of inputs rather than the objective elements of the inputs represents the stimulus for responding. It acknowledges a range of human motives that is wider than the tissue-deficit drives. It focuses on attempted need satisfaction as the organizing principle for voluntary behavior. And it addresses the behaviors that have become either automatic or automatized and have, to a greater or lesser extent, moved out of the arena of voluntary responding.

**Self-Determined Behavior**

Self-determined behaviors involve people's deciding how to behave based on their expectations about how to achieve satisfaction of their needs. The theory utilizes an information-processing framework. The central nervous system, called the central processor, obtains stimulation through the sense receptors and organizes it into units that have meaning in terms of existing cognitive structures and affective processes. This interpretive process is an active one, as we have learned from the Gestalt psychologists such as Koehler (1947); the central processor arranges bits of information into recognizable wholes.

An information-processing approach typically has viewed the person as a passive receiver and processor of information (see Ryan and Deci, in press). As such, the organismic theory, though using an information-processing framework, stands in contrast to other information-processing theories. I consider the organism to be active such that motivational and affective processes lead it to seek relevant information, to block out unwanted information, and to organize and interpret information in unique, though understandable, ways.

The information-processing model involves the use of informational inputs to make decisions about how to behave and to guide the organism toward the completion of the chosen behaviors and the satisfaction of salient needs. This process of guidance is based on the use of expectancies to which one compares one's existing state and decides how to continue. Miller, Galanter, and Pribram (1960) discussed the way in which this occurs and proposed what they called a TOTE unit to describe the process. People's behavior is purposive and aimed toward the attainment of some standard; periodically they *T*est their existing state against the standard; if there is a discrepancy, they *O*perate to reduce the discrepancy; again they *T*est; and if there is a match they *E*xit from the sequence. The standards can be conceptualized usefully as cognitions, though they may be based in affective processes or tissue deficits. The completion of a TOTE cycle also may be compared to the completion of a gestalt (Koehler 1947) or the satisfaction of a quasi-need (Lewin 1951). People strive to complete TOTEs or to finish business.

This process of TOTE-governed behavior represents the structure of behaving that is energized by the ongoing, cyclical, intrinsically motivated process of seeking and conquering challenges (Deci 1975)—that is, of selecting a standard that is optimally discrepant (Hunt 1965) or moderately assimilable (Piaget 1952) and then behaving to reduce the incongruity or accommodate to and assimilate the material. Behaviors motivated by tissue deficits (drives) may be similarly understood using the TOTE unit as a general structure. Here the expected satisfaction of the drive is the standard against which people compare their existing state and then operate to achieve the standard if there is a discrepancy between the state and the standard. The basic structure of the TOTE process is illustrated in figure 3-1.

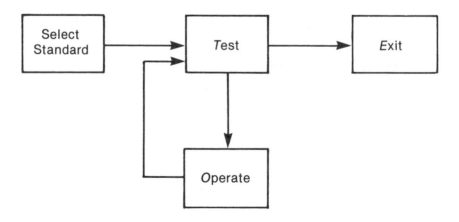

Source: Miller, Galanter, and Pribram 1960.

**Figure 3-1.** A TOTE Unit

Self-determined behavior is characterized as an entire sequence that commences with informational inputs and terminates when its purpose has been achieved, (that is when the motive or motives at the heart of the sequence have been satisfied). In actuality, behavior is ongoing, yet breaking the ongoing flow of behavior into such sequences allows a causal analysis of behavior.

The first phase in a sequence of self-determined behavior is the receipt of stimulus inputs by the central processor. These inputs of information come from three sources: they may be sensations received from the environment through the sense receptors; they may be internal sensations from the tissues of the organism; or they may be bits of information accessed from memory storage. One might, for example, see a pizza parlor and smell pizza cooking; this is information from the environment. In addition one might register a disequilibrium in blood sugar level and gastric motility; this is information from organismic tissues. And one might become aware that it has been five hours since eating; this is information from memory.

Self-determined behaviors do not necessitate external stimulus inputs to begin a sequence. Information from internal sources (the needs of the organism as they exist in the physiology and memory of the organism) may initiate a sequence that includes searching the environment for relevant stimulus inputs.

Informational inputs from the person and/or the environment enter conscious awarenesses and are interpreted as the potential for need satisfaction. For example, the inputs mentioned above would be interpreted as hunger and would leave the person desirous of satisfying the hunger. I shall refer to this second phase in a sequence of motivated behavior as the awareness of potential satisfaction. Kagan (1972) defined this cognitive representation of a future state as a motive. I shall use the term *conscious motive* interchangeably with *awareness of potential satisfaction*. Later I introduce the term *nonconscious motive*, so I shall typically specify whether a motive is conscious or nonconscious. In cases where it is clear that I am speaking of conscious motives, I may simply use *motive* since it is less cumbersome. In cognitive theories, nonconscious motives are not considered, so there is no need for the specification of types.

Conscious motives are the standard for the operation of a TOTE unit, to which I shall refer as the outer TOTE unit. The sequence now has its purpose: to achieve the satisfaction of which the person became aware, that is, to satisfy the motive. The term *(conscious) motive* as used here is an awareness or a cognition. The term is used by some people to refer to dispositions of the organism, for example, the achievement motive. I am not using it that way. These enduring dispositions are the things that I refer to as needs of the organism, such as the hunger need or the need for achievement. These dispositions exist in the tissues and memory of the organism. I shall refer to this set of dispositions as one's need structure. Thus a need structure is composed of needs that exist in the tissues and memory of the organism; is modifiable through experiences; and provides informational inputs that the central processing system interprets, in conjunction with inputs that it receives or selects from the environment, as conscious motives (as awarenesses of potential satisfaction).

The reason for distinguishing motives from needs is to emphasize that self-determined behavior is a function of a conscious awareness. These awarenesses, of course, derive from underlying properties of the organism here referred to as needs, and these needs exist in the form of a structure. (I am referring to the structure as a need structure since it is composed of needs, although I have somewhat misleadingly referred to it as a motive structure in much of my previous writing.)

Once people have become aware of potential satisfaction, they select behaviors that they expect will lead to the desired satisfaction. They choose what to do or, as some theorists would say, they select a goal. The goal would be either the completion of the selected behaviors in the case of intrinsically motivated behaviors, or the completion of the behaviors and the attainment of a reward in the case of extrinsically motivated behaviors. A goal, therefore, would be the plan to complete a behavior or a set of behaviors, perhaps in conjunction with an extrinsic reward; it should not be confused with the motive or the desired satisfaction. For example, a "hungry" woman has a motive to satisfy the hunger; she is aware that she could achieve a desired state in which there was quiescence in terms of hunger. The motive is to achieve that satisfaction. The specific means of achieving the satisfaction is irrelevant at the motive phase, though it emerges as centrally relevant at the goal-selection phase. The woman might decide to go out for an elegant Japanese dinner as a way of satisfying the motive. The plan to have the dinner is the goal. Eating a hamburger and french fries at home would be a different goal and would just as easily satisfy the hunger motive, though the woman may prefer one over the other for various reasons. In the case of intrinsic motivation, the motive is to feel competent and self-determining; the goal might be to climb a mountain or build a bird feeder.

One expects that the goal completion will produce the desired satisfaction; indeed the goal was selected because the person expected it to produce the satisfaction. Yet one decides in an uncertain and ambiguous world, so it may be that one's expectations will not be realized, goal completion may not lead to the desired satisfaction. If it does not, the person will return to select another goal, utilizing the new information. Again, of course, the selection will be based on expectations that the new goal will lead to the desired satisfaction.

This third phase in the sequence of self-determined behavior, behavioral decision making (or goal selection), is the common element of the various cognitive theories of motivation (for example, Lewin 1938; Atkinson 1964; Vroom 1964). People decide what behaviors to undertake (the goal) in pursuit of satisfaction of their motives. The selection of behavior becomes a second standard for the governing of a second TOTE unit, which operates within the first feedback loop (or TOTE unit). The larger feedback loop, called the outer TOTE unit, has the motive as its standard and exits when the satisfaction is achieved. The inner feedback loop has the goal as its standard and exits when the goal is achieved (that is, when the behavior is completed, and in some cases when the reward is received). The TOTE unit with the goal as its standard operates wholly within the TOTE unit that has the motive as its standard. First, the person selects a motive or set of motives; this sets up the overriding TOTE feedback loop. Then the person selects a goal that is intended to satisfy the motive(s); that sets up the inner TOTE feedback loop, which operates in a more immediate sense to govern the person's behavior. The goal was selected because the person expected that completion of the goal would lead to the desired satisfaction. If the person were correct, then goal completion would terminate the inner feedback loop and subsequently terminate the outer feedback loop. If the person's planning were incorrect, the goal attainment would terminate the inner loop, but it would not terminate the outer loop because the goal would not produce the desired satisfaction. Thus the overriding unit would still be operative and would lead the person to select a new goal and set up a new inner TOTE unit in anticipation that the attainment of this goal would produce the desired motive satisfaction.

Let me refer to the hunger example to illustrate. A woman who is said to be hungry is experiencing a motive; she is aware of some future satisfying state. Thus the motive is the standard for the outer TOTE unit. Then the woman decides to go for a Japanese dinner. That is the goal. She will continue to behave until she has accomplished the goal; she will get dressed up, travel to the restaurant, and so on. The goal of having the Japanese dinner organizes her behavior and therefore is the standard for the inner TOTE unit. When she leaves the restaurant, the inner TOTE unit will be completed, but she may or may not have completed the outer TOTE unit; she may or may not have satisfied her hunger. If she has, she is done with the motive for the time being; if not, she may select a new goal aimed at the same motive satisfaction. Perhaps she will decide to go for an ice cream sundae, in which case that is the new goal. One would hope that with the completion of that goal and that inner TOTE unit, the motive would also be satisfied and the outer TOTE unit would be terminated as well.

One can deduce easily that the fourth phase in the sequence of self-determined behavior is the purposive behavior aimed at achieving the goal. As people behave, they will be comparing where they are to where they want to be (the goal). Upon completion of the goal, the behavior will terminate. In cases where there is an extrinsic reward as an aspect of the goal, there are really two steps involved: completing the behaviors and obtaining the reward. In cases where there are no extrinsic rewards, the completion of the behaviors is the only aspect to the fourth phase. There has been a great deal of research on this phase of the sequence. As early as 1908, Yerkes and Dodson reported that performance will be maximized when the level of motivation is at an optimum—not too low or too high. That indicates that the quality of the goal-directed behavior is influenced by the strength of the motive. Locke (1968) has reported that the nature of the goal will influence performance (the behavioral phase). He stated, for example, that specific goals lead to better performance than do vague goals such as "to do as well as possible." More recently, McGraw (1978) has reviewed the literature on the effects of extrinsic rewards on performance. He concluded that rewards tend to facilitate performance on overlearned behaviors, but they impair performance on behaviors that require creativity, conceptualizing, and learning.

The fifth and final phase of the skeletal model is the satisfaction of the motive. If the expectations that led to the goal selection were correct, the satisfaction will follow immediately from the goal completion; if not, satisfaction will not follow and a new goal may be selected that is expected to produce the desired satisfaction. The outer TOTE unit guides one toward this motive satisfaction. The five phases that comprise the skeleton of this theoretical approach are diagrammed in figure 3-2.

Will was defined earlier as the capacity to choose behaviors in accord with one's thoughts, feelings, and motives. One can now see that the sequence of self-determined behavior that I outlined above has will as a key element. Central to the theoretical approach is the idea that people can decide how to behave and that the decisions are based on their thoughts about how best to satisfy their motives.

In addition to selecting behaviors, one's will has the additional task of managing motives. Frequently people are aware of more than one motive at a time. While it may be possible to select a goal that will satisfy all of these motives simultaneously, typically that will not be the case. People must therefore decide which one or ones to attempt to satisfy at that time; the others must be held in abeyance. When there is only one motive, there is less need to recognize people's capacity for willing. However, with several motives, one must sift among the motives and select the one or ones that will be operative, and hold in abeyance the motives that were not chosen for satisfaction. It is particularly the function of holding motives in abeyance that necessitates the concept of will.

The decision among motives will depend on a variety of factors. At times of homeostatic crisis such as a very empty stomach or a very full bladder, one typically attends to that salient motive. If at such times one does not, the will must work hard to keep those motives in check. Similarly at

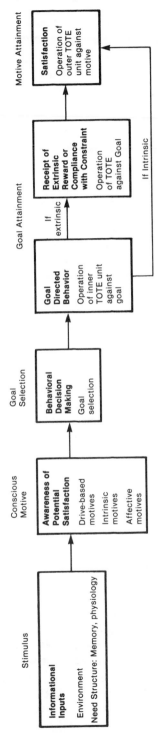

**Figure 3-2.** Basic Structure of an Organismic Theory of Self-Determined Behavior

Note: Informational inputs activate the formation of conscious motives. Goals are then selected that are expected to lead to satisfaction of the motives. Then the person behaves to attain the goals. When the goal is extrinsic, the person completes the behavior and gets the reward; when intrinsic, the goal is just the completion of the behaviors. Finally, when the goal is attained, the motive is satisfied (if the goal was properly selected) and the sequence terminates.

times of intense affect—what Simon (1967) called real-time needs—that affect typically will energize behavior. If not, the will must work hard to keep the affect in check. The decisions are based on the information available at that time. One might put off eating even when very hungry if an important outdoor job is nearly finished and it is about to rain. Or one might remain calm in a very frightening situation if one believes that getting upset would aggravate rather than help the existing situation. Typically one attempts to satisfy as many motives as possible and as efficiently as possible.

The motivational basis for the process of deciding is intrinsic motivation, the ongoing need of the organism to feel competent and self-determining. Intrinsic motivation provides energy for a variety of activities and processes of the organism, including decision making and holding excess motives in abeyance. Intrinsic motivation energizes one's will. When one is hungry, one can refrain from eating out of the need to be self-determining. One does not have to give in to drives or emotions when one believes it is disadvantageous to do as the drive or emotion impels one to do. When one successfully abstains, one will be rewarded intrinsically with the feeling of competence and self-determination.

In addition to energizing the covert process of decision making, which is integral to all voluntary behavior, intrinsic motivation may energize play, learning, and other overt behaviors that are suited to a person's capacities and interests. Within the organismic model, the motive that is ongoing—unless interrupted, for example, by a tissue imbalance or emotion—is the awarenes that one can feel competent and self-determining. When this is the salient motive, people will choose to engage in behaviors that provide them with a challenge that is optimal for their capacities. The conquering of this challenge, which is the aim of the purposive behavior phase of the model, leads to the desired satisfaction and terminates that sequence.

### Automatized and Automatic Behaviors

The preceding outline of self-determined behavior focused on voluntary behaviors that were consciously chosen in the service of motive satisfaction. Many behaviors, however, are not of that type. Many have passed out of the arena of voluntary responding and have become either automatic or automatized. For example, when one climbs a flight of stairs, one's feet move as is required to get one up the stairs. The overall behavior of climbing the stairs may have been consciously decided, but the molecular behavior of stepping was not. Often people develop what are colloquially called habits, in which, for example, they take a drink every time they pass a certain water fountain. Eventually they may get to the point of taking a drink at the fountain with only the slightest awareness of having done so;

the behavior has become automatized. Eating and smoking may become automatic; people sometimes report after they have eaten or smoked something, "I couldn't stop myself." They may even eat or smoke without being aware that they did so.

Schneider and Shiffrin (1977; Shiffrin and Schneider 1977) have distinguished between automatic detection and controlled search as modes of information processing. Subjects were shown to employ these two modes, an automatic mode and deliberate one, in their attention and learning experiments. Thus these researchers were making the distinction between intentional and automated responding at the level of cognitive processing that I am making at the level of overt behavior.

Langer (1978) made a similar point by suggesting that many behaviors are mindless, done without thinking. She reported a study (Langer, Blank, and Chanowitz 1976) in which it was hypothesized that people will behave thoughtlessly unless their habits are inadequate for the occasion. In that experiment, subjects were using a copy machine, and the experimenter interrupted, requesting to copy either five or twenty pages. There were three conditions crossing the small versus large request: a simple request with no explanation; the same request with a redundant explanation, "May I use the Xerox machine because I have to make copies?"; and the same request with an explanation containing real information, "May I use the Xerox machine because I'm in a rush?" The authors reasoned that in the second condition the explanation is totally redundant. Thus if the information was being processed, subjects would respond in this condition just as they would in the first condition, which had no explanation. On the other hand, if they did not process the information fully, they would respond just as they would in the third, "real explanation" condition. Further they suggested that people would respond mindlessly so long as something about the situation was not intrusive or disruptive. Thus, while a small request for five pages should trigger a mindless response, a large request for twenty should be more disruptive and thus direct attention to the request. This led to the prediction that in the small-request conditions, subjects in the redundant-explanation condition would behave like subjects in the real-explanation condition since the structure of the request was the same in both conditions. However, in the large-request conditions, subjects in the redundant-explanation condition should behave like the no-explanation condition since the experimenters were providing no additional information. The results showed exactly what was predicted, leading the authors to conclude that people engage in minimal information processing unless the situation somehow demands that they attend and make conscious decisions.

I agree that people often will behave mindlessly when the situation allows; however, the need for competence and self-determination sometimes will lead people to make conscious decisions even when mindless behavior would have been adequate given the situational demands.

Nisbett and Wilson (1977) have reported experiments indicating that subjects often are unaware of stimuli that produced particular behaviors and are unaware of the behaviors themselves. They suggested that people do not have access to the cognitive processes that determine behavior, so they were, in essence, asserting that all behaviors are automated and that self-awareness is simply an inference.

In a reply to Nisbett and Wilson, Smith and Miller (1978) asserted that although some behaviors are executed without the behaver's having access to the determinative processes, others are decided upon quite consciously. They reanalyzed the data from a study by Nisbett and Bellows (1977), which Nisbett and Wilson had used to support their argument, and Smith and Miller found evidence that subjects can have access to the informational determinants of their behavior. Thus Smith and Miller were suggesting that Nisbett and Wilson were reporting an interesting phenomenon but were overstating its occurence, much as I just suggested that Langer's assertion, while interesting, was also an overstatement.

### Becoming Automated

For a response to be performed mindlessly, it must be overlearned. Each of us has put one foot in front of the other, in the activity called walking, so many times that the process requires no attention, unless, for example, we are walking on a rough, novel terrain. For ten-month-old children, the activity requires the greatest of attention, and even then they may teeter or fall. The activity has not yet been thoroughly learned. Thus the basic requirement for automated responding is that it utilize overlearned behaviors, which then may become linked together. For someone learning to drive, steering requires attention, shifting gears requires attention, and operating the clutch requires attention. Each of these activities gradually becomes overlearned, and then the set of activities becomes automated.

Behavior becomes overlearned through repetition. The behavior must be repeated many times in the presence of some constant stimulus input—whether environmental, imaginary, or kinesthetic. In such situations, some sort of reward is involved. The reward may be extrinsic, like candy or praise, or it may be some internal process such as intrinsic gratification or anxiety reduction or avoidance. Many of our little habits, like tapping our fingers on the table—behaviors that Csikszentmihalyi (1975) analyzed as microflow experiences—are, or were initially, of the anxiety-reduction or avoidance variety. All of these repetition experiences begin as chosen activities aimed at goal attainment in the service of some extrinsic, intrinsic, or affective motive. Through repeated experience, they become overlearned. They require less and less of one's attention as they become automated and are governed by stimuli and habits.

This process of repetition acquisition is referred to by behaviorists (such as Thorndike 1913; Skinner 1974) as conditioning. I shall not use the term *conditioning* since it implies a passive mechanism rather than an active organism. I assert that these overlearned behaviors begin as chosen behaviors and may move out of the realm of being chosen when they have become overlearned.

The capacity for mindless responding is an interesting double-edged sword. On the one hand it is extraordinarily important, for it frees one's attention and will for new concerns. When one does not have to attend to putting one foot in front of the other but rather lets automatized walking take over, one's attention is available for whatever else interests one. On the other hand, it also interferes with one's self-determination, for nonchosen behaviors may become rigid and difficult to change. For example, some people keep the magazines on their coffee table lined up perfectly. When a magazine gets out of line, it is returned to its proper place. It is possible for such a person to enter the living room while talking to a friend, go to the coffee table, straighten the magazines, and not even realize that he or she has done it. This may be useful insofar as the magazines got straightened without even interrupting the conversation, but to the extent that the person "has to" straighten the magazines, the person has lost freedom of choice. The person has become a pawn to some mechanism that controls the behavior.

Both automatic or automatized responses require consistency in the situation. If the initiating stimuli are not present, the behavior will not be emitted, even if it is appropriate. For example, suppose there is an all-glass door that you open and walk through regularly. A sign is taped to it about eye level. Having walked through that door dozens of times, you approach it, see the sign and, without thinking, reach up and push the door open. One day, when the sign has been removed, you may walk into the door because the cue for the automized behavior of opening the door is absent. Further, if the situation has changed so that the environment does not respond to one's automated behavior in the way to which one is accustomed, one may become anxious and frustrated. One of the remarkable aspects of self-determined behavior is its flexibility. As the situation changes, the person is responsive and makes the required adjustments. Automatized and automatic behaviors, however, are characterized by their inflexibility; they do not respond adaptively to sudden changes. In such situations, the person may become disoriented and emotional, responding with mild annoyance or extreme rage (Mandler 1975).

When a situation changes, automatized and automatic responding will need to be reprogrammed, or as Abelson (1976) would say, one must learn new scripts to govern the behavior. Reprogramming is the function of the will. When one becomes aware that an automated behavior no longer is serving the purpose for which it was acquired and that maintaining the response pattern is inefficient, one may choose to reprogram the pattern. Typically that means deciding to focus attention on reprogramming, which may require repetition of the required response or restructuring reward contingencies so the desired response will be instrumental for some type of motive satisfaction. Responses that have been used often over a long period may require greater attention to be reprogrammed; those that are less well established may be more easily reprogrammed. In some situations the person will prefer simply to deprogram a response to allow freedom for exploration rather than to program a replacement response. One would direct attention to stopping the automatized response so the exploration could occur. For example, suppose someone has acquired an avoidance response to classical music such that one automatically does not listen when classical music is being played. Deprogramming that response, so one can explore the music, requires that one attend at the point in which the automatized blocking out of the stimulus occurs. Then one can attend to the music rather than blocking it out. In time one might discover an interest in the music that motivates the exploration, though at first one must be quite deliberate in attending to it.

Automatized behaviors may occur without the person's being aware of them. For example, locking the door to your apartment may become so routinized that if you were stopped a minute after you left the apartment and asked whether you had locked it, you would have no recollection of having done so. You may answer yes, banking on the fact that you always lock your door, but you would have no awareness of having done so this time. Changing an automatized behavior, such as locking the door, that occurs with little or no awareness may require quite a concerted effort, but the difficulty is simply one of remembering to do it. One must mobilize one's capacity for self-determination in a very focused way.

*Automatized versus Automatic Behavior*

Some behaviors can be reprogrammed readily. For example, when you change from a car with a standard transmission to one with an automatic transmission, it may take some repetition before you refrain from reaching for the clutch, but the transition is likely to take a relatively short time and to go quite smoothly. People who have been driving with a standard transmission longer will probably take longer to reprogram, though even then the transition is not likely to be problematic.

For the person who straightens magazines without thought, an attempt to stop doing so is likely to be quite problematic. If he or she can refrain, it is likely to cause considerable anxiety, and the person may give in to the urge to straighten them and then report, "I had to do it. I couldn't stand them that way."

I suggest that there are two types of automated or mindless behaviors; I shall refer to them as *automatized* and *automatic*, respectively. At an operational level these two types of behaviors will be distinguished on the basis of the ease with which they can be terminated or reprogrammed. Those behaviors that are easily changed will be called *automatized*; those that are not easily changed and are likely to recur spontaneously when they are changed will be called *automatic*.

The words *automatized* and *automatic* are often used interchangeably, yet I am using them to refer to different types of behaviors. Superficially the two types of behavior appear the same; they are routinized behaviors performed with a minimum of attention. But in other ways they are quite different. Automatized behavior is easily self-determined; automatic behavior is not. The term *automatized*, being a derivative of the verb *to automatize*, connotes activity and suggests that the process of automatizing is done actively in the service of one's capacity for self-determination. The term *automatic* connotes a passive mechanism, something that one does not do but that gets done. One does not will automatic behaviors, nor can one easily undo them.

Behaviors such as shifting gears in a car are automatized. These behaviors are often subroutines in a larger sequence of behavior. One decides to drive to the store and utilizes automatized shifting as a subroutine in the behavioral sequence of going there. Or one decides to climb the stairs and walks as part of the larger sequence of getting upstairs. Behaviors are automatized in order to free one's attention and will for other concerns. They are acquired to allow one to be competent and self-determining. With an array of automatized behaviors, one can take on challenges, achieve difficult goals, and work effectively in a complex environment.

One can acquire automatized responses for either intrinsic or extrinsic reasons. For example, one may acquire many automatized moves while playing basketball for the pure fun of playing. Or one may acquire certain automatized moves while being forced to play the piano. Once an automatized response has been acquired, later it may be utilized for either intrinsic or extrinsic reasons, regardless of the motivation that was involved in its acquisition. For example, the basketball player may use the intrinsically acquired, automatized responses when competing for money. Or the piano player may utilize the extrinsically acquired, automatized techniques while playing the piano for fun. The mark of an automatized response is that it is performed involuntarily (in the sense of not being chosen at the time), yet it can easily be brought under voluntary control, either to remain in the realm of self-determined behavior or to be reprogrammed.

The second type of nonintentional behaviors is the automatic behaviors. Behaviors such as compulsively straightening magazines or eating and smoking when one is trying not to are automatic. They are extremely difficult to change and may be quite maladaptive since they cannot be easily reprogrammed to accomodate to changing circumstances. Therapy typically involves working to change automatic behaviors. I shall now suggest that automatic behaviors are controlled by nonconscious motives.

In chapter 1 we considered Hilgard's (1977) research on hypnotism and pain, which indicated that behaviors may be controlled at a non-conscious level as well as a conscious one. The behaviors that I have characterized as automatic—not under the voluntary control of one's will—are controlled by motives that are not conscious. Suppose a child continually is denied affection and nurturance. With time that need may be suppressed, that is, held out of conscious awareness, and may motivate behaviors such as overeating. Or consider a young boy who was frequently hit by a babysitter. This child might associate his parents' leaving him with being hit and develop automatic behaviors, such as cringing, hiding, or getting upset, whenever a significant other leaves him. On the surface the behavior looks irrational, is not understandable, and seems unmotivated. In fact, it is quite understandable and follows straightforward motivational principles, but the motivation is operating out of conscious awareness.

Automatic behaviors are difficult to change because they are determined by these nonconscious motivational processes. The information that they utilize is often faulty, and since it is held out of awareness it is not readily verified. Much of it is acquired before children reach the level of formal operations (Piaget 1952) so it involves nonlogical conclusions and inaccurate associations.

Automatic behaviors may be acquired gradually as an unsatisfied need is suppressed, or they may be acquired quickly as a result of some intense emotional experience. For example, if while walking into a department store one is accosted, the terror and rage that are elicited may create a pattern of avoiding department stores or even all stores. This pattern is not chosen; the person would report something like, "I cannot bring myself to go into one of those places." The avoidance behavior keeps one from reexperiencing the unpleasant feelings—it is motivated—but it tends to be rigidly automatic rather than willed. Generally these behaviors require therapeutic experiences involving catharsis and reinterpretation of information in order to change.

*Automatized, Automatic, and Chosen Behaviors*

The theoretical framework described earlier and represented in figure 3-2 is a model of voluntary responding. It emphasizes conscious motives and choice of behaviors. Motives are awarenesses of human needs, and behaviors are goal directed in the service of those awarenesses. Automatized and automatic behaviors work differently. Consider first the case of automatized behavior. Here a person becomes aware of a motive and then proceeds to satisfy it without consciously choosing a behavior. One might, for example, be aware of the discomfort of a full bladder and the desire to end the discomfort (the motive is conscious) and then, without deciding to do so, proceed to a restroom and urinate. Alternatively, as with climbing the stairs, one is aware of the motive and decides to climb the stairs and then invokes the automatized behavior of walking.

In terms of the organismic model, automatized behavior may follow from the motive, bypassing the decision-making and goal-directed behavior, and proceed directly to the satisfaction. This is represented schematically in figure 3-3 as bypass I. Additionally automatized behavior may be invoked following the decision making and either may replace or work in conjunction with the deliberate goal-directed behavior. Hence the schematic also shows inputs to automatized behavior from the goal-selection phase.

When automatized behavior totally bypasses the goal-selection phase, the inner TOTE loop is inoperative. People do not choose the behaviors; they follow directly from the conscious motive and terminate when the motive is satisfied. Since automatized behaviors are not chosen, they are not considered self-determined. Even when they follow goal selection, they are not themselves chosen but are subroutines of chosen behaviors. Going upstairs is chosen, but the automatized behavior of walking is not. Nonetheless even though they are not chosen, they are readily deautomatized or reprogrammed because the person is aware of the motives that energize the behavior, and therefore the motives may serve as a cue to reprogram.

With automatic behavior, there is no awareness of motives, and there are no goals. Therefore not only are the goal selection and the inner TOTE loop bypassed, but so are the awareness of potential satisfaction (the conscious motive) and the outer TOTE loop (bypass II in figure 3-3). Stimulus inputs from the person or the environment activate nonconscious motives that initiate behavior. Termination will occur when the nonconscious motive is satisfied. Satisfaction of the nonconscious motive is different from satisfaction of a conscious one since the behaviors may be substitute behaviors (such as eating to satisfy a nonconscius need for affection) and therefore not really satisfy the underlying, nonconscious motive; however, for simplicity, I shall end bypass II at the satisfaction of the nonconscious motive.

With automatized, automatic, or self-determined behaviors, a behavior may terminate before satisfaction is achieved if some stimulus event (either internal or external) becomes so salient as to break into the ongoing sequence and begin a different sequence.

Often automatic and automatized behaviors are said to be under the

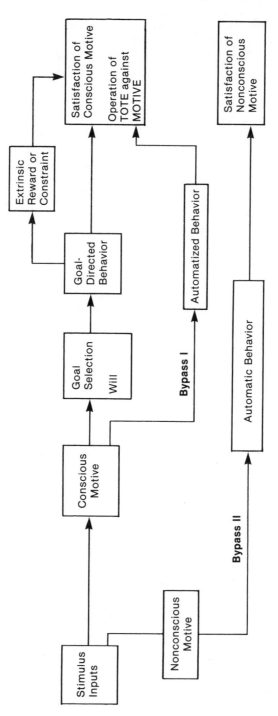

**Figure 3-3.** Automatized Behavior and Automatic Behavior

Note: This schematic representation shows how automatized and automatic behaviors relate to the theoretical framework of voluntary, self-determined behavior.

control of stimulus events since there appears to be a high degree of covariation between the stimulus situation and the behavior. However, although explaining a behavior in terms of stimulus events may account for a significant portion of the variance in the behavior, the explanation tells only part of the story. The behavior would not occur if the person were not predisposed to behave in that way in those stimulus situations. The behavior must be motivated in some way if it occurs. For predictive purposes, a focus on the stimulus events may work well, but for understanding the behavior, equal attention to the person will be necessary. Behaviors that are automatic are motivated by nonconscious motives, and it is for that reason that the motivational elements in the person are difficult to study. Behaviors that are automatized are motivated by either intrinsic or extrinsic motives that are energizing the behavioral sequence of which they are an aspect. One of the important reasons for focusing on the motivational as well as stimulus variables that interact to determine the behavior is so the behavior can be brought back into the realm of self-determination. While control of stimulus events may be useful for controlling the behavior, there are many circumstances in which changing the stimulus events is difficult. By focusing on the motivational components of the response, a person can understand the meaning of the response and gain control over it.

**Motivational Subsystems**

In chapter 2, I introduced the concept of motivational subsystems, suggesting that there are three such subsystems: intrinsic, extrinsic, and amotivational. When the intrinsic motivational subsystem is operative, the person may be engaging in either self-determined behavior or automatized behavior. In its purest form, the person might be engaging in some play or exploratory behavior that was chosen (self-determined) to satisfy the conscious motive to feel competent and self-determining. These behaviors undoubtedly would include many automatized subroutines (for example, to climb a mountain, one must walk) though the overall organization would be chosen.

*Overt Behavior, Covert Processes*

The intrinsic motivational subsystem has been brought to bear on two levels of human functioning. We have considered overt behaviors that are intrinsically motivated, and I have also suggested that some covert processes are intrinsically motivated. In chapter 2 I suggested that intrinsic motivation energizes the covert processes of choice. Additionally, I assert, the intrinsic motivational subsystem provides energy for holding motives in abeyance, searching for relevant information, and directing the reprogramming of automatized responses. Thus all self-determined behaviors involve some intrinsic motivation. Whether the overt behaviors that are chosen are play behaviors (intrinsically motivated) or drive-based behaviors (extrinsically motivated), there is necessarily some intrinsic motivation involved if the behaviors are chosen (self-determined) rather than mechanistically performed (automatic). Thus, eating as well as playing can be self-determined, yet if it is it will involve some intrinsic motivation to energize the covert processes, as well as the extrinsic motivation that is the primary energizer of the overt behavior of eating.

The extrinsic motivational subsystem, in its pure form, will energize either automatized or automatic behaviors. Automatized responses—like shifting gears—can be invoked at any time in a sequence of extrinsically motivated behavior, whether the overriding behavior is automatic or self-determined. Automatized behavior also can constitute the overriding behavioral sequence, as, for instance, when a man realizes that he is hungry (the motive is conscious) and then, without deciding and with little awareness, proceeds to the refrigerator to get something to eat. Automatic behaviors are typical of the pure form of extrinsically motivated behavior. For example, people who seem obsessed with making money or controlling others are extreme in the centrality of the extrinsic motivational subsystem, and their money-getting or controlling behaviors are automatic.

I am not saying that extrinsically motivated behaviors cannot be chosen; often they are. The point is that insofar as they are chosen, there is some intrinsic motivation involved. Most behaviors are not organized purely by only one of the three subsystems but involve a mix of two. Much extrinsically motivated behavior involves self-determination, yet an elaboration of the extreme conditions of intrinsic, extrinsic, and amotivational subsystems has explanatory utility for it provides the framework to assess the degree to which the various subsystems contribute to a given behavior.

Extrinsically motivated behavior is automatic for the child. In response to internal stimulation, a child cries and sucks when it is hungry. Only later can a child bring self-determination—intrinsically motivated decision making and delay of gratification (holding motives in abeyance)—to bear on satisfying extrinsic needs. To the extent that children develop the capacity to self-determine, they will be responsive to internal cues and will choose behaviors that lead to gratification. To the extent that their sense of self-determination does not develop, they will become more responsive to external cues (doing what they are made to do) and will engage in automatic behaviors. The latter is considered a pure form of the operation of the extrinsically motivated subsystem; the former is considered an interaction of the operation of the extrinsically and intrinsically motivated subsystems.

In its pure form, the amotivational subsystem involves no behavior. People who feel helpless and hopeless tend to be passive and tend not to behave. Sometimes when people feel hopeless and are somewhat passive, they will also be engaging in some automatic behavior like scowling at the person whom they blame for their situation. This would constitute an interaction of the amotivational and extrinsic subsystems. This, like the mix of the intrinsic and extrinsic subsystems in self-determined, extrinsically motivated behavior, can be understood only if the nature of the three motivational subsystems is clearly defined its pure form. The relationship between the motivational subsystems and the three types of behavior appears in figure 3-4.

### Perceived Locus of Causality

When the intrinsic motivational subsystem is operative, the perceived locus of causality is internal. When intrinsically motivated, people are responsive to internal, motivational cues, and they see the environment as being responsive to their initiations. Internal, person factors constitute the perceived cause, and outcomes constitute the perceived effect.

When the extrinsic motivational subsystem is operative, the perceived locus of causality is external. When extrinsically motivated, people are largely responsive to external cues. External cues, such as reward contingencies and constraints, constitute the perceived cause, and the behavior constitutes the perceived effect. Conceptually behavior would be said to be controlled by the interplay of environmental factors and nonconscious motives, yet the perceived causality is said to be external since the motivational determinants are out of conscious awareness.

With the amotivational subsystem, the perceived causality would be impersonal. Behavior and outcomes are perceived as independent—such people believe that they cannot attain desired outcomes—so there tends to be no voluntary behavior.

### Sense of Competence and Self-Determination (Willfulness)

Willfulness is an individual difference variable that reflects the extent to which one utilizes one's will. Clearly the strongest sense of competence and self-determination, or willfulness, is associated with the operation of the intrinsic motivational subsystem. Accompanying this subsystem would be feelings of both self-determination and competence. People choose how to behave and manage their motives, and their self-determination leads them to activities that are moderately challenging and that they can master.

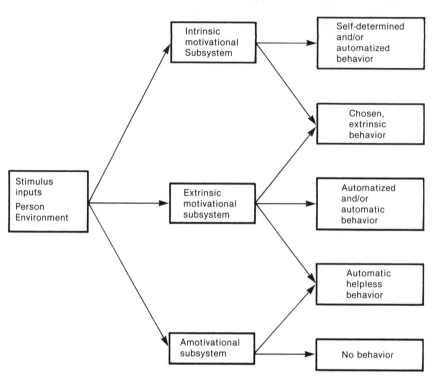

**Figure 3-4.** Relationships among the Motivational Subsystems and Types of
         Behavior

The extrinsic motivational subsystem tends to be associated with a lesser
degree of willfulness. People operating out of this subsystem are less self-
determining since their behavior would tend to be controlled by the environment and nonconscious motives. They could, however, be quite competent
though not self-determining. To get rewards and satisfy constraints, people
often must perform very effectively.

The amotivational subsystem is associated with the least willfulness.
People would feel neither competent nor self-determining in relation to
their situation; indeed that is the basis of their inactivity.

The central functions of the will are to manage motives and choose
behaviors. Strong forces from internal or external sources that are the basis
of motives often must be held in check for the person to function effectively. Motives that are based in strongly salient drives will interrupt a
behavioral sequence unless they are managed effectively by the will. To the
extent that one does not have a strong sense of competence and self-
determination, one would be unable to manage those motives. Therefore

such motives tend to be blocked from awareness. Put somewhat differently, one will tend not to attend to stimulus elements that one cannot deal with. This can be seen as a process of filtering that is performed by the extrinsic and amotivational subsystems. Some inputs will not pass through the filter to form motives; instead they will be blocked from awareness and be the basis for the nonconscious motives that energize automatic behaviors. Shevrin and Dickman (1980) similarly suggested that motivational factors such as avoidance of anxiety and guilt will affect whether stimulus elements break into conscious awareness. The extent to which one filters out stimulus inputs, I hypothesize, is directly correlated with one's sense of competence and self-determination. There will be least blocking from awareness of motives when the intrinsic subsystem is operative, moderate blocking when the extrinsic subsystem is operative, and most blocking when the amotivational subsystem is operative.

**Cognitive Evaluation Theory**

Within the context of the organismic theory of motivation, we can observe the operation of the processes involved in cognitive evaluation theory. Research has explored the effects of rewards, controls, and feedback on people's intrinsic motivation. I suggested that when people's intrinsically motivated behavior is rewarded or controlled, an instrumentality tends to develop between the activity and the reward, such that the activity becomes reevaluated as a means toward some extrinsic end rather than simply an interesting activity in its own right. The external factors facilitate a shift from the intrinsic to the extrinsic motivational subsystem as centrally operative. Like Heider (1958) and deCharms (1968), I referred to this occurrence as a change in perceived locus of causality, since there seems to be an adjustment in people's perception of causality from internal (I do it because I like it) to external (I do it for the external reward) that accompanies the underlying motivational change. When this process occurs, people are left with decreased intrinsic motivation and a decreased sense of competence and self-determination. Conversely when external factors promote choice and are responsive to a person's initiations, they will facilitate a shift from the extrinsic to the intrinsic motivational subsystem. The perceived locus of causality will become more internal.

The process of change in perceived locus of causality can be conceptualized as a feedback process that begins in the linkage between behavior and extrinsic rewards, or the absence of such a linkage, and feeds back information to one's need structure and motivational subsystems. The subsystems in turn affect the motives, decision making, and behavior. The change in perceived locus of causality process is represented in figure 3-5 as feedback channel 1.

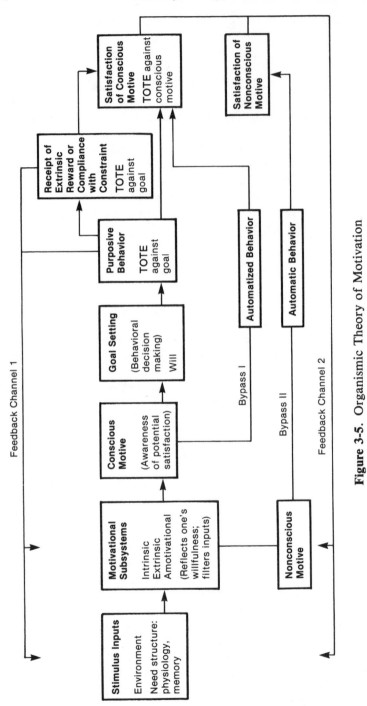

**Figure 3-5.** Organismic Theory of Motivation

The second proposition of cognitive evaluation theory states that intrinsic motivation will be affected when an experience of efficacy or inefficacy affects a person's perceived competence. This process can be represented as a feedback channel that takes information from the satisfaction phase (as influenced by the performance phase) to the need structure and motivational subsystems. The motivational subsystems in turn affect motives, goal setting, and behavior. Much like the feedback process that is characterized as a change in perceived locus of causality, this feedback process works either to increase or decrease one's intrinsic motivation and willfulness. The satisfaction of one's intrinsic motives is the feeling of competence and self-determination that in turn strengthens one's intrinsic motivation for the activity and one's general sense of competence and self-determination. This makes one more ready to continue seeking challenges; it leaves one feeling better about oneself as a capable human being; and it enhances one's ability to choose meaningfully among behavioral alternatives. Repeated failure to satisfy an intrinsic motive can leave one with the feeling of incompetence and helplessness, which then weakens one's intrinsic motivation for the activity and one's general sense of competence and self-determination. This failure to conquer the last challenge makes one more closed to seeking further challenge; it leaves one feeling worse about oneself and less clear and decisive about setting behavioral goals. In short, positive information about one's competence and self-determination strengthens one's willfulness, while negative information erodes it. The process is depicted schematically as feedback channel 2 in figure 3-5.

# 4 Emotional Processes in the Organismic Theory

Emotions are related inextricably to motivation and self-determination. Emotional processes, like motivational ones, cross-cut all areas of psychology; they are studied in physiological, cognitive, social, developmental, and therapeutic psychologies, to name a few. And emotions are ever-present in daily living; one can observe emotions, both subtle and intense, in every walk of life. Emotions may be experienced internally without leading to overt behavior sequences, or they may be an integral element in a sequence of motivated behavior. They may be involved in self-determined, automatized, or automatic behaviors. In this chapter we will consider the concept of emotion, focusing particularly on its relation to self-determined and automatic responding. The framework for interpretation will be the organismic theory of motivation.

As with the matter of will, the first psychologist to write lucidly about the emotions was James (1884, 1890). For him, and for Lange (1885) who wrote at about the same time, an emotion was conceptualized as the feeling of bodily changes that occur in response to some stimulus object. An important element of his theory was that these bodily changes occur reflexively once the stimulus object is perceived. In turn, one becomes aware of these bodily changes and that awareness is the emotion. For example, if someone comes up behind you and pokes something into your back, the kinesthetic sensing of the poke leads immediately to such things as pulling away, increased heart rate, a change in your breathing pattern, and a change in facial expression. These bodily changes, movements, and tendencies toward action are then experienced as an emotion, probably startle, fear, or both. According to James, one does not pull away and breathe differently because one is afraid; rather one reflexively pulls away and breathes differently, and the experience of doing that is the emotion. The key point in this is the placement of bodily changes before the mental event called emotion rather than after it. It is not the case, said James, that the perception of a stimulus object leads to a mental event called emotion, which leads in turn to expression of the emotion.

James's assertion of the awareness of bodily changes being emotion is fundamentally sound. Without the bodily changes, there is no emotion, just thought. An emotion involves an organismic reaction to a stimulus object, and the reaction occurs throughout the tissues of the organism, not just in the thought processes. James made the point that the body is like a sounding board and that an emotion affects all aspects of the organism. This point too is a very important one and emphasizes the holistic nature of the human organism.

The element of the theory that has received greatest criticism is the assertion that all emotion is fundamentally a reflexive response. Many theorists have asserted that some process of evaluation, interpretation, or appraisal is interspersed between the perception of the stimulus and the emotional response. It seems to me that there is some truth on each side of this debate. In James's behalf, one need only think of neonates who respond very rapidly to stimulus events with the more coarse emotions, such as fear, joy, and startle. It is difficult to imagine some intervening evaluative process between a stimulus event and the immediate fear response of an infant. The response seems to be reflexive. As the child matures, the constellation of emotional responding beomes decidedly more complex. Evaluative processes enter into the picture in at least two ways. First, an immediate intuitive interpretation may mediate between the stimulus event and the organismic response. And second, a later, more elaborate evaluation of the situation and one's arousal may influence one's affective response. For example, one may experience an initial feeling of startle in response to a stimulus and after further evelution experience anger, fear, or relief.

Even in adults, some emotional responding may be largely reflexive. Emotions such as startled fear may continue to be reflexive and occur with minimal cognitive activity. Zajonc (1980) has argued that affective reactions often occur with little cognitive or perceptual interpretation, and those that involve a minimum of cognitive activity are different from those that involve more extensive cognitive activity. Mandler (1975) similarly distinguished automatic affective responses from those that involve transformations of inputs through extensive cognitive evaluations. Nonetheless, while reflex-like emotional responding may occur in adults, with maturation, evaluative processes play an increasingly central role in emotional responding.

There were other points to James's theory of emotions. He emphasized that emotions are responses, yet these responses may follow either an actual stimulus event or the memory or imagination of an event. Recalling a past event may set off an emotional response as strong or stronger than the response to the actual event. James made the point that one does not readily remember one's emotions; rather one more readily recalls stimulus events and then reexperiences the emotional response. This point has been emphasized in certain approaches to therapy. For example, in Gestalt therapy (Perls 1973), central importance is placed on experiencing emotions in the present—even emotions associated with past events—rather than talking about past emotional experiences. This is often accomplished by having the client image or reenact the past event and then actually relive the emotion. In so doing, the emotion typically will be as vivid as the original experience.

Not only can memories of past events elicit emotional responses, images of events that have not occurred can do the same because of the human capacity to reason. Based on similar past events, one can imagine some future event and have it be as clear and excitatory as remembered past events.

James also asserted that all bodily changes (which underlie emotions) are felt immediately as they occur. Surely, however, this is not so. One of the core ideas of psychoanalytic theory, and one that in principle seems immune to refutation, is that emotions are often suppressed or repressed. Excitation often occurs that is not experienced consciously; people block awareness of bodily changes that are the basis of emotion. I am reminded of an anecdote that occurred in a therapy group. One man was responding to another in a rather adamant way, while at the same time believing and insisting that he was not angry. Another person said to him, "If you could just see yourself right now, what you would see is an angry man." It may be true that all bodily changes are accessible to one's awareness, though it is certainly not true that they are always in one's awareness. Further, it often takes considerable work before certain feelings can be let into awareness.

James made the interesting and important point that emotions blunt themselves through repetition. Events that repel one at first will become less objectionable with repeated exposure. At first, events, whether pleasant or unpleasant, may be quite disruptive to one's instrumental or rational responding. Gradually, however, one comes to take them in stride. Few medical students encounter their first cadaver without considerable autonomic involvement; yet, in time, the physician is able to make incisions in people and corpses alike with little, if any, emotional response. James suggested that this blunting is caused by two processes: normal accommodation or habituation in which the human is able to adapt to discrepant inputs, and a tendency toward economy in the nerve paths, which are involved in responses to repeated exposures. This second tendency, according to James, is the basis of increased efficacy. The phenomenon of adaptation to emotion-eliciting events is widely recognized by therapists and is the basis of such procedures as desensitization (Wolpe 1969).

Since in James's conceptualization, emotional responding is a set of reflexive processes, one might expect wide differences among individuals, for individuals' reflex patterns vary greatly. This raises the intriguing question of the genesis of particular reflex patterns. James's answer to this question was one of the weaker elements of his theory. He began by utilizing the work of Darwin (1872) to make two points. First, many reflexes, which are experienced as emotions, are inborn and are vestiges of responding that was biologically useful for the individual or species. The baring of one's teeth in fear or anger played a survival function at one time in the evolutionary sequence when biting was a primary form of attack. Following on the first principle is what James called the "principle of reacting similarly to analogous feeling stimuli." Across senses there are perceptual impressions that seem to tie together and thus produce similar reflexive responding. Something that smells or sounds sweet may produce the same reflexive activity as something that tastes sweet. Finally, James asserted that although some emotional responses can be understood in terms of these two principles, many cannot. These other responses are what he called quasi-accidents in the wiring of the central nervous system. The nervous system, being extraordinarily complex, is subject to mechanical reactions that are permanent to the organism yet are nonutilitarian in nature. These are unintended consequences of the way the complex system was wired.

I do not find James's account of the epigenesis of emotion to be very convincing. Surely some emotional reactions are remnants of survival responding, yet the cross-modality and quasi-accident explanations seem to account for little variance. This, in itself, need not vitiate other aspects of James's theory, for the principle of classical conditioning, later introduced by Pavlov (1927), would be quite useful in describing the onset of emotional responding within a reflexive framework for understanding emotions. Still, the matter of epigenesis, together with the obvious fact that cognitive mediation occurs in much of our emotional responding, makes James's assertion that all emotional reactions are reflexive quite untenable.

The important elements of James's theory for our understanding of emotions are that emotions are based in physiological changes and the experience of those changes; that they may be stimulated by events, memories, or created images; that they involved the whole organism; and that with repeated exposure one accommodates to arousing stimulus events.

## Cognitive Mediation in Emotions

In contrast to James's focus on reflexive responding, more recent theories of emotion tend to place emphasis on some form of cognitive mediation (see Arnold 1960; Izard 1977; Lazarus 1968; Schachter 1966; Tomkins 1965) between the stimulus event and the emotional response.

For Arnold, one of the early theorists in this tradition, emotion is a human experience. It is not, she asserted, simply a set of physiological changes or patterns of automonic excitations; it is what the person experiences while the changes and excitations are occurring.

Arnold (1960) suggested that all emotions have a stimulus object—whether actual, imagined, or remembered, whether concrete, vague, simple, or complex. This object is perceived by the person; that is, the object is apprehended as an object, in the objective sense. One may perceive a fist moving toward oneself or a state of affairs like the possibility of failing an examination. Arnold then pointed out that this objective perception is appraised by the person as it stands in relation to the person. The appraisal gives the object meaning for the person, and one's emotional response follows the appraised meaning of the stimulus object. The percepton of the moving fist is simply a perception until one recognizes that it is moving toward oneself and will lead to a collision. At that point, one has appraised the event and understands the relationship between the event and oneself. The emotional response then will follow. The relation of the object to the self may, like the object itself, be very vague. Simply seeing a fist moving toward another may arouse an emotion through identifying with the about-to-be-struck person. Following an appraisal, a person is in a psychological sense either drawn to or repelled from the stimulus object. This impulsive, psychological movement toward or away from an object is, accoding to Arnold, the emotion.

She emphasized that the initial appraisal may be immediate and intuitive. It is not something that is deliberate or mulled over. One has the intuitive sense of doom or delight and responds instantly. Young children, she said, have this capacity for intuitive appraisal, just as do adults, though, of course, some learning goes into knowing which objects are attractive and which harmful. When a child touches a flame for the first time, the child withdraws instantly. Arnold argued that this withdrawal and the emotional experience that accompanies it follow the child's intuitive appraisal that the flame is hurtful.

James would have argued that one reflexively withdraws. At this most basic level of emotional responding, I find the two explanations essentially indistinguishable. Whether one chooses to call the process involved in a child's withdrawal from a candle flame reflexive or intuitively appraised seems largely a matter of vocabulary; however, there may be criteria of evaluation that favor one choice of words over the other. For example, in some emotional responding, the evaluative process is less immediate, less intuitive. A reflexive explanation of those respondings would be less satisfactory. Hence, for the sake of parsimony and theoretical consistency, one might choose the intuitive appraisal vocabulary for the more basic respondings. For me, it is important to distinguish those emotional responses that are immediate and intuitive from those that follow a more deliberately evaluative process. Whether one chooses to call the immediate responding reflexive or appraised is inconsequential. It is in this sense that in the most basic responding, and especially for young children, James's reflexive theory seems adequate and insightful.

Arnold did make the important distinction between intuitive appraisal and reflective judgment. With increasing cognitive capacity, one's reflective judgment (that is, one's understanding) of a stimulus event increases. We reason whether something is in our interest, and an emotional response may follow accordingly. Arnold emphasized that when a stimulus object is perceived, the intuitive appraisal is immediate and reflective judgment follows. Therefore an immediate appraisal may cause an initial withdrawal, while the subsequent reflective judgment leads one to approach.

Arnold's definition of emotion involves a psychological movement toward or away from the stimulus object. This she referred to as an action tendency. These tendencies, she said, are such that they lead to action, for the emotion is accompanied by a set of physiological changes that are painful or uncomfortable if action does not follow to relieve them.

To recapitulate, Arnold made the important distinction between immediate intuitive appraisal of a stimulus event and the more deliberate reflective judgment. I likened the intuitive appraisal to what James called reflexive responding. Arnold proposed that intuitive appraisal happens first and that reflective judgment may follow, in some cases correcting the original appraisal.

In many situations there is immediate appraisal of (or at least an immediate emotional response to) the stimulus event; however, this need not be the case. Some stimuli may be affectively neutral such that an emotional reaction does not occur until the reflective judgment has been made. When one first sees a painting in a museum, there may be no emotional response to it. It takes time to allow in and reflect on the images before one experiences an emotional reaction of pleasure or displeasure, joy or disgust. Interestingly this reflective process may be either intuitive and phenomenal, or cognitive. For example, upon viewing a painting, one might think, "I like the angular relationship of the red and green as a focal point of . . ." In response to this reasoned judgment, one experiences an emotional response. On the other hand, one may view the painting more holistically and without words or concepts intuit a liking or disliking. This process is reflective and takes time, yet it is experientially different from the more reasoned evaluation.

## The Self

At the heart of cognitive theories of emotion is some form of evaluative judgment. In some way one must know whether a stimulus is attractive or harmful. Those theorists who focus on the evaluative process—whether as an intuitive process or a thoughtful one—tend to invoke some form of the self as a standard for evaluation. Rogers (1951) used the idea of self-concept, suggesting that emotions are evoked when one's perception of a stimulus relates more centrally to one's self-concept. One feels joy, for example, when one's perception of an event supports one's concept of self; one feels anger or fear when one's perception of the stimulus threatens one's self-concept. In a similar vein, Beck (1976) spoke of personal domain, composed of everything in which one has some involvement. At the center is one's concept of self, including personal and physical attributes, goals, and values. Surrounding the self-concept, yet still within the personal domain, are objects, people, and ideas that relate to the person; these include relatives, friends, chairs, books, national allegiance, and so on. Beck stated that one's emotional response depends on whether the stimulus event enhances or diminishes one's personal domain. Events that subtract from one's personal domain cause sorrow, those that endanger it cause fear, those that attack it cause anger, those that increase or inflate the value of the domain cause joy, and so on.

Beck's conceptualization describes the antecedents of particular emotions rather than just emotions in general. His theory is one of deliberate cognitive processing so it closely parallels the reflective judgment aspect of Arnold's theory, but it fails to address the more immediate intuitive-appraisal aspect of the human emotional response.

## Arousal and Cognition

One of the most cognitive, least intuitive theories of emotion was proposed by Schachter and his associates (1966; Schachter and Singer 1962). Schachter asserted that emotions are a function of physiological arousal and a cognitive evaluation of the situation that elicited the arousal. Following the earlier work of Duffy (1962) and Lindsley (1957) who had defined emotion as simply arousal or activation, Schachter proposed that stimulus events produce a general excitation that the person then labels as joy, anger, or whatever seems appropriate for the situation. Thus, for example, joy and anger may be understood as the same internal response that is given a different label and hence is said to be a different emotion.

Schachter and his colleagues did a number of empirical investigations that led to this theoretical point of view, the most cited of which is the Schachter and Singer (1962) study. The essence of their research was that subjects who were given epinephrine injections and exposed to a person who was modeling euphoria reported being happy whereas those who had been given the epinephrine and exposed to an angry model reported feeling angry. The phenomenon that Schachter and his colleagues have isolated and that is also described by Mandler (1975) is interesting. People do sometimes look to external cues to understand their emotional arousal; however, it is, I suggest, only one aspect of emotional responding rather than its core. Zajonc (1980) reported that people often experience emotions with no "reflective judgment" about the event. He found, for example, that subjects expressed preferences for stimulus elements to which they had been exposed previously over ones to which they had not been exposed previously, even though they showed no recognition of those elements. Thus, he asserted, these subjects seem to have acquired an affective reaction to the elements without cognitive awareness.

Presumably there must be some cognitive activity, since the stimulus event must be perceived and encoded, though this appears to go on at a preconscious level of processing. Research and theorizing on attention have indicated that much of the initial processing of stimulus events is preconscious (Broadbent 1958; Treisman 1964). This preconscious evaluation, which need not produce recognition, is the intuitive appraisal. This type of cognitive activity appears to be sufficient for emotional responses (Zajonc 1980), though the more reflective cognitive activity emphasized by Schachter and by Mandler also enters into some emotional responses.

Schachter's and Mandler's theories seem to suggest that emotional responses require an evaluation of the stimulus field to determine what emotion is appropriate. Mandler stated that this approach can be understood in terms of self-attributions (Nisbett and Valins 1971), whereby the emotional experience amounts to an inference about oneself based on an evaluation of the circumstances in which one feels arousal. These theories seems to explain the emotional responding of the extrinsic motivational subsystem but fail to deal with the emotional responding of the intrinsic motivational subsystem.

Emotional reactions are partially a function of reflective judgment, what Schachter called cognition. The reflective judgment may be the primary mediator of the emotional response, as, for example, in the case of the emotional reaction to the museum painting. Alternatively the reflective judgment may replace or reinforce an antecedent intuitive appraisal that followed immediately and nondeliberately from the stimulus event, as, for example, in the case of the fist moving toward one, where the immediate response of fear and startle might be replaced by pleasure if reflective judgment lets one see that it is a friend's fist being swung in affection and jest. When reflective judgment precedes an emotional reaction, the judgment may be phenomenal (intuitive) or more deliberately analytic.

Schachter seemed to be describing those responses in which the primary mediator was deliberate, thoughtful reflective judgment, based on information from the environment. I am suggesting that this type of emotional responding occurs when, for some reason, the respondents do not utilize their internal cues—what Polanyi (1958) called personal knowledge—to mediate their response but instead rely on information from the environment and from their ideas of what they should feel in that situation. For example, the man in the therapy group thought that he should not feel angry under those circumstance, so he did not feel angry. To the extent that one has blocked awareness of internal cues, one relies on external cues and makes deliberate, self-conscious judgments that mediate the experienced emotion. This is likely to happen, for example, in a situation of evaluation apprehension. When people are concerned about how they are supposed to feel, they tend to ignore the internal cues of their intuitive appraisal and rely on external cues that tell them the so-called appropriate response. This is not an uncommon process, but neither is it the essence of emotional responding.

Schachter and his colleagues were observing this phenomenon in their experiments. Experimental settings are often experienced by subjects as restrictive, and it is probable that their experimental setup created an evaluation apprehension. Hence, those subjects who were experiencing arousal from the injection that they did not understand may have judged the situation in a highly self-conscious way and responded in accord with their judgments. It is widely understood that people can feel emotions when they begin to think them. Actors and actresses, for example, often report that when they get into their characters, they actually feel the emotions that they are portraying. And those performances in which this phenomenon occurs are the most convincing ones.

The capacity for thoughtful, reflective judgment to mediate emotional responding allows people control over their own emotions and behaviors. To understand that all swinging fists are not intended to hit one affords one the kind of self-control that is an aspect of maturity and is important for harmonious interpersonal relations. On the other hand, it also allows for self-deceit. One may think that one feels a certain way and then behave accordingly, yet underneath there is some other feeling that is not being recognized. A common example of self-deceit in emotional responding may be instructive at this point. In many societies children are taught that certain emotions are good and others are bad. Anger, for instance, is generally seen as a bad emotion except in certain justifiable circumstances. This learning prompts people to ignore their intuitive response to a stimulus event, to disregard their internal cues, to focus on the "appropriate" response, and hence to deceive themselves into believing that they feel one thing when in fact their intuitive emotional response is another. Much of the therapeutic process involves uncovering the intuitive emotional responses that people have failed to recognize.

## Perturbation?

One of the frequently debated points in the psychology of emotion is the extent to which emotions are disruptions to rational functioning. On one side of the issue, Young (1961) and Maier (1949) suggested that emotional responding is disturbed, goalless, expressive responding, while Arnold (1960), Leeper (1948), and other asserted that emotions organize and direct goal-oriented responding.

Young (1943, 1961) has long asserted that emotions are acutely disturbed human processes that occur as a response to some situation and are expressed in a variety of physiological changes. The physical changes are governed by the autonomic nervous system, and the ensuing behavior is characterized by a diminution in control by the cerebral cortex and an increase in responding that is organized subcortically. While emotions are responses to particular events, continued Young, there may be underlying conditions in the person that increase the likelihood of these events and that extend the duration of the disturbance for periods of days, weeks, or months.

Young pointed out that emotional responding often shows recognizable patterns in responding. For example, startle responses include a quick, muscular jerk; hostile responses include a baring of the teeth, a focusing of the eyes, and so on. Yet Young also criticized the views of emotion that define it as patterned responses (Watson 1919), since these views disregard the disorganized nature of emotions and fail to distinguish emotions from other patterned responses such as sneezing.

For Young the idea of emotion stands in contrast to rational, goal-oriented responding. It is responding that is a reaction to some immediate stimulus event, interrupts ongoing motivated behavior, and is characterized by disorganization. He suggested that if emotional responding were purposive or goal directed, there would be no need for the concept of emotion; motivation would suffice as an explanation.

Young did point out that emotions are not the only affective processes. Other types of feelings such as sentiments, moods, and interests are less intense forms of affect and do not have the same disruptive effect as emotions.

Leeper (1948) sharply criticized the work of Young and other authors such as Shaffer (1936) and Woodworth (1940) who considered emotion a disturbance. Leeper asserted that they have failed to provide an adequate definition of disorganized behavior and that they use the term inconsistently. He asserted that the idea of emotion as a perturbation is inconsistent with the data on the matter. While it may be true that an emotional response interferes with proceeding activities, this does not mean that the responses are disorganized. On the contrary, he proposed, they are highly organized responses; emotions tend to organize behaviors that are consistent with the emotion. He used stage fright for a pianist as an example. Stage fright may in fact interfere with the response of playing the piano, but it organizes the response of avoiding the stage appearance; it organizes behavior consistent with the fright. Leeper augued that emotions therefore should be considered motivational. His point is similar to Simon's (1967) view of emotion as a response to a real-time need that interrupts the ongoing, less salient activity and organizes a subroutine to deal with the immediate stimulus event. Leeper suggested that when emotions are viewed as motivational phenomena, educators and parents will be faced with the task of developing an emotional richness in life rather than, as the perturbation theorists would suggest, minimizing emotional responding.

Following on Leeper's essay, Webb (1948) defined emotions as responses that are not readily seen as drive based and that have a lawful relationship to measurable properties of some stimulus. The point was the same. Emotions should be seen as motivational in nature, though they are not drive based. Webb's definition, which was formulated within a Hullian framework, attempted to provide the basis for empirical research on the motivational nature of emotions.

The debate over whether emotions are perturbations is characteristic of psychological debates that are formulated in either-or terms. Clearly there is utility in having proponents of opposing positions hold firmly to their viewpoints as a way of clarifying issues. Here we see just such a situation. An interesting point about this debate, and others like it, is that each side, while holding strongly to its position and derogating the other, also seems to recognize and incorporate the essence of the other position into its own. The two opposing positions are not so very different. It is a matter of both-and rather than either-or.

First, Young has stated that not all affective processes are disruptive. Hence we have more of a definitional disagreement than anything else. If he were to define emotions more broadly, as most other authors do, to include these other affective processes, then we would be left with the point that sometimes emotional processes are disorganized. Further, Young suggested that even the disruptive emotional episodes include adaptive responses; for example, frightened people often run from the frightening stimulus event. These is disruption of ongoing behavior, yet an appropriate response also emerges.

Now consider Leeper's work. He acknowledged that the stage fright interfered with the behavior of playing the piano and motivated escape behavior. He also acknowledged that in the cases of extreme emotions, there are disruptions that interfere with doing the activity; trying too hard to win a game may interfere with playing well.

Thus, it appears that apart from the rhetoric, the two positions bear some similarity and point to the truth of the matter. To a greater or lesser extent, emotional responses are perturbations that interrupt less salient behaviors. They may be quite disruptive of the goal-directed activity already in progress, as stage fright and trying too hard are. While Leeper saw stage fright as motivating escape behavior, therefore being organized, it is hard not to consider it as disruptive for it puts the person in a debilitating conflict. The person may neither flee the stage nor play as well as he or she might otherwise do; in short, the stimulus event of facing the crowd has caused a perturbation. The person shakes, forgets, and stumbles. Cortical control has given way partially to autonomic responding and subcortical control.

On the other hand, emotional reactions are often minimally disruptive (or perhaps interruptive is a better word) and initiate goal-directed responding. If while walking along daydreaming, someone sees a building of unusual and interesting architecture, the interested response (an emotion) may interrupt the daydreaming (hence it is minimally disruptive) but it may also motivate a goal-directed inspection of the building and perhaps also a study of the architect.

Thus I am suggesting that emotions may be highly disruptive, in which case they would interrupt the preceding activity and impair performance at the time the emotion is occurring; or they may be at most mildly interruptive of the prior activity and facilitate performance of some activity while the emotion is occurring.

**Repression**

One attribute of recent cognitive theories of emotion is the focus on cognitive or conscious evaluation of stimulus information from the environment and/or the person's internal processes (physiological changes and memory). While this is an important aspect of the overall picture of the emotion, it fails to consider something to which all dynamically oriented clinicians give much of their attention: emotions that occur or exist out of conscious awareness. These are often referred to as repressed emotions, though other labels, such as blocked emotions, are also given to the same or similar phenomena. The idea of repression evolved in the psychoanalytic tradition and was one of the important elements of Freud's conceptualization. Freud (1959a) suggested that repression is a state into which an impulse (a desire for emotional expression) goes when it meets with a resistance, the aim of which is to make the impulse inoperative. The function of repression is to keep a need or emotion out of awareness.

Such a concept is inconsistent with the cognitive theories that require conscious processing of information (reflective judgment) and suggest that emotions are conscious experiences of a reaction to some stimulus event. Without the conscious experience, there can still be a reaction to the stimulus event. Intuitive appraisal occurs out of conscious awareness and can lead to the physiological changes and action tendencies that characterize emotional reactions. These reactions may well be blocked from conscious awareness and would need to be inferred from observations or measured with various recording devices such as a polygraph. As Shevrin and Dickman (1980) stated, whether stimuli and responses break into consciousness depends on stimulus factors such as loudness, state factors such as fatigue, and motivational factors such as avoidance of anxiety.

Rapaport (1971) made the point that the term *emotion* is used to refer to a specific, time-limited phenomenon, such as feeling angry when someone bumps into you, and also to refer to the ongoing dynamics that underlie emotional phenomena. Emotions that are denied immediate expression may cause a chronic alteration to the physiological and psychological processes and thus cause what are typically called emotional disturbances. Thus, he was suggesting that repressed emotions alter one's psychological structures and lead to certain kinds of responding.

In psychoanalytic psychology, emotions begin in unconscious processes and are discharges of psychic energy that express an instinctual conflict. When the resistances or anticathexes of the ego and superego win out over the id's desire for drive gratification, the emotion is repressed. This involves displeasure since there is an accumulation of tension, yet it also involves an overriding pleasure that derives from the achievement of the aims of the resistance.

Repression and related concepts are extremely important for an understanding of emotion and motivation. It seems clear that some motivational and emotional processes exist out of awareness and that these nonconscious processes may persist through time and energize what I refer to as automatic responding. Attention to this phenomenon is especially important for clinical psychology since these automatic behaviors are involved in maladaptation.

To accept the idea of nonconscious or repressed emotions does not require that one accept the psychoanalytic definition of emotions. I suggest that emotion does not begin as an unconscious, conflictual process. Rather it begins as either a conscious or nonconscious reaction to some stimulus event. The reaction follows intuitive appraisal and/or reflective judgment and may initiate and energize subsequent behavior that is either automatic or self-determined.

**Emotion Defined**

An emotion is a reaction to a stimulus event (either actual or imagined). It involves changes in the viscera and musculature of the person, is experienced subjectively in characteristic ways, is expressed through such means as facial changes and action tendencies, and may initiate and energize subsequent behaviors that are either automatic or self-determined. An emotional reaction (which need not include overt behavior) involves the entire organism; as James suggested, the organism is like a sounding board for the emotion. Changes in breathing and heart rate, for example, reverberate throughout the organism, though one is not always aware of these effects. An emotion may or may not be consciously experienced. Nonconscious emotions are reactions to a stimulus event that involve changes in the viscera and musculature but are not experienced in awareness.

Generally emotional reactions are followed by overt, motivated behaviors, which may be either automatic or self-determined. In the case of automatic responses, the emotional reaction remains nonconscious and initiates some action sequence that is not chosen. In the case of self-determined responses, the emotional reaction provides information that is interpreted as a motive, leads to the selection of a goal, and initiates the subsequent goal-directed behavior.

Generally (rather than necessarily) emotional reactions will initiate overt behavior. The tendency is for behavior to follow, yet, as with motives, the will may operate to hold emotions in abeyance. One may experience an internal reaction and deliberately refrain from acting on it. The deliberateness involves the operation of will. People may even attempt to block any outward, expressive reflection of the changes in the viscera and musculature that are involved in the emotional reaction. For example, one may attempt to maintain a poker face in an emotion-evoking situation. This, too, is a function of the will. When the emotional reaction is stronger, the will must work harder to block the expressive or motivated behavior and as a result is less likely to do so successfully.

Emotional reactions involve an evaluative component. This evaluation may be immediate and highly intuitive (in other words, reflexive in nature), or it may be reflective and thoughtful (in other words, cognitive in nature). The intuitive appraisal occurs nonconsciously and is the initial element in emotional reactions. In automatic responding, there is only intuitive appraisal, which then initiates the automatic response sequence. The stimulus event is perceived, followed by a nonconscious appraisal, and subsequently by the behavior. Typically the stimulus event will be consciously perceived, though it need not be, as the subliminal perception experiments have demonstrated (Dixon 1971). The mediation between stimulus event and behavior will be nonconscious, which is a defining element of automatic behavior. And, finally, the overt behavior may or may not be consciously experienced, for example, a person may be aware of overeating without knowing why, or the person may eat without even being aware of eating. Self-determined behavior that follows an emotional reaction necessitates cognitive, reflective judgment as a mediator. The stimulus event is interpreted consciously; it becomes the basis of a subsequent motive and the subsequent goal-directed behavior. Reflective evaluation gives a cognitive understanding to a stimulus event and may lead to behavior that is consistent with the understanding.

The capacity for reflective evaluation provides humans with greater control over their responding; people who understand a situation as non-threatening, whereas an intuitive appraisal might interpret it as threatening, are in greater harmony with the environment and can be said to have greater control over their responding. On the other hand, the capacity for reflective judgment to mediate emotional responses may produce self-deception and facilitate maladaptation. For example, suppose a stimulus event occurs and one's intuitive appraisal produces an emotional response of anger. Further, suppose one has learned that anger is not an acceptable emotion and the learning has led the person to block the angry response from awareness. The person may evaluate the stimulus event reflectively so as to cause the response of, say, contentment. The experienced response is contentment, but underlying the experienced response is an emotion that is nonconscious and may be the basis for maladaptive, automatic responses.

Three primary dimensions have been useful for descriptively characterizing emotions: intensity, hedonic value, and the degree of perturbation. Some theorists (such as Young 1961) have used these dimensions as defining characteristics of specific emotions, asserting that individual emotions are responses that can be defined in terms of their values on these dimensions. Other theorists (such as Izard 1977) have asserted that each emotion constitutes a qualitatively different experience and therefore is not definable in terms of these dimensions. Each point of view has merit. While each emotion involves a qualitatively different experience, emotions can be described meaningfully on these dimensions. Sadness, anger, and joy are qualitatively different as classes of responses. Further, within any class, individual responses differ quantitatively. The three dimensions of emotion are useful in a descriptive sense for characterizing differences within classes as well as between classes of emotions.

Analogously, humans, dogs, and rats are different as species, and individuals differ within species. Descriptions such as size and weight are useful for distinguishing individuals within each species and also among species, even though values on these dimensions do not define the species.

The first descriptive variable that has been used with emotions is intensity. Some reactions are quite subtle and involve very slight changes in the person; others are extremely intense and involve drastic changes in one's physiology and a compelling conscious awareness. Sometimes the extent of intensity is reflected in different names. For example, we might say a person experiencing mildly pleasant affect is pleased or delighted whereas a person experiencing strongly pleasant affect is joyful. And a joyful response may itself vary in intensity. Stronger emotions are more readily observable since the expressive organismic responses such as facial changes are more pronounced. Stronger emotions require more will to be controlled or directed.

Second, emotional responses have hedonic value. They are experienced either as pleasant and desirable or unpleasant and undesirable, and any type of emotion may be more or less pleasant or unpleasant. The pleasant emotions sometimes are referred to as positive and the unpleasant ones as negative. I am reluctant to use these words, however, because *positive* and *negative* imply evaluation—good and bad. I believe that the labeling of certain emotions as negative perpetuates an attitude that they are bad and therefore encourages the process of not recognizing these so-called negative emotions. This process of blocking awareness may lead to automatic responding that is maladaptive for the individual. Thus I shall refer to emotions as having pleasant or unpleasant hedonic value, and I shall avoid the labels of positive and negative.

Third, to a greater or lesser extent, emotions will involve perturbation or disorganization in responding. Greater perturbation involves less cerebral control of the responding and greater subcortical organization of the behavior. It is important, nonetheless, to recognize that even the so-called disorganized responses can be seen as being or having been crudely purposive (though not, of course, in the cognitive or goal-directed sense) for they too involve intuitive or reflexive action or action tendencies that are consistent with survival or past learning in light of the stimulus event. For example, anger may involve lashing out at the predator, and fear may involve flight for escape. The emotional responses either will be serving a (need-satisfaction) survival function in the present or will be a rigid response that at one time was adaptive for that environment but that may be maladaptive because the response has remained while the environment has changed.

It is interesting to consider the relationship between the intensity of a response and the degree of disorganization. First, we recognize that one's response to a stimulus event will tend to become less intense with repeated exposure. People tend to accommodate to a stimulus as they encounter it repeatedly. The degree of intensity may also affect the extent to which one's response is disorganized and one might speculate that this relationship is curvilinear. Yerkes and Dodson (1908) reported an inverted U relationship between intensity of a motivating stimulus and learning time. This study has often been generalized to the law of an inverted U relationship between motivation and performance: as motivation for an activity increases, performance will increase up to some optimal level, at which point performance will decrease with increases in motivational strengh. Adapting that principal to the current situation leads to the speculation that as the intensity of one's response increases, cerebral organization may increase up to some optimal level, beyond which point increases in intensity will cause greater disorganization. I know of no direct evidence for the speculation, though it is an interesting point for exploration.

Emotions are immediate reactions to a stimulus event that may or may not initiate subsequent behavior. Emotional traits are more or less stable individual differences referring to the tendency to experience a particular emotion. We speak of angry people or happy people, meaning that the people tend to be angry (or happy) often. Things that do not seem to affect most people might make others angry (or happy).

Emotions are highly interrelated to other human processes. For example, we have seen that emotions are influenced by cognitive evaluations; similarly emotions affect cognition. The way one thinks is influenced by how one is feeling. So, too, perceptions are antecedents of emotions, but emotions also influence perceptions. One may see an event differently when one is happy and when one is sad. And the same holds for memory, motivation, and behavior.

## Motivation, Emotion, and Behavior

Motivation and emotion are closely interrelated. Throughout this book and an earlier one (Deci 1975), the reward for intrinsically motivated behavior has been said to be the feelings of competence and self-determination. In psychoanalytic psychology (Freud 1959a), behavior is said to be motivated by instrinctual drives, which have both an ideational representation and an affective component. Many theories of emotion include the notion of action tendencies, which is motivational in nature. These are but a few examples of the interplay between motivation and emotion.

The next section examines closely the ways in which affective processes are involved in the motivation of behavior. First, however, it is important to note that while the two groups of processes are intertwined, heuristically it is useful to classify them as separate, though related phenomena. Motivation is based in a person's need structure—that part of the person that exists in memory and physiology and is composed of needs of the organism. These needs are enduring, relatively stable aspects of the person that emerge into awareness on some type of regular, cyclical basis independent of any eliciting stimulus event. One gets hungry whether or not one sees food or food cues; one needs to undertake challenges and have stimulation whether or not a challenge or source of stimulation is present. Indeed the nature of motivation is such that one seeks out such things as food and stimulation when a need is salient, and needs become salient even if they are not prompted by a stimulus event. Emotion begins as a reaction to some stimulus event that involves physiological changes and subjective experience. It may, though it need not, initiate subsequent behavior; however, it does not operate in the cyclical fashion of pushing into awareness independent of stimulus events.

In a sense, the distinction between motivation and emotion is arbitrary. We shall see that affect is an integral element in the organismic, motivational theory; however, it seems useful to make the distinction since the psychology of emotions typically has encompassed different phenomena and processes from the psychology of motivation. By recognizing the distinction between the two sets of phenomena, they can be brought together into an integrative theory of human behavior.


## Self-Determined Behavior

The organismic theory of motivation (schematically represented in figure 3-5) suggests that motives are awarenesses of potential satisfaction—in other words, cognitive representations of some future, satisfied state. Conscious motives are formed out of stimulus inputs from the environment and from one's need structure, the latter existing in one's physiology and memory. Motives lead people to set goals or plan behaviors that they expect, given their limited information, to lead to the desired satisfaction. Once the goal has been set, the person engages in the behavior and, if the planning was correct, will experience the desired satisfaction when the goal is reached. The satisfaction may follow directly from the goal attainment or may be mediated by an extrinsic reward. This description is of self-determined behavior—behavior chosen based on one's motives and the information available to one.

Emotions are reactions to stimulus inputs. People feel anger, joy, fear, disgust as a result of some juxtaposition of a stimulus (actual or imagined) and themselves. The emotion (unless it is a nonconscious emotion, which does not figure into this discussion) is experienced in conscious awareness. Thus, an emotion, like a motive, develops out of stimulus inputs and exists in one's awareness. However, the focus of a motive is achieving a future state; the focus of an emotion is the present stimulus event. An emotion is not a motive, but a motive may follow directly from an emotion. Emotions are, in part, cues that call up motives. When one man (person A) is angry at another (person B), an aggressive motive may be summoned, which might in turn lead A to set the goal of punching B or of criticizing him in his absence. Or if a woman (person C) sees a very unusual magazine cover, the interest that is stimulated (an emotion) may call up an intrinsic motive that leads her to the decision to thumb through or read the magazine (the goal). In these cases the emotional reaction served as a cue; it elicited an awareness of potential satisfaction, which began a sequence of motivated, self-determined behavior.

Once a motive has been established, the person aims to achieve the satisfaction that he or she had anticipated in the motive phase. This motive attainment occurs through the satisfaction of a human need. Recall that needs—for food, competence, sex, and so on—are enduring aspects of the person that exist in the person's need structure. These needs are the basis of motives, those transitory awarenesses of potential satisfaction that set a sequence of behavior into action. Thus, to achieve satisfaction means to gratify the underlying need. With need gratification comes an emotional experience. Satisfaction of a motive is accompanied by a subjective feeling or an affective experience. Thus, emotions also enter the theoretical framework at the point of termination. It is widely accepted that motive satisfaction is a pleasantly affective experience. For example, Freud believed that pleasant affect follows tension reduction, which, of course, occurs when a drive is gratified. Young (1943) also said that an emotion is involved in the satisfaction of a motive. The rudimentary elements of the relationship between emotion and self-determined behavior appear schematically in figure 4-1.

*Automatized and Automatic Responding*

Often people's behavior is not chosen or self-determined but rather occurs in an automatized or automatic fashion. In some cases they are mediated by the awareness of a motive and in some cases not. These behaviors appear schematically in figures 3-5 and 4-2 as bypasses I and II.

Different schools of psychology use different psychological processes to describe what I have called the automated behaviors. In behavioral psychology the processes of classical and operant conditioning provide an account. There, however, all behaviors are said to be conditioned; there is no concept of chosen, self-determined behavior.

In psychoanalytic psychology, behavior is said to be unconsciously motivated. Automatic responding would be seen as fixated behavior, which is motivated out of an unconscious conflict between id and ego (or superego) forces. In cognitive psychology, it would be seen as programmed behavior with certain properties, such as highly limited search procedures. And in humanistic psychology, automatic responding tends not to be considered in the theories; rather it is seen as the villain, which therapeutic and growth procedures are aimed to dispel.

In organismic theory, automatic behaviors are a subset of the behaviors that are not consciously chosen. Generally one does not choose to scream at someone who accidentally bumps into one on a crowded street; the response, if it occurs, is automatic. Automatic responses are closely tied in with the emotions. Disorganization or perturbation leads to automatic responding. Behavior is less under the control of cortical processes and more under the control of subcortical processes. They can be said to be under the control of the interplay of a stimulus event and nonconscious motives and emotions. These automatic behaviors tend to express the affect. As the degree of perturbation increases, the probability of automatic (as opposed to automatized and self-determined) behaviors increases.

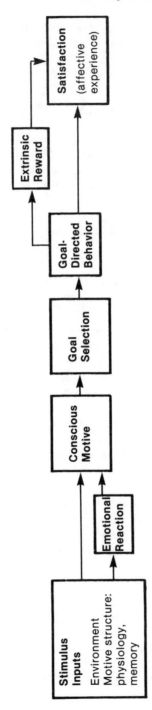

Note: Conscious emotions are reactions to stimulus inputs, which are experienced in conscious awareness and which serve as cues that call up motives. The motives in turn lead to goal selection and subsequent behavior. All motives, however, are not preceded by emotional responses, as indicated by the direct link between stimulus inputs and motives. Emotion also enters the framework when motives have been satisfied.

**Figure 4-1.** The Role of Emotion in Self-Determined Behavior

Expressive responding may follow conscious awareness of the emotion and of a concomitant motive, in which case it would be automatized behavior, or it may not be mediated by conscious awareness, in which case it would be automatic behavior.

*Frustrated Goals and Motives*

When a motive is satisfied, the satisfaction involves a pleasurable affective response. Now suppose that a motive is not satisfied. This could occur in one of two ways; either the person attains the goal but finds that satisfaction does not follow, or goal attainment is blocked. For example, the intrinsically motivated person C person picked up the magazine with the interesting cover. The motive was to feel the satisfaction that comes from learning something interesting. She then set a goal of reading the magazine. She selected this goal with the expectation that reading it would lead to the intrinsic satisfaction of having learned something interesting. She read the magazine but found it trivial and boring, so she did not experience intrinsic satisfaction. The goal was achieved, but the motive was not satisfied and the underlying intrinsic need was not gratified. Or, suppose the magazine did turn out to be quite interesting. She began it and got quite enthused, only to turn the page and find that the middle ten pages had been torn out. Here the path to her goal had been blocked, so the goal could not be attained.

In situations where a need is not satisfied by the chosen goal or where attainment of the goal is blocked, one could respond in one of two types of ways, or a combination of both (see Mandler 1975). One could become frustrated and emotional, perhaps displaying aggression (Dollard et al. 1939), or one could see it as a problem to be solved and either set a new goal that would satisfy the salient need or find a way to circumvent the barricade. In a case where the goal had been attained but the motive was not satisfied, one could respond with bored frustration (an emotional response) or could choose something else to read that looked interesting (a purposive) response of selecting a different goal aimed to satisfy the same motive). In the case where the goal attainment was blocked by the missing pages, the woman could respond by throwing the magazine on the floor and yelling at the miserable creep who tore out the pages (an emotional response), or she could find another copy of the magazine or a different magazine with a story on the same topic (a purposive response of circumventing the barrier).

To summarize, when motive satisfaction is not attained, there are various responses that characteristically follow: the person might become frustrated and engage in expressive, often aggressive behavior aimed at the source of frustration; the person might become frustrated and displace the resulting emotional, aggressive response onto an innocent other; the person might select a different goal aimed at satisfying the same motive; and in the case where the goal was blocked, the person could search for an alternate path to the goal, one that would circumvent the barricade.

The former two alternatives involve emotional responses; the latter two, rational, goal-directed responses. Now consider two interesting questions: Are the behaviors that follow the emotional responses self-determined and goal directed? Under what circumstances are people likely to respond in the former two emotional ways versus the latter two ways in which the original motive and/or goal continue to guide the behavior?

In addressing the first question, Maier (1949, 1956) argued strongly that the behavior following frustration is not goal oriented, though Leeper (1948) asserted that it is. Maier reasoned from data obtained in learning studies with animals that showed that the responses to frustration occur spontaneously, are apparently unreinforced, persist for an unusually long period, and may be immune to change when new information is presented. He asserted that the unusual, abnormal fixation that often occurs indicates that the behavior is of a sort different from goal-directed behavior.

Recall that Leeper's explanation of C's frustrated, agressive response to the missing pages would be that a new goal replaced the former one—a goal of, say, reducing the tension of frustration. Let us consider the incident in light of the current framework of motivated behavior and make several important points. First, if a goal is blocked and the person responds emotionally, that response is a side track from the motivated sequence that was in progress and is therefore interruptive. The previous goal and motive that were guiding the behavior will, at least temporarily, move into the background. Further, the emotional response may, though need not, lead to the awareness of a new motive, which then sets up a new sequence of behavior. This would be akin to what in computer language would be called a subroutine. Presumably when the new sequence is completed, the person would return to the initial sequence, once again guided by the previous goal and motive.

This explanation has not, however, addressed the question of whether the frustrated behavior is goal directed or, in the terms of out overall discussion, self-determined. The answer depends on whether a motive develops and is followed by the selection of a goal. In other words, is the person subject to the existing information and using that for flexible goal selection? Typically the answer appears to be no, as Maier's animal studies have shown. When one responds to a blocked goal or motive in a frustrated way, the behavior is often automatic and follows directly from the frustration. Sometimes, however, the answer would be yes, for people who experience frustration may resist a tendency to become disorganized and may respond to the frustration either by selecting an appropriate goal under the circumstances or by proceeding with the previous goal by solving the problem creatively. In other words, people may experience frustration and still proceed directly to attain the goal or select a new goal to satisfy the same motive without engaging in expressive, frustrated, automatic behaviors.

There arises a problem of terminology at this point. Many authors (including Maier) use the term *motivated* to refer to chosen, goal-directed responses. Others (for example, Freud) use it to refer to behaviors governed by unconscious processes. And still others (Leeper is one) use it to refer to any behavior, including frustrated, emotional, expressive behavior. I would consider all of these motivated behaviors. However, I distinguish three kinds of motivated behavior: self-determined behavior, which is the chosen, goal-directed behavior that is flexibly responsive to changes in information; automatized behavior, which is not chosen but follows directly from the conscious awareness of a motive; and automatic behavior, which is non-consciously motivated and therefore appears to follow directly from the stimulus event.

Let us now consider the second question posed earlier: when will a person respond to a blocked goal or motive in the more rational, goal-directed way versus the emotional, expressive way?

One element of the answer to this question is the process of accommodation. Recall James's (1890) suggestion that with repeated exposure to a stimulus event, one's response becomes blunted. To the extent that the blocked path is familiar, either because it has occurred before or a similar event has occurred before, the person's response will be less disruptive and more directed toward solving the problem. Further, individuals have different thresholds for tolerance of frustrating events; given the totality of their makeup (genetic endowment and learning history), some people have developed a greater capacity for encountering barricades to goal attainment without experiencing frustration and upset. Further, any individual will vary from time to time in terms of how much goal blockage can be tolerated without causing frustration and upset. When other aspects of the person's life are operating smoothly, the person is likely to have a higher frustration tolerance than when other aspects are themselves in a chaotic state.

The nature of the frustrating situation may also be an element in the person's response.* One might speculate, for example that there would be less emotional upset when alternative paths to the goal are readily available. And, further, this may interact with the importance of the goal. One would think that more important goals would cause greater frustration; on the other hand, one might also expect the person to work hard to circumvent the blockage to an important goal. Perhaps an important goal that could be circumvented readily would lead to the least frustration, and an important goal

---

*These speculations were suggested to me by Victor Vroom.

that could not be easily circumvented would lead to the most. I know of no empirical evidence that bears directly on these speculations, though they are quite intriguing.

### Emotions and the Motivational Subsystems

Different motivational subsystems—intrinsic, extrinsic, and amotivational—involve different types of affective experiences. Let us consider these in turn.

The intrinsic motivational subsystem is based in the intrinsic need for competence and self-determination. It involves the strongest sense of competence and self-determination, which means that it employs the energy of intrinsic motivation for the covert, psychological processes of choice and managing motives. Given this capacity, the person is able to deal with strong emotions by managing them and the accompanying motives as well as by selecting appropriate behaviors given a cognitive evaluation of the situation. There would be primary attention to internal cues for the identification of emotions, and those cues would be evaluated in conjunction with information from the environment and memory to determine the behavioral response. Behavior would be self-determined, and the intuitive and phenomenal evaluations that consititute the emotion would be important informational sources for the selection of behaviors.

The extrinsic motivational subsystem is based in tissue-deficit drives and acquired extrinsic needs, such as the need for money or power. Its focus is on receipt of extrinsic rewards and compliance with extrinsic constraints. It is responsive primarily to external cues that signal the routes to extrinsic gratification. When purely extrinsically motivated, people may feel very competent if they do well what they need to do to get rewards and comply with constraints, though they will not feel self-determining since their behavior is largely controlled by the interplay of environmental factors and nonconscious motives rather than conscious choices. Their sense of competence and self-determination will tend to be lower when they are extrinsically motivated than when they are intrinsically motivated.

Given the external focus of the extrinsic motivational subsystem, emotions tend to be based on rather deliberate reflective judgment. People will tend to feel those emotions that are appropriate for that situation, emotions that are consistent with the extrinsic contingencies. The phenomenon described by Schachter (1966) and his colleagues is the archetype of the emotional reactions of the extrinsic motivational subsystem. Direct access to internal cues is blocked, and one therefore feels emotions in accord with what the environment dictates. It is interesting to note that a person may, based on the reflective judgment of the extrinsic motivational subsystem, report feeling one thing, say contentment, and simultaneously engage in automatic behavior that is consistent with the underlying feeling that has been blocked from awareness, say anger. Thus a person might be banging a fist on the table or be ravenously eating, or making caustic, sarcastic remarks while feeling content.

This distinction between the emotional processes of the intrinsic and extrinsic motivational subsystems can be seen in this hypothetical example. When someone is accosted or grossly insulted, the intrinsically oriented response might be to experience rage, feeling, for example, as if he or she wants to kill the other person. The person, however, would behave as is appropriate given the rage and the situation. The extrinsically oriented response would involve interfering with the experience of rage, since one's sense of self-determination is not strong enough to manage the true emotional reaction. The problem with the latter approach is that the blocked emotion will feed into the motivation of automatic behavior. With awareness of the emotion and motive, the person is determining the behavior; with blocked emotions and motives, the behavior is determined by nonconscious processes and tends to be maladaptive.

Finally, the amotivational subsystem tends to be accompanied by the feelings of despair and hopelessness. One is unmotivated to behave out of a belief that desired outcomes are unattainable. Emotions tend to be blocked, and when there is behavior it tends to be automatic and based on a mix of the extrinsic motivational subsystem with the amotivational subsystem.

To recapitulate the role of emotions in motivated behavior, consider the organismic framework (see figure 7-3, p. 168) Stimulus inputs from the environment and from one's memory or physiology instigate the operation of one of the motivational subsystems (or mixture of them). Emotions are experienced in ways characteristic of the operative subsystem. Information either passes freely into awareness to be experienced as an emotion that may lead to self-determined behavior, or it may be filtered to be congruent with the demands of the extrinsic or amotivational subsystems. In the latter case, the experienced emotion will differ from the underlying emotion that is blocked from awareness and that prompts an automatic response (bypass II). A conscious emotion may serve as a cue for the creation of a motive, which in turn may lead to automatized behavior (bypass I), or it may be the antecedent of goal selection and goal-directed behavior. If the automatized behavior was accurately programmed, it will lead to motive satisfaction (a pleasant affective experience). In the case of goal-directed behavior, it may lead to goal attainment and motive satisfaction (a pleasant affective experience) or the goal may be blocked. In this latter case, a subroutine would be initiated that may lead to subsequent automatic behavior, automatized behavior, or self-determined behavior.

**Other Theories of Emotion and Motivation**

Two other general theories of emotion have been proposed that bear similarity to the organismic theory of behavior. Lazarus and his associates (Lazarus 1968, 1974; Lazarus, Averill, and Opton 1970) have developed a complex response theory of emotions, and Izard (1977) and Tomkins (1962, 1963) have developed a differential emotions theory.

Lazarus's theory suggests that emotions are a reflection of a person's adaptive interaction with the environment, an interaction to which the person brings a set of competencies, beliefs, and needs. The theory is based on the idea of cognitive evaluation, much like Arnold's theory.

Lazarus defined emotion as a complex disturbance involving subjective experience, physiological changes related to action tendencies, and expressive and goal-directed behavior. The nature and intensity of the emotion depend on cognitive appraisal of the stimulus input in relation to the organism's well-being. In lower animals this appraisal is built into the nervous system; in humans, thought processes play a major role. The physiological perturbation arises from the tendency toward action.

Already we see many commonalities with the framework presented in this book. Both consider the nature of the organism's adaptive interaction with the environment based on the competencies, needs, and beliefs of the organism. Both view emotions as reactions involving physiological changes and subjective experience. Both recognize that cognitive evaluation plays a major role in human emotional responding but that the more basic reflexive or intuitive element also plays a part. Both attend to the nature (or hedonicity), intensity, and degree of disturbance in the response. And both explicate the expressive as well as instrumental quality of responding.

The emotional-response system of Lazarus and his colleagues divided an emotional response into three parts (or subsystems). The first, the stimulus properties, suggests that the perception of a stimulus event is not a passive process but involves an active interchange between perceived and perceiver. The stimulus event has certain characteristics that convey constant information; for example, a loaded gun pointed at someone conveys specific information independent of the perceiver and situation. Stimulus events also convey information that is not specific to the stimulus event but depends on the perceiver's relation to it; for example, the stimulus may be novel or familiar to the perceiver. And finally, the perceiver's initial response to the stimulus event influences the continued perception of the event; for example, if your immediate response to an event is fear, you see the event through the eyes of a frightened person, in which case the event will look very different than it would to a joyful person.

The second phase of the model involves cognitive appraisal of the stimulus event and an invocation of coping strategies congruent with the appraisal. This phase gives meaning to the stimulus event. A person evaluates whether the event is cause for threat or nonthreat, fear or delight; and the person proceeds to one or more of three coping strategies. In some cases, the appraisal determines that no emotional response is required. For example, as you stand on the sidewalk waiting to cross the street and see a speeding car coming down the street, no emotional response is necessary; you simply wait for the car to pass and then cross the street. In other cases, the appraisal leads to direct action tendencies (withdraw or approach) and/or cognitive processes such as distortion or suppression. Lazarus and associates have referred to the evaluation as primary appraisal. They pointed out that the primary and secondary appraisal are often so inter-twined as to be indistinguishable.

The third phase is called response categories. Lazarus and associates distinguished three: cognitive, expressive, and instrumental. A person may respond without overt behavior simply by reconstructing the stimulus event. One might conclude, for example, that some threats of punishment from a teacher or parent are meaningless. Note, of course, that this conclusion response may either be correct or incorrect; nonetheless it concludes the event for the time being at least. Alternatively a person may respond overtly either expressively by getting very diffuse and shaky, for example, or in-strumentally by engaging in some purposive, goal-directed response.

Again, one can draw parallels between Lazarus's formulation and the one outlined in this book. While the scope and focus of the two theories are different in many ways, there are important similarities in their treatment of the relationship between emotion and behavior. Lazarus's comments about the stimulus event are important, although I have not focused much atten-tion on stimulus properties in my analysis. Further, while Lazarus's distinc-tion between primary and secondary evaluation is somewhat different from the distinction I drew (in line with Arnold) between intuitive appraisal and reflective judgment, the scope of psychological activity encompassed in the two theories is quite similar. The distinction between expressive and in-strumental behavior is also similar, though I have referred to expressive responding as automatic responding or automatized responding. Finally, I have not referred to cognitive responses as a specific category of respond-ing, although the cognitive-reappraisal response in Lazarus's system is a form of reflective judgment. I have noted that when the extrinsic or amotivational subsystems are operative, humans often work to put or keep aspects of the stimulus event and their own reactions out of awareness, which is a phenomenon similar to what Lazarus called the cognitive ego mechanism coping strategy and the response of unrealistic cognitive reap-praisal.

Differential emotions theory was presented by Izard (1977) and in part developed by Tomkins (1962, 1963). This theory is unique in its specificity and intriguing in some of its postulates. Emotion is said to be a complex process involving neurophysiological, neuromuscular, and phenomenological aspects. A given emotion begins when a stimulus event is perceived and instigates activity in the limbic system and/or cortex. These neural impulses are organized subcortically to produce facial expression through instigation of the motor system. Each of the basic, discrete emotions (Izard said there are ten) has a characteristic pattern of muscular activity in the face. The facial expressions are then fed back to the cortex where they are integrated to form the phenomenological experience of some differential emotion.

Notice the key role played by facial activity in this theory and the specific absence of visceral, autonomic activity. Izard asserted that the visceral activity, and indeed the physiological changes that echo throughout the organism, follow from the experience of emotion rather than cause it. He placed facial changes, rather than visceral changes, as the basis for a subjective experience of emotion. As such, he stands in clear contrast to the 1890 theory of emotions presented by James, though interestingly, as Izard pointed out, in James's earlier (1884) statement of the theory, voluntary muscular activity was included as an aspect of the bodily changes whose perception constitute emotions. Izard has focused on the voluntary muscular activity of the face as the bodily changes that form the foundation of emotional experience. He did add that visceral activity is an important element of the total emotional experience for it provides cues to awareness that are quite salient. Further, it is an important factor in the activity that is initiated by the emotion. For Izard, emotions are considered the principal motivating phenomena. He distinguished emotions from drives and considered both to be affective states. His basis for distinguishing the two is the cyclicity involved in the tissue deficit of drives. Each specific emotion is the basis for subsequent behaviors consistent with the emotion.

Cognition need not come into play in the experience of emotion, asserted Izard. The cortical integration of facial expression into subjective experience may occur without cognitive mediation. However, cognition then plays a key role in the transformation of experienced emotion to motivated behavior. Evaluation and expectation play a role in behavioral selection.

Differential emotions theory places emphasis on the interactive nature of drives, emotions, and cognition as means of amplifying, attenuating, or inhibiting each other in the ongoing experience and behavior of the human being.

Differential emotions theory has both similarities to and differences from the present organismic theory of behavior. Both give emotions a role in the motivation of behavior, though Izard's theory gives it a more prominent place. Both make a distinction between needs and emotions; Izard separates the basic drives from emotions, calling both affective, whereas I have contrasted needs to emotions. In doing so, I have used a broader category of needs, encompassing psychologically based as well as tissue-deficit-based needs, thereby including as needs some phenomena that Izard would call emotion. Intrinsic motivation as a phenomenon and system is considered emotional in Izard's theory. For Izard, a cognitive-affective interaction that precedes and initiates behavior is similar to what is referred to as a motive in the organismic theory. Further, Izard placed primary emphasis on facial expression as the basis of emotional experience, whereas I have included it with other muscular and visceral changes as the inputs to the subjective experience of emotion.

Izard's theory differed from earlier theories such as Young's (1961) in that Izard considered emotions to be organizers of motivated behavior rather than disruptive responses. Also he considered each emotion to be qualitatively different rather than just quantitatively different on salient dimensions such as intensity. Yet on both of these matters, an integrative rather than contrasting point of view seems appropriate. Emotional reactions do interrupt ongoing behavior and may even be quite disruptive, yet they are often the basis for subsequent goal-directed behavior. Further, each emotion is a qualitatively different experience, but the dimensions of intensity, hedonic value, and degree of disruption have served satisfactorily as descriptors of emotions.

Izard made some interesting points about what I have called nonconscious emotional reactions, although he implied that they occur less often than I have suggested. He explained that feedback from facial expressions may not reach consciousness if more salient demands, resulting from some other emotion or drive, set up an inhibitory process. I would add that cognitive structures can serve the same inhibiting function. Further, he suggested that when the neural and facial components fail to achieve consciousness, they may result in one of two outlet processes. They may be directed into the reticular activation process resulting in nonspecific arousal, which then affects autonomically activated organs. This plays a key role in psychosomatic illness. Second, the neural and facial activity may reach a sufficient level of integration as to be a specific, nonexperienced emotion. In such cases it may be stored in memory and subsequently recalled and experienced. Later, thoughts of a partiuclar stimulus event may call up the experience of a particular emotion that one did not experience at that time.

**Part II
Self-Determination and
Organismic Well-Being**

# 5

## The Loss of Self-Determination and Well-Being

Perhaps the two most important, and interrelated, points in this book are that self-determination has important motivating properties and that being denied the opportunity for self-determination results in the loss of organismic well-being. The first part of this book presented an explication of the role of self-determination in motivational processes. This second part is concerned with the role of self-determination in organismic well-being.

### Empirical Evidence

In recent years there have been numerous empirical studies, with people as well as animals lower on the phylogenetic scale, that have explored some aspect of the relationship among self-determination, motivation, and well-being. These studies have varied in their vocabulary, theoretical constructs, and psychological viewpoints, yet they all lend support to the notion that self-determination is crucial for healthy organismic functioning. One general paradigm for these experiments is that experimental subjects are given an opportunity to utilize a modest amount of additional self-determination relative to the control subjects. They may be allowed to choose what tasks to work with, be given control over some small aspect of their lives, or be given tasks on which the probability of success is quite high; then the groups are assessed on some relevant dependent measure such as intrinsic motivation, performance, or self-confidence. Alternatively the experimental group is denied some opportunity to be self-determining, for example, by being given tasks that are insoluble, and then the groups are assessed on some dependent measure. With human subjects, the manipulation of giving rather than denying additional self-determination typically is used for obvious ethical reasons. To study the effects of denied opportunities for self-determination, research is done with subjects whose baseline opportunity for self-determination is very low, and then some subjects are given greater choice or control, so that in a sense the control group (functioning at baseline) becomes, in theory, the experimental group.

We did one study (Zuckerman et al. 1978) on the effects of self-determination in which college students who were asked to work on a set of interesting puzzles either were allowed to select which puzzles to work on or were assigned those puzzles selected by another subject. Thus there were two groups doing the same tasks, but subjects in one group were given choice over the task and those in the other group were not. The results indicated that subjects in the choice condition were more intrinsically motivated for the activity than those in the no-choice condition. In a somewhat similar experiment (Swann and Pittman 1977), young children either were led to believe they had a choice over their play activities or they were not led to believe this. Once again, those who believed they had greater choice displayed greater intrinsic motivation than those who did not.

Choice has also been shown to affect subjects' performance in learning situations (Perlmuter and Monty 1977). In a modified paired-associate learning paradigm, yoked pairs of subjects were compared on their learning performance. One member in each yoked pair was allowed to select either the stimulus nonsense syllable (Perlmuter and Monty 1973) or the response nonsense syllable (Monty and Perlmuter 1975), while the second member was assigned the syllable selected by the yoked partner. Consistently those subjects who were given choice learned faster than did their no-choice counterparts. These and similar findings simply corroborate what has been advocated in applied areas for some time. In education, theorists such as Bruner (1962) have suggested that freedom to choose and explore is important for motivation and learning; in organizational psychology, participative management and job enrichment are based in the idea that greater self-determination improves motivation and performance (McGregor 1960).

Theoretical as well as empirical work has indicated that increased self-determination leads to enhanced motivation and performance. Additional research has shown that when people feel as if they have control in a situation, they can tolerate various aversive stimuli such as overcrowding or noxious sounds. In one of a series of studies, Glass and Singer (1972) asked subjects to work on various tasks in a room where loud, cacophonous sounds filled the air. One group of subjects had no control over the sound and had to tolerate it; a second group could control it with a button; a third group was told that they had access to someone who could control it, though they were asked not to use this means unless necessary. The subjects with no control over their surroundings did markedly worse on complex tasks and liked the situation less than did either the subjects with the control switch or those who believed they could get control if necessary. Similarly Sherrod et al. (1977) reported that subjects in an aversive noise situation showed increasingly poorer preformance as their degree of control over the noise decreased. Pennebaker et al. (1977) found that subjects exposed to bursts of unpleasant noise reported more physical symptoms such as headaches when they believed they had less control over the noise.

Rodin, Solomon, and Metcalf (1978) have shown that people who feel as if they have some personal control find crowded spaces less aversive. Subjects standing in front of the control panel of an elevator reported feeling less crowded than those standing in a different corner, even when the elevator was equally densely populated and other people were equally close to the subjects. Langer and Saegert (1977) reported that subjects who had increased cognitive control over a crowded situation (derived from greater information about the effects of crowding) were more effective and less stressed than those who had less cognitive control.

We have seen that increased self-determination enhances motivation and performance and that when subjects have the perception of control over aversive stimulation, the stimulation seems less stressful, interferes less with task performance, and causes less physical symptomatology. Let us now review the effects of loss of self-determination on motivation, performance, and well-being. Here we shall see that the loss of self-determination has serious and far-reaching consequences.

## Denial of Self-Determination

Seligman (1975) has considered this matter from a behavioristic perspective. He reasoned that when people are in situations where outcomes are independent of the people's responses, they will lose motivation, display impaired learning, and in some cases show a fear response. Helplessness is the experience of being in a situation with response-outcome independence, and according to Seligman, people have a drive to avoid helplessness.

Seligman and his colleagues have done a series of studies, largely with dogs and rats. The typical paradigm involves subjecting the animals to some aversive stimulus in a situation where no response will terminate that aversive stimulus, including responses that previously had done so. Thus, for example, dogs learned to escape from shocks by pressing a panel; they were then given shocks again, but the panel pressing produced no relief. The animals stopped responding, began cowering in the corner, and failed to respond even when the panel pressing would allow escape. Seligman emphasized that it was not the aversive shock itself that produced this response, for other animals who were shocked as much but had response-outcome dependence in their situations did not show the same unfortunate responding. It is, he continued, the lack of control over the aversive events rather than the aversive events themselves that impairs motivation and performance and produces fear.

Hiroto (1974), one of Seligman's collaborators, did a similar experiment with humans and demonstrated that lack of control will affect their learning as well. Students were subjected either to uncontrollable loud noise, controllable loud noise, or no noise. They were then asked to use a finger shuttle box while there was noise in the background. Moving across the shuttle would turn off the noise, yet those subjects who had previously had uncontrollable noise were significantly poorer at learning that they could control the noise than were the other two groups.

These and a variety of related experiments are very important, for they have demonstrated quite clearly that helplessness impairs performance and motivation. However, I find Seligman's theoretical treatment of the data somewhat inadequate. First, he suggested that organisms have a drive to avoid helplessness. Leaving aside his atypical use of the term *drive*—which is generally reserved for the tissue-deficit needs such as hunger—he has framed the drive in a negativistic way. The need, I assert, is not to avoid helplessness; it is to be effectively self-determining. A person who has never experienced helplessness will not know of the need to avoid it, yet that person will be striving actively to experience competence and self-determination. Considering the need to be one of helplessness avoidance gives the matter an incongruous tone of reactivity rather than activity. The core of self-determination involves acting on the environment to feel intrinsic gratification. When people are unable to behave in a competent, self-determined way, they feel helpless and display the responses described by Seligman. Although Seligman (1975) framed the theory in operant language, he did suggest that cognition (the belief that I am helpless) mediates between the nonresponsive environment and the impaired responding. Mediating cognitions do play a crucial role; however, emotional and motivational factors are also aspects of the helplessness phenomenon and need to be included more directly.

Stotland and Blumenthal (1964), for example, found that providing subjects with a choice about what order they would be administered test items significantly reduced their anxiety. They still expected to take the same tests as the no-choice subjects, but the modest self-determination exercised in selecting the order was enough to have an impact on their anxiety. Even in Seligman's studies, helpless animals and humans displayed emotional responses; yet he treated those as dependent variables rather than causally mediating events. It is important to understand the interplay of anxiety, fear, and emotionality in situations of noncontrol or helplessness, for they are the basis of much pathology, maladjustment, and general organismic ill-being.

Schulz (1976) found that residents of an old folks' home who could predict and/or control the schedule of visits to them by college student visitors were better off physically, psychologically, and behaviorally than other residents who were visited with the same frequency but with no predictability or control. Subjects who were visited but who had no predictability or control were no better off than others who were not visited. A matter as seemingly small as predicting or controlling the time of visits led to the people's taking less medication than the other groups, being rated healthier and more zestful by observers, perceiving themselves to be happier and to have more hope, being more active and making more future commitments, and reporting less time of being lonely and bored. These findings were demonstrated even more dramatically in an unexpected result that appeared in a follow-up study (Schulz and Hanusa 1978). In data collected twenty-four to forty-two months after the termination of the study (and hence the termination of the controllable visits), subjects who had had control or predictability over the visits seemed to be worse off than subjects who had not been visited or who were unpredictably visited. The subjects who had been able to control or predict the time of the visits evidenced dramatic declines from having been better off than the no-control and no-visit groups during the period of control or prediction to being worse off than the other two groups following the termination of the visits. Apparently having been given a little control (or predictability), in a situation where they had presumably accommodated to the no-control nature of the institution, had been very important to them, so the loss of it had quite a significant impact.

Langer and Rodin (1976) found similar results using a different paradigm in an old folks' home. In their study, two groups of subjects received short lectures from a familiar staff member. In one group he emphasized that they had influence over their own lives, suggesting that they could decide to visit friends, rearrange the furniture in their rooms, and so on. In the other group he emphasized that it was the staff's responsibility to make the home an enjoyable place and to do whatever possible for the residents. Also in the first group, subjects were told that a movie would be shown on two nights and they could decide if they wanted to see it and, if so, on which night. Subjects in the second group were told that they would be assigned a night to see it. Finally, all subjects were told that they would be given plants for their rooms; those in the first group were told that they could select the one they wanted, and in fact decide if they wanted one, whereas those in the second group were simply given one. The former group was told that caring for the plant was their responsibility, whereas the latter group was told that the nurses would care for it.

The results of the Langer and Rodin study corroborated those of Schulz's study. Subjects for whom self-responsibility had been emphasized and who had been given opportunities for choice and control displayed a greater sense of activity and well-being. In an eighteen month follow-up, Rodin and Langer (1977) found that the beneficial effects of the self-responsibility treatment continued. Those who had been given greater control were still healthier and happier.

While the Rodin and Langer findings of a continued treatment effect at first might seem inconsistent with follow-up data from Schulz's study that showed the negative effect, careful consideration suggests that the results are in fact quite consistent. In the Schulz study, subjects were given control (over the time of visits) and then the control was removed. The additional control improved well-being, and the subsequent loss of control reduced well-being to below baseline. Having had the control and then lost it made its absence particularly troublesome. In the Rodin and Langer study, the manipulation was a lecture stressing how many opportunities subjects had for control of their own lives. This learning was not terminated (in the way that control was in Schulz's study) even though there were no additional lectures on self-responsibility. Further, the plants that the residents had been given to be responsible for were still theirs if they wanted them, so they still had a cue related to the self-responsibility lectures and they still had something to be responsible for. Hence the beneficial effects continued because the enhanced opportunities for self-determination continued.

The negative impact of being given control and then having it usurped was also highlighted in a study by Perlmuter, Monty, and Cross (1974) using a modified, paired-associate learning paradigm. They found that subjects, who were asked which of five response syllables they preferred to learn and were then assigned one to learn that was not among the five, performed worse in their learning than subjects who were not asked about their preferences. Subjects given such a choice who then learned the chosen syllables performed better than those not asked about their preferences. In sum, lack of self-determination over aspects of one's life is quite detrimental, and it is particularly so when one has been taunted with the opportunity for self-determination and then had it denied.

*Illness and Death*

The highly negative effects of loss of self-determination are even more dramatically demonstrated by the so-called unexplainable deaths. Lefcourt (1973) reported witnessing a case in which a female who had been mute for ten years lived in a hospital ward for hopeless cases. By chance she was relocated briefly to the ward for people soon to be released. Within two weeks she regained speech and became gregarious. Shortly thereafter she was returned to the hopeless ward, and within a week this woman, who had been judged by doctors to be in excellent medical health, died. Many similar cases exist (see Engel 1971) in which people who seem to be in good health die unexpectedly and unexplainably (in the medical sense) when they are in situations that are stressful because of their lack of control. Frankl (1959), in a description of his experience in a World War II concentration camp, asserted that the survivors were the people who managed to maintain a sense of willfulness. He reported observations of many people for whom death followed almost immediately when they gave up hope.

Evidence that loss of self-determination and the corresponding hopelessness can cause serious physical illness and death is not only anecdotal. Schmale and Iker (1966) reported an investigation of women who had shown slight irregularity in cervical cells. These women were then separated into those who had experienced significant personal losses in the preceding six months and those who had not. Of those who had experienced loss, 61 percent developed cervical cancer; of those who had not experienced loss, only 24 percent developed cervical cancer. This study suggests that the lack of control over significant outcomes, as evidenced by personal loss, may predispose people to serious organismic malfunctioning.

In a survey study at an old folks' home, Ferrari (1962) found that virtually all of the people who had reported upon entering that they had no choice about being institutionalized had died within three months, whereas virtually all of the people who had reported having had choice about being institutionalized were still alive at the end of the same period of time. Glass (1977) has summarized several other research studies that have linked stress (which can be thought of as the inability to control significant outcomes) to illness (especially coronary disease) and death.

Although much of the evidence is anecdotal or from case studies and surveys, the weight of it seems clear. When people experience loss of self-determination, when they believe they cannot control aspects of their lives and achieve desired goals, when they feel helpless, they display various manifestations of maladaptation and illness, and in extreme cases they may die.

*Helpless: All or None?*

In cases where severe illness or sudden death occur, the situation typically appears utterly without hope. Life in a concentration camp and forced institutionalization in an old folks' home are both grim circumstances, ones in which there seems to be nothing to live for. More frequently, however, people experience intermittent feelings of helplessness, and typically of a much milder intensity. The consequences, similarly, would be more mild: irritation, mild depression, or nervousness, perhaps accompanied by somatic manifestations of a mild form.

Seligman (1975) has likened the state of helplessness to that of depression, suggesting that depression can be viewed as a passive, stressful reaction to a nonresponsive environment. I agree that people's responses to a loss of self-determination may be depression, though there are a variety of other disorders that may also follow this loss. In Seligman's animal experiments, the nonresponsiveness of the environment was total, there was a high level of aversive stimulation, and there were no other behavioral options available. It was inevitable that the animals would cease all responding except expressive emotionality. However, in most actual situations with people, the environmental nonresponsiveness is less extreme, and people may develop other modes of coping with the stress. For example, they might aggress against the uncontrollable element or displace the aggression onto a friend.

## Self-Determination or Control?

Self-determination is an important motivating force, and the loss of it has various harmful consequences. Many of the research studies, however, have been formulated in terms of control: the need for control, the feeling of control, the effects of loss of control. That raises the question of whether control and self-determination are the same. Generally control refers to a person's achieving a particular outcome; it may be operationalized as success at an activity, being the boss, or making decisions for others. While this is related to self-determination, it is not the same thing. Self-determination means the freedom to decide for oneself—the freedom to choose one's own behaviors in accordance with one's inner needs, feelings, and thoughts. Being a boss or succeeding at a task (which is called being in control) will often leave people feeling self-determining, yet one need not be the boss, or succeed, in order to feel self-determining. Further, being in control does not guarantee self-determination, for people often feel trapped in positions of control.

The point, clearly, is that control and self-determination are not the same, at least as the terms have typically been used. Often self-determination is afforded through control, but control is not necessary for self-determination nor does control assure self-determination. People need to be self-determining; self-determination is necessary for well-being. But people do not always need to be in control; what they need is the freedom to decide for themselves whether to be in control.

People sometimes want to be cared for, to have others be in control. One may at times prefer to be a passenger than to be the driver, even though the driver has more control. And one may prefer to sit with feet up, sipping a gin and tonic, while someone else takes control of the dinner preparations. At times, too much control is anxiety producing and may have detrimental effects (see Averill 1973).

Some people might say that the person who is sitting with the gin and tonic is in control. The problem here is one of vocabulary. Control typically means being in charge of the situation, actively controlling what gets done. Self-determination, by contrast, means deciding whether to be doing something actively, whether to be in control of the situation. Thus, for example, I would say that the passenger would be self-determining but not in control (assuming, of course, that the passenger had chosen that role). And the gin-drinker would be self-determining but not in control unless he or she was "making" someone else do the cooking or telling the other what or how to cook. In the case of telling the other what to do, the gin-drinker would be in control as well as being self-determining.

In the studies on control that I reviewed, control was shown to have beneficial effects. I suggest that that it is because the control either left the people feeling more self-determining or helped to relieve some stress. Having control is particularly important where one's self-determination has been threatened. In crowded places or noisy rooms, in psychological laboratories or institutional settings, people often feel evaluation apprehension, self-consciousness, or claustrophobia. Some sense of control becomes crucial when the environment is such that self-determination is very difficult. To feel self-determining, one must be effective in one's interactions with the environment; one must see results of one's actions. Hence when someone is placed in a nonresponsive environment (as, for example, in Seligman's animal experiments), one is left without a feeling of self-determination, one is helpless, and one needs control as a means of feeling self-determining.

In the Rodin et al. (1978) crowding study, the control afforded subjects in a filled elevator was simply standing in front of the control panel. This is not control that in any meaningful sense affects their situation. Yet it apparently afforded the subjects a feeling of control that moderated the stress of the crowded elevator. Some exercise of control or some sense of control, even if it is really irrelevant, may help to ameliorate the feelings of helplessness that occur when one has lost the opportunity to be self-determining.

At times, one may "fail" at an activity (that is, not have control) and still feel effective and self-determining. If you are undertaking a challenge that you know is a bit beyond your capacity and you do well but do not conquer the challenge, you may still feel satisfaction. One sometimes hears athletic coaches, following the loss of a big game, say, "We really played good ball, I'm proud of the players, but the other team just outplayed us." The team decided to take on a challenge, the players did well at it, and they were left feeling competent and self-determining even though they did not win.

One can observe in some people an intense need to be in control; they seem always to need control. Some others do not always need control, but at times they seem to need it intensely, perhaps being very rigid and authoritarian. I assert that the intense need for control is a response to an inner feeling of not being self-determining. As people feel less self-determination, they often feel a heightened need to control the situation.

These people might be in control, but they would not be self-determining. At times the intense need for control may become pathological, as in the power mongers.

**Inner Control**

Controlling a situation may give people a sense of self-determination, and people seem to need more of this control when their feelings of self-determination have been threatened. But there are other ways to achieve feelings of self-determination. In the Eastern philosophies, the emphasis is placed on the inner experience of control rather than on controlling the situation. One is said to achieve a sense of self-determination (perhaps even satori) by concentrating on inner rather than outer control. It seems safe to say that the world will never be free of disasters, illness, and other stressful events. The route to peace in such stressful situations, according to Eastern philosophy, is through an inner accommodation to these stimulus events that cannot be controlled (see Suzuki 1970). Kelly (1955) made a similar point by suggesting that self-determination is not so much a freedom from constraints as it is an acceptance of those constraints in the individual's system of constructs.

One's interpretation of stimulus events plays a role in one's achieving inner control. For example, suppose your car breaks down on the way to a meeting and you miss the meeting. Later the committee chairperson yells angrily at you for missing it. You might interpret the yelling as confirmation that you are a bad person and cannot control your life, in which case you might feel helpless. Or you might interpret it as indication that even though the chairperson is upset and angry, you did the best you could given the situation. In the latter case, there would be no helplessness; you might feel sorry about inconveniencing the chairperson, but you would not be upset and helpless.

Often the fear, panic, and feelings of helplessness that accompany events result more from one's idiosyncratic interpretation of the event than the event itself. A person may misinterpret a rather responsive situation as being nonresponsive. The person would fear helplessness and might behave in a way that makes the environment nonresponsive. An example of a misinterpretation of an event actually creating the aversive event would be a person who interprets a mild chest pain as an antecedent of a fatal cardiac arrest, and as a result of the interpretation experience severe anxiety that brings on a heart attack, even if the initial pain had been just heartburn.

An understanding of situations can provide cognitive control (see, for example, Averill 1973; Langer and Saegert 1977) and may ameliorate the stress associated with the situation. Langer, Janis, and Wolfer (1975), for example, have shown that stress is substantially reduced for surgical patients when they are provided with information that helps them cope with the difficult situation. Of course, it is also true that some stimulus events are more difficult to accept (to experience without severe stress) than others. Knowing that you will be sick for one week is easier to adapt to than knowing that you will be sick for a year. Even so, an understanding of the situation and the concomitant reduction of uncertainty will help restore the person's feeling of self-determination because it clarifies the constraints and possibilities with which he or she must work.

Self-determination (the flexibility in individual responding) is not solely a matter of acting on the environment to bring about changes; it is in part a matter of accepting the unchangeable elements of the situation and accommodating effectively to them. An effective accommodation involves treating constraints as information to be used in making decisions about how to satisfy needs. Constraints typically limit the options available to one, and effective accommodation means selecting from available options in a way that maximizes motive satisfaction. One can also create new options for oneself, thereby enhancing the choice, but the point is that certain desired things sometimes are not available, and that fact requires accommodation. If you head for the library to study and find it closed, you may accommodate effectively (for example, by borrowing the needed book from a friend and finding a quiet place to study), or you may be upset and ineffective (for example, by breaking a window in the library and angrily going to a nearby bar to spend the evening in upset). Recognizing that one cannot attain certain goals or achieve certain ends can be either highly stressful or relatively nonstressful depending upon one's interpretation and accommodation.

Cognitive control or internal accommodation can compensate for one's inability to control significant events and thereby leave one with a feeling of self-determination. A man who learns that he has only three years to live can accept the fact and make the most of the three years by feeling affect, satisfying motives, and accomplishing goals—in short, accommodating and being self-determining—or he cannot accept it, by being stressed, feeling frustrated and upset, and acting maladaptively—in short, not accommodating and behaving automatically.

## Reactance

The idea that a seemingly nonresponsive environment will leave people helpless and paralyzed seems counter to our widely held belief in the survival instinct. One might expect that if your freedom were threatened, you would fight to preserve it, rather than slouching in a corner. Just such a hypothesis has been proposed and validated by Brehm (1966, 1972). He suggested that threats to one's freedom arouse a motivation, which he termed reactance, to protect or restore the freedom. If, for example, two options are equally attractive—you cannot decide between a blue car and a red one—and then one of the two options is eliminated—the red one did not come through on the shipment as expected—the eliminated item tends to become more attractive. You are likely to prefer the red car even though you were deadlocked until you heard that you no longer could choose the red one. You might subsequently find yourself traveling a hundred miles to a dealership in the next city to look for a red one. At least you are likely to grumble to the dealer if you agree to take the now less-preferred blue one.

The level of one's experienced reactance depends, according to Brehm, on several factors: (1) the belief that you had freedom in that realm; (2) the severity of the threat (if you expected no curfew and were told by a parent to be home by 1 A.M. you would experience less reactance than if you were told to be home by 10 P.M.); (3) the importance of the freedom being threatened (you might scarcely care if you return to your apartment to find that the superintendent has, without consulting you, replaced the light fixture in your closet, whereas you might be quite distressed if the fixture over the dining room table were changed); and (4) the implication of this threat for future freedoms (if you were assigned to lecture on a topic that you did not like, you might let it pass if you know it will not happen again, whereas you would put your foot down hard if you thought it would set a precedent).

Hammock and Brehm (1966) found that if people expected to have a choice among several options, they experienced reactance when they were assigned an outcome even if it was the one they preferred. However, Lewis and Blanchard (1971) reported that subjects who were assigned outcomes they preferred experienced greater control (hence, less reactance) than subjects who were assigned outcomes they dispreferred.

The predictions from reactance theory and from learned helplessness theory seem quite contradictory. Wortman and Brehm (1975) have suggested, however, that people's reactions to situations in which they have no control—whether it be reactance or helplessness—will depend on mediating factors. They believe that when people expect control, loss of that control will arouse reactance; however, when they expect no control, they will respond helplessly. Thus when people are exposed to uncontrollable situations, at first they will be strongly motivated to gain control; however, with repeated exposure to the situation, gradually they will learn that they cannot gain control and will respond with diminished motivation, performance, and health. Further, and unfortunately, the helplessness generalizes to similar situations so that people may act helpless even when they could control the situation (Seligman 1975). Wortman and Brehm added that important outcomes will cause greater reactance at first and then greater helplessness after repeated uncontrollability.

I find the analysis of Wortman and Brehm very cogent, though I think that for some people reactance motivation will persist longer than they seem to indicate. People often exercise their freedom quite creatively within relatively nonresponsive environments. For example, workers who are given menial jobs within a highly authoritarian setting may turn their reactance into attempts to beat the system. Because they cannot legitimately gain control, they develop schemes that in many cases are counter to the organizational goals but that give them a sense of control. Or they may develop informal social structures within which they have freedom and respect.

## Freedom: Reality, Perception, Deception

The issue of whether freedom can actually exist in human responding or whether it is simply an illusion is both fascinating and complicated. In a philosophical sense, the answer to whether there is actual freedom is unknowable; it is only assumable. In a psychological sense, the answer must come from empirical data. Thus freedom must be defined in a way that allows for an empirical test. In this book, self-determination is the concept that operationalizes freedom. Self-determination means that internal states such as motives, thoughts, feelings, and choices are causal antecedents of behavior. Thus the data reviewed so far provide unequivocal evidence that there is freedom of the sort that I have referred to as self-determination. When people believe they have freedom (Steiner 1970), when they believe their behaviors will have an impact (Rotter 1966), they behave differently, they feel different, and they experience a different sense of well-being than when they believe they are not free and that the world is nonresponsive to them. This is evidence that people can be free, for it demonstrates that internal states—thoughts, feelings, desires—can have a causal impact on behavior.

It is clear from various studies that people must perceive that the environment will respond to them (they must perceive that they have the opportunity to be self-determining) in order to remain motivated and healthy. People who are in an environment that is responsive (that is, one where they have freedom) but who do not perceive the responsiveness (that is, they do not perceive that they are free), will behave like people who are in a nonresponsive environment (one in which they are not free). Thus, actual freedom (control or response-outcome dependence) is not enough; there must be perceived freedom (perceived control or perceived response-outcome dependence) as well. People may have a variety of options in a highly responsive environment, but if they do not believe they are free, if they do not feel free, they will not behave like free people; they will not be self-determining.

There remains the more knotty problem of whether perceived freedom is enough to ensure motivation and health or whether there must be actual freedom as well. There are several elements in the answer to this question. First, it is clear from the data that over the short run, perceived freedom is enough; there need not be actual freedom. For example, in our study (Zuckerman et al. 1978), subjects were given actual choice about puzzle problems, and this was shown to increase their intrinsic motivation for the activity; and in the Swann and Pittman (1977) study, subjects were given perceived choice but not actual choice, and still their intrinsic motivation increased. Numerous other experiments have shown the same result; in fact, the common paradigm in social psychology for studying choice is to give the illusion of choice rather than actual choice. Subjects are told, for example, "You are free to select whatever task you would like to work on, but as long as you are sitting in front of task B, why don't you start with it." These so-called illusion-of-choice studies yield results that would be expected in actual-choice situations.

On the other hand, this illusion-of-choice effect will last only until the person tries to use the choice and finds that it does not exist, that the environment does not respond. It may take a few tries before the person abandons the perception of freedom, but it will soon vanish. This point is similar to Wortman and Brehm's (1975) point that people will try to regain freedom until they are convinced that they cannot get it, and then they will experience helplessness.

If people are led to believe that they have freedom and then find out that they do not, they may be worse off than they would have been without believing it in the first place. This hypothesis received support from the Schulz and Hanusa (1978) and Perlmutter et al. (1974) findings that gaining and then losing choice may be worse than not having it.

The realization that the perception of freedom and control affects behavior has led some theorists to suggest a kind of misattribution therapy in which they give a client false information about the cause of a disturbance as a way of ameliorating the distress. Yet this seems to be extremely risky, for if the clients learn that they have been deceived by a person whom they trusted, even if the person was attempting to help, the consequences could be quite profound. Further, one aspect of self-determination is the accommodation to the realistic constraints in a situation. When trusted authorities misrepresent the nature of these constraints, people are denied important information that is necessary for a healthy self-determination.

Another aspect of the answer to whether perceived choice, in the absence of actual choice, will ensure well-being is that people may deceive themselves in thinking they have choice when they do not. As a way of maintaining self-esteem or reducing cognitive dissonance (see Aronson 1969), people may convince themselves that they are self-determining.

Alcoholics, heavy smokers, and overeaters often believe that they could stop drinking, smoking, or overeating if they wanted to. They have created perceived self-determination without actual self-determination. Yet this self-deceived freedom does not ensure well-being; indeed it is likely to perpetuate ill-being since it is a cover-up for malfunctioning and it prevents people from seeking help.

Many of the data on cardiac disease and sudden death (see Glass 1977) come from successful people such as business executives who have considerable control and who perceive themselves to be self-determining. Yet much of their behavior is automatic rather than self-determined; they are pawns to external rewards and constraints while believing (self-deceiving) that they are free and self-determining. This interpretation leads to the conclusion that a self-deceived perception of freedom is not enough for well-being.

**Motivational Subsystems**

When people are in environments that are not responsive to their initiations, they tend not to be self-determining; they tend to operate out of either the extrinsic motivational subsystem or the amotivational subsystem. Most of the research on helplessness and lack of control relates primarily to the operation of the amotivational subsystem. When the amotivational subsystem is solely operative, there would be no behavior; people would be passive; they would believe there is no use in behaving. The dogs in Seligman's studies could be described as being in the amotivational state; they were inactive. The most extreme case of the amotivational state would be death, as we saw in the sudden-death cases.

Typically people do not become wholly inactive; helplessness is not all or none. Instead they experience helplessness, but they engage in some amount of automatic behavior such as displaced aggressive acts or overeating. These situations involve the mixture of the extrinsic and amotivational subsystems (figure 3-4) yielding automatic, helpless behavior. People in the amotivational state feel and perceive themselves as if they were nonself-determining. Their perceptions may not be veridical, but the error is likely to be an underestimation of their opportunities for self-determination, as has been demonstrated by the fact that helplessness generalizes to situations where there is response-outcome dependence (Hiroto 1974).

Studies of hard-driven people who develop coronary disease or die suddenly show a primary operation of the extrinsic rather than the amotivational subsystem. When the extrinsic system is operative, people are quite active rather than passive. When the extrinsic system is solely operative, people are behaving automatically; they are not self-determining. However, they may be in control of situations. The point is that even those behaviors are determined primarily by the interplay of extrinsic cues and non-conscious motives. Further, people, when the extrinsic system is operating and they are behaving automatically, may report that they are being self-determining. This is what I referred to previously as self-deception. Thus I hypothesize that when the amotivational subsystem is operative, people will tend to underestimate their possibilities for self-determination, whereas when the extrinsic motivational subsystem is operative, people will tend to overestimate their possibilities for self-determination.

The concept of self-deception is difficult for experimental psychologists to deal with, for it is not readily accessible; it must be inferred. On the other hand, clinicians find that some such concept is invaluable, indeed necessary, for integrating clinical evidence. The concept was particularly useful in accounting for the relationship between highly extrinsically motivated people and illnesses such as those reported by Glass (1977).

Let me elaborate on how to distinguish a self-deceiving, automatic behaver from the self-determiner (especially one operating from a mix of the intrinsic and extrinsic subsystems referred to in figure 3-4 as chosen, extrinsic behavior). Self-determined behavior is flexible; it changes as information changes. In fact, people will seek relevant information to make informed decisions. When behaving automatically from the extrinsic subsystem, people will be less flexible and less responsive to relevant information. Indeed they will resist information that is inconsistent with their automatic behavior. Recently McGraw and McCullers (1979) presented data that supported this assertion. They found that when subjects were paid (thus the extrinsic subsystem) to work on a series of nine Luchins (1942) water-jar problems, they had a more difficult time breaking set than subjects who were not paid (thus the intrinsic subsystem). On nine problems, the solution to the problem of ending up with a given quantity of water involved using a formula of $B - A - 2C$. Rewarded and nonrewarded subjects did equally well on the problems, but on the tenth problem, which required the much simpler solution of $A - C$, the rewarded subjects did significantly worse. The extrinsic subjects were not as flexible in dealing with the new information; they found it harder to break their set of $B - A - 2C$.

## Biased Perceptions of Self-Determination

Recent research has indicated that people sometimes overestimate their freedom and other times underestimate it. For example, Langer (1975) found that people often feel more free than they actually are. She reported that people who engaged in purely chance tasks such as cutting a deck of cards or drawing lotteries often believed their likelihood of winning to be above chance level. In fact, it was not so much the actual probabilities of winning that affected people's confidence as it was extraneous factors such as competition, familiarity, and choice. When people competed against a nervous opponent rather than a confident one, they believed their chances of winning were higher even though it was a purely chance event. Similarly when they had choice—for example, when they selected their own lottery ticket rather than simply being given one—they felt as if their chances of winning were higher even though the event was chance. People are often so eager to have control that they believe they have it when in fact they do not. This focus on external, extraneous cues occurs primarily when people are operating from an extrinsic motivational subsystem. For example, when they do not have a strong sense of competence and self-determination, they will tend to be extrinsically motivated and will assess their degree of control, choice, or freedom on the basis of external cues.

Biased perceptions of freedom sometimes involve underestimates (rather than overestimates) of one's possibilities for choice and control. Subjects who have no control in one situation may generalize the belief in no control to other situations. Other studies have even shown that learned helplessness, lowered expectations for one's performance, and poorer performance can be induced simply by having subjects witness others doing poorly (Brown and Inouye 1978), by having them observe, though not actually experience, a noncontingency between responses and outcomes (DeVellis, DeVellis, and McCauley 1978), or by assigning them a label of inferiority (Langer and Benevento 1978).

In sum, there are many factors other than the actual possibility of choice, the actual probability of success, or the actual degree of control available that influence people's perceptions of their own freedom or control. This discrepancy between actual and perceived freedom may be one of overestimation, which tends to be associated with the extrinsic motivational subsystem, or underestimation, which tends to be associated with the amotivational subsystem.

## Individual Differences in Self-Determination

People often misassess their opportunities for self-determination, perceiving that they have either more or less opportunity than is actually the case. Several studies have focused on situational factors that have had a significant impact on people's perception of greater or lesser control—such as having failed at a similar task previously, competing against a confident versus an anxious other, or being labeled a failure. Personal factors also influence whether people perceive a situation as one that affords them control or is nonresponsive to their initiations. The same situation may leave one person feeling helpless but motivate another to solve the problem. Previously I suggested that different motivational subsystems will lead to different reactions to situations. I now raise the interesting question of what personality characteristics (in other words, relatively stable traits) will affect people's perceptions of a situation and their responses to that situation.

Rotter (1966) has suggested that people have different generalized expectancies about the relationship between behavior and reinforcements. Some people tend to believe that reinforcements are largely a matter of chance; fate either delivers them or it does not. People's behavior is seen as having little to do with whether they receive rewards. Such people feel that it is no use to try to influence the political process or to try to make friends. Whatever happens will happen. These people are said to have an external locus of control, for they believe that the control of reinforcements is external to themselves. Other people tend to believe that there is a close correlation between their behavior and the reinforcements that follow. If you engage in the appropriately instrumental activities, you will receive the desired rewards. In general, they expect a high degree of relationship between responses and outcomes, so they are more likely to try to influence the political process or to make friends with people whom they find attractive. These people are said to have an internal locus of control, for they believe that control of reinforcement is internal to them; it resides in their behavior.

This construct is a generalized one; that is, it is an orientational tendency. Highly internal people do not believe that all rewards are closely correlated with behavior, but in the absence of contrary information, they are likely to operate with the assumption of behavior-reward dependence. Applying the construct to the question of why different people respond differently to the same stimulus event (with some people acting helpless and others being motivated to achieve) suggests that people with an internal locus of control are likely to respond by attempting to conquer the challenge or overcome the source of frustration, while people with an external locus of control are likely to respond with diminished motivation and performance. Externals tend to believe that responses and outcomes are independent, so they are quick to pick up on cues that suggest it and then respond helplessly. Hiroto (1974) has provided some evidence for this hypothesis. In his study of controllable noise, Hiroto found that subjects with an external locus-of-control personality were more likely to become helpless than subjects with an internal locus-of-control personality. (For other related studies see Lefcourt 1976.)

Thus, we see that people have different general beliefs about the relationship (or lack thereof) between behavior and rewards, and these beliefs influence how they respond to a stimulus event.

The distinction of internal versus external locus of control made by Rotter, and paralleled by Seligman's distinction between helpless and nonhelpless people, is very important; however, it is important to make a finer dinstinction in people's orientations toward control and causality. To do that, I shall consider the concept of locus of causality (Heider 1958; deCharms 1968; Deci 1975), which began in the literature on attribution processes, and relate it to the concept of locus of control. In Rotter's theory, the term *locus of control* is used; people are classified as having an internal versus external locus of control. In causality theory, the term *locus of causality* is used, and people are characterized as having a personal or impersonal locus of causality (Heider 1958).

Rotter distinguished internal from external control on the basis of one's belief in the relationship between one's own behavior and reinforcing consequences. Internal-control people believe in a relationship between their behavior and reinforcements; external-control people believe that reinforcements are chance occurrences and that their behaviors do not produce desired consequences. In the language of attribution theory (Heider 1958), external-control people would be said to experience impersonal causality. Events are not caused by their intentions but rather by some unknown (impersonal) forces in the environment.

Internal-control people believe in a relationship between behavior and reinforcements. For them behavior is caused by personal intentions. The attribution theory terminology for internal control would be personal causality. Thus personal versus impersonal causality parallels Rotter's internal versus external control and Seligman's helplessness versus nonhelplessness.

Personal causality should be broken down further into internal causality and external causality (Deci 1975). Both of these are types of personal causality, for both are mediated by motives, whether conscious or nonconscious. They are personally caused, but the object of the intentions is different. In internal causality, the person selects goals for which the rewards are primarily intrinsic; heuristically, the behaviors are internally caused. In external causality, the person behaves to satisfy motives for which the rewards are primarily extrinsic, (such as money or power); heuristically the behaviors are externally caused by the rewards or controls in the situation. Another way to make this distinction is to say that with internal causality, the person is the cause of behaviors and outcomes are the effect, whereas with external causality, outcomes are the cause of behaviors and the person is the effect. In both cases there is dependence between behaviors and outcomes, but in an experiential sense one could say that the initial element in the causal sequence of internality is a personal need, whereas the initial element for externality is an external cue, such as a reward or constraint.

Internal versus external causality is not the same as internal versus external control. Internal versus external locus of control parallels personal versus impersonal causality. External control and impersonal causality do not involve mediation by motives or intention. By contrast, both external causality and internal causality are mediated by motives; thus they are personally caused. The locus of control for either internal or external causality would be internal. The confusion arises because of the similar vocabulary of the two theories. Personal causality (internal or external causality) involves the belief in a correlation between responses and outcomes (thus it parallels Rotter's concept of an internal locus of control) while impersonal causality involves the belief in response-outcome independence (Rotter's external locus of control or Seligman's helplessness). Table 5-1 displays the relationship among these various concepts.

## Causality Orientations as Personality Types

The three beliefs about the nature of causality—internal, external, and impersonal—constitute a cognitive component of the pure-form operation of the three motivational subsystems—intrinsic, extrinsic, and amotivational.

**Table 5-1**
**Relationship among Locus-of-Control, Locus-of-Causality, and Helplessness Concepts**

| | Locus of Control (Rotter, 1966) | Locus of Causality (Heider, 1958 Deci, 1975) | Helplessness (Seligman, 1975) |
|---|---|---|---|
| Behavior and outcomes are independent | External control | Impersonal causality | Helplessness |
| Behavior and outcomes are dependent | Internal control | Personal causality (External causality if motivated by external constraint or reward) | Not helplessness |
| | | Personal causality (Internal causality if intrinsically motivated) | |

Every person has all three subsystems, with the concomitant views of causality; however, people vary greatly in the extent to which the various subsystems are operative and in the extent to which the various perceptions of causality are central. I now propose to characterize people on the basis of the relative operation of their three subsystems and on their correspondingly predominant beliefs about causality. There are three types of personality described by the three causality orientations. People can be characterized as having an internal-causality orientation (they are internals), an external-causality orientation (externals), or an impersonal-causality orientation (impersonals).

*The Internal-Causality Personality*

These people operate primarily from the intrinsic motivational subsystem. When they are seeking extrinsic rewards, there is a mix of the intrinsic and extrinsic subsystems, such that the extrinsically motivated behaviors are chosen. They tend to perceive the locus of causality to be internal, and they tend to feel self-determining and competent. The most natural form of personality is one characterized in large part by internal causality. It is a mode of functioning that utilizes a maximum of personal knowledge (Polanyi 1958). Perls (1973) referred to it as organismic functioning. One operates more holistically in the sense of allowing more information into conscious awareness. One is to a greater extent in the state of subjective experience (May 1967) and is more likely to experience what Csikszentmihalyi (1975) called flow, that "unified flowing from one movement to the next." Such people would have a greater awareness of basic human needs and emotions and would have a greater clarity in utilizing this information to make behavioral decisions. One would, for example, be more aware of the organismic need for food and respond to the need rather than to eating habits. One would recognize one's anger more clearly and deal with it more adaptively. One would have less need to project disliked and unknown parts of oneself and would instead accept them and manage them accordingly. One would accept oneself for who one is. These descriptions are phenomenological in nature; what they mean in terms of the organismic framework is that such people would have a strong sense of competence and self-determination and a high degree of willfulness. Information from one's motive structure and the environment would instigate the intrinsic motivational subsystem and pass freely into conscious awareness to form motives. There would be less blocking of emotions, so they too would be allowed into conscious awareness and would provide the basis for motive formation. One would have a stronger sense of will; in other words, one would make more behavioral decisions and be more self-determining, and, finally, there would be less automatic, maladaptive responding motivated by non-conscious motives and emotions. Much behavior would be automatized, for automatization is necessary and useful, but internal-causation people would be more able to bring that behavior back into the realm of self-determination either to reprogram it or to govern it with decisions. Thus internal causality would involve much automatized behavior but a minimum of automatic behavior.

Sometimes it is suggested that an internal orientation is harmful because it leads people to blame themselves for failure. But that is a misconception of internal causality. True internals are not concerned with blame and fault; they are interested in understanding how and why they failed so they can succeed next time. They would ask, "What did I do, given the enivironment as it exists, that contributed to the failure?" Then if they find that there is nothing they can do to succeed given the situation, they would accommodate to the situation and look for success elsewhere. The idea of blaming oneself is a characteristic of the amotivational subsystem and the impersonal-causality orientation.

Internals display flexibility and responsivity to the environment. When the situation allows intrinsically motivated behavior, it would be forthcoming; when the situation requires extrinsically motivated behavior, that would be forthcoming, but it would tend to be the chosen extrinsic behavior that involves extrinsically motivated overt behaviors and intrinsically motivated covert, cognitive processes (information selection and choice).

## The External-Causality Personality

The external is archetypically represented by the highly driven overachiever. These people are always striving for more. They believe in a response-outcome dependence and are forever responding in an attempt to achieve another outcome. Their focus is external; they look for indicators of success (wealth, accumulation, titles) and do what they need to get them. They are not unlike a dog on the treadmill of yesteryear.

External personalitites display what Glass (1977) and others have referred to as a Type-A behavior pattern (Jenkins, et al. 1967). It is characterized by considerable urgency, increased aggression, and excessive competition. The Type-A behavior pattern is said to be a response to stress or to lack of control. The external personality is a rather stable orientation involving a high degree of Type-A behaving, and this personality orientation results from an underlying lack of self-determination. For externals, there is an ever-present stress from the continued failure to satisfy their underlying intrinsic need for self-determination. People who display the Type-A behavior pattern have been found to be twice as likely to have coronary disease as others (Glass 1977).

External people operate primarily with an extrinsic motivational sub-system. They can be distinguished by their inflexibility in responding and in processing information. The pure-form operation of the extrinsic subsystem involves considerable automatic behavior, which is specifically characterized by its inflexibility.

The external orientation is somewhat deceptive, for externals often appear to be self-determining; they frequently make choices. But their decisions tend to be based on external cues and criteria, and their primary deficiency is in managing motives rather than selecting behaviors. Externals always seem to have to be striving for extrinsic goals; their behavior is controlled by the extrinsic rewards and cues. Their striving for rewards dominates their awareness. Sometimes people may choose behaviors to satisfy extrinsic motives, but they do not choose the motives. The motives are strongly determined by external cues. This point is illustrated by people who cannot take a vacation; they get very anxious and distraught when they are away from the office. They cannot hold in abeyance motives like the desire for power, money, or status.

I speculate that the people who jumped from skyscrapers during the stock market crash during the Great Depression were very high externals. External factors so determined their behavior and their self-worth that the sudden loss of those external cues and indicators of worth left them helpless and unable to cope. They plunged into the amotivational state and ended their lives.

To a large extent, people with an external-causality orientation have lost touch with their basic organismic needs, such as for food, competence, and self-determination. They behave automatically, and their behavior appears to be governed by external cues. In actuality, of course, the behavior is governed by an interplay of external cues and nonconscious motives. These people seem to have a high need for control as a cover-up for their low sense of self-determination.

The matter of self-deception is relevant to the external orientation, for this orientation involves the greatest self-deception. There is a tendency to hold motives and emotions out of awareness—for example, to attend not to their feelings of nonself-determination but instead to those of control. The blocking of motives and emotions from awareness is an active process that is a function of the extrinsic subsystem. Interestingly the information being blocked is accessible to awareness, and indeed the process of blocking information from awareness necessitates knowing the information (at a preconscious level) in order to block it out. Thus self-deception is a process performed by the extrinsic (and amotivational) subsystems that typifies externals (and impersonals). It involves believing some things about oneself and presenting those things; contradictory things are known preconsciously and blocked from awareness.

In psychoanalytic theory, the ego is said to repress unconscious material. This concept, however, presents a logical inconsistency, for something cannot be repressed if it is not known in some sense. The motivational subsystems select information for awareness; that which is blocked and the criteria for blocking are accessible to awareness—they are "known"—but not attended to. Psychotherapy involves directing attention to the blocking processes so that information will be allowed into awareness where it can be managed more effectively. It is characteristic of internals, and is therefore a goal for therapy with externals (or impersonals), that they are aware of motives and emotions, they are aware of learned admonitions, and they utilize a strongly developed sense of self-determination to manage these forces in effective ways.

### The Impersonal-Causality Personality

These people have learned to be helpless; typically they display the behaviors elaborated by Seligman (1975). They have experienced continually thwarted attempts at self-determination, and they have learned that the environment is not responsive to their initiations. One such person once said to me, "I've lost the desire to make choices. I feel like I'll exist as long as my body holds out, but I won't participate." Such people evidence little self-determination, and their behaviors are largely automatic. The amotivational subsystem is predominant for impersonals, though their automatic, helpless behavior (see figure 3-4) involves a mixture of amotivational and extrinsic subsystems.

These three personality types represent pure forms—most people will not fit exactly into one category. Models such as this one provide theoretical tools that allow us to study behavior and design interventions for therapy and education.

### Self-Determination, Competence, and Personalities

At times, the distinction between internals and externals may seem difficult to understand because externals who operate from the extrinsic subsystem may be highly competent individuals and may appear to be making choices. But their choices are controlled by external cues rather than an awareness of organismic needs, so the real lack of choice appears in their inability to manage needs and motives. Unlike internals, they have to be doing what they are doing.

Table 5-2 describes the personality orientations in terms of competence and self-determination. Since the three orientations parallel the three motivational subsystems that exist within every person, the table similarly describes aspects of a person's subsystems. Internals are described as competent and self-determining; externals as competent but not self-determining (they behave very effectively but are governed by external cues); and impersonals as neither competent nor self-determining. The combination of self-determining and incompetent does not persist over time. If one initiates and continually fails, one will not remain self-determining; either the person will give up initiating and comply (be extrinsically governed and become external) or will continue to fail and end up feeling helpless (amotivational and impersonal). Given my definition of willfulness as being based in a sense of competence and self-determination, it is clear that internals on average would be most willful; externals, moderate; and impersonals, least. However, externals often will display much of the "determined gritting of one's teeth" type of willing that May (1967a, 1967b) referred to as willpower, although they will evidence very little of the other type of willing that involves steering oneself toward the gratification of organismic needs.

The table suggests that self-determination is more fundamental than competence for intrinsic motivation. In fact, a study by Fisher (1978) corroborated this by showing a correlation between competence and intrinsic motivation in conditions of personal causation (self-determination) but no correlation between competence and intrinsic motivation in the absence of personal causation.

In a sense, I have overemphasized the difference between competence and self-determination. When free to initiate, people will tend to develop competencies, so the two will be closely linked. But the point is that one can control people to be competent, and indeed this is the core of extrinsic motivational techniques and the external orientation.

**Table 5-2**
**Causality Orientations**

|  | *Self-Determining* | *Nonself-Determining* |
|---|---|---|
| *Competent* | Internal | External |
| *Noncompetent* | Unstable state | Impersonal |

# 6 Development and Self-Determination

The development of competence and self-determination is intertwined with that of personality and cognitive structures. This chapter considers the development of one's sense of competence and self-determination (one's willfulness) and the corresponding development of personality orientations. Recall that the internal-causality orientation involves a high level of willfulness; the external-causality orientation, a moderate level; and the impersonal-causality orientation, the lowest level.

One's level of willfulness and one's causality orientation may change somewhat throughout life as one has experiences of efficacy and inefficacy. However, the first dozen years of life are extremely important, for they seem to leave one with a rather enduring sense of competence and self-determination and with what might be termed a baseline causality orientation. While one's willfulness and orientation may change somewhat, adults are clearly less maleable than children, so later changes tend to be smaller and less dramatic.

Just as we are neither as free as we like to think, nor as determined as we fear (Tomkins 1969), we are neither as plastic as some would have us believe (Kagan 1978) nor as determined by our early experiences as others have suggested (Freud 1924, 1955). The remnants of early experience exert influence throughout our lives, yet these influences are better viewed as general orientations than as determinants of specific behaviors. In spite of these orientations, will, that capacity for choosing behaviors and managing motives, provides the freedom from specific determination by early experiences.

Healthy development involves establishing an autonomous mode of interacting with the environment such that one chooses behaviors that allow satisfaction of one's needs while at the same time respecting the people and material in one's environment. This requires that parents and other significant people in a child's environment provide a setting in which the child is allowed freedon to explore within clear boundaries. Children must discover things for themselves if they are to be self-determining in later years. At the same time, they must also come to a reconciliation with the demands of the environment. They must achieve a certain degree of impulse control that allows harmonious interactions with their surroundings.

The simple, behavioristic prescription for achieving one's developmental goals in raising a child is to reward desired behaviors and extinguish undesired ones. This approach, however, has two main difficulties. First, healthy development involves the strengthening of certain psychological processes rather than specific, reinforceable behaviors. The problem of how to strengthen processes such as trust or self-determination is sufficiently complicated that the reinforcement paradigm is not adequate as a means of conceptualizing the matter. The second difficulty with a reinforcement approach is that rewards often decrease intrinsic motivation and internal causality. Rewards are controllers of behavior, and people may as easily fight against the controls by doing other behaviors and aggressing against the controller as allow themselves to be controlled. In a similar vein, when people are denied desired rewards their frustration does not necessarily extinguish the behavior; it may lead them to change their goals, lash out at the source of frustration, develop rigidities in behaviors, and so on. The consequences of being denied the opportunity to be competent and self-determining are quite profound.

People play an active role in shaping themselves, in part by responding to the stresses of biological and environmental forces. All people do not respond the same to stimuli, and any person's response becomes incorporated into the person so as to influence later behavior and later development.

**Stages of Personality Development**

Freud's theory of personality development is organized around the libido, that source of highly mobile (or dynamic) energy that is the basis of sexuality. According to Freud, libido makes demands on the human psyche and motivates one's interactions with the environment. During early years, these interactions are the basis of human development. The libido, being a mobile source of energy, changes its location in predictable ways such that different regions of the child's body are the center of erogenous excitation at different periods in early life. With each region of excitation, said Freud, comes a psychological conflict, and the ways in which these conflicts are resolved or not resolved are the factors that create one's personality and determine later behavior. The three major crises occur during the first six or seven years of a child's life and correspond to three regions of sexuality: the mouth, the anus, and the genitals. Each region, being the focus of sexuality for one developmental stage, is the battleground for a struggle between urges and inhibitions, and the resolution of the struggles is said to create a behavioral prototype that persists into adulthood and influences one's interactions with the world.

Freud correctly isolated three key phrases of development in the first half-dozen years of a child's life, yet his strict focus on the sexual component of development has obscured an understanding of the development of self-determination and will. White (1960) and Erikson (1950) have added competence and interpersonal components to Freud's sexual focus and therefore have helped to elaborate the issues involved in the development of self-determination.

White asserted that a strictly libidinal model cannot explain children's emotional development adequately. While excepting the basic ideas of Freud's theory, White proposed the addition of competence elements to the analysis of development. He asserted that a development model must recognize the existence of competence motivation and attend to the type of mastery experiences that are central for a child at various stages in development.

Competence refers to one's capabilities for interacting with the environment in ways that allow one to exist and develop. Humans must learn skills for effective interacting, and this learning is what is meant by competence development. The motivation comes from intrinsic motivation. White (1959) referred to it interchangeably as competence motivation and effectance motivation. In discussing intrinsic motivation, I emphasize both its competence and its self-determination aspects. The two are closely related though partially separable. Effective interacting implies both, yet in White's (1960) discussion of competence and psychosexual development, he focused more on competence as it relates to skill acquisition in eventual preparation for an adult work life. Thus his discussion was somewhat narrow in its explication of the relationship between intrinsic motivation and development.

Intrinsic motivation is involved in exploration, manipulation, and a host of other non-drive-reducing behaviors. While it is surely the case that much learing occurs from the processes of drive reduction, it is equally the case that much activity of an exploratory and playful nature occurs at precisely those times when one's basic drives seem well sated. These activities are not random, idle movements; they are carefully organized, serious endeavors that promote competence and leave the child feeling efficacious. One difficulty in the analysis of these behaviors motivated by intrinsic motivation is that they frequently operate in conjunction with other motivational processes. The case of interested exploration may be a pure case of intrinsic motivation, yet all too often the case is not pure. Nonetheless a careful analysis of competence-related phenomena based in intrinsic motivational processes seems extremely important.

Erikson's theory was also based in the psychoanalytic tradition, though his primary elaboration of Freudian psychology is in terms of the social influences that interact with drives. His developmental theory bears much relationship to Freud's and the first five core conflicts parallel the five stages in Freud's theory of psychosexual development. The principal difference is that Erikson's theory is not so narrowly based in libidinal concerns but is pointed in terms of the nature of the core conflict of a developmental epoch as applied to a wide variety of settings. The first four stages are of primary interest for our concerns with the development of self-determination.

*The First Year*

According to Freud, sexuality is centered in the mouth during the first year of a child's life. It is the primary organ for interacting with the environment and is the home of libidinal excitation. Sucking, which occupies much of the child's time during the first few months, provides nourishment, as well as contact with mother. Teething, the first major trauma (following birth itself) with which an infant must deal, occurs in the oral region, causing pain and providing the mechanism for aggressive expression.

The libido model focuses on feeding. Children's experiences with feeding are said to orient their later interactions with the world, and their developing attitudes toward their mothers and the feeding experience are said to be the prototype for their attitudes toward other objects as well. Their confidence in their surroundings, as well as their sense of self in relation to the surroundings, is said to develop out of their feeding experiences. Although feeding is the focal activity, the drive that is used in the analysis of the development is not hunger but the libido. The libidinal energy of the oral region becomes cathected to certain objects, most notably the mother and her breast. These objects will forever be the only suitable objects for nurturance and oral libidinal gratification. The growing child must find appropriate substitute objects to achieve the desired satisfaction. Thus, according to Freud, the type of relation between the child and its mother and her breast becomes the pattern for relating with objects onto which the libidinal energy has been displaced.

White pointed out that there is much more to a child's first year than just the gratification of oral stimulation. Children of a few months tend to play with their bottles and food in a way that indicates greater interest in manipulation and playfulness than in oral satisfaction. Further, as Hunt (1965) has noted, children around the first month demonstrate a rudimentary kind of intentional behavior aimed at maintaining or creating pleasurable stimulation of many kinds other than oral; for example, children of this age like to be rocked and bounced. This maintenance of pleasurable stimulation serves an important adaptive function; it helps in the coordination of sensory and motor modalities and elementary self-control. By the ninth month, children are actively seeking novel stimuli to expand their ability to handle the environment. They have become actively curious and seek situations that produce learning and growth. By this period, children are spending several hours a day at play, and they are beginning to display an insistence on doing things for themselves whether in the realm of feeding or otherwise.

All of these behaviors are directed and may occur with considerable force. They clearly represent a primary agenda for the baby, and their gratification seems to be a feeling of efficacy. While feeding is an important part of a child's experience in its first year, so too are a whole range of other behaviors which are motivated by the needs for competence and self-determination. Children's successes and failures, their opportunities or lack thereof to explore and play, all influence their sense of themselves and the way in which they approach the world around them. As several writers (Bruner, Jolly, and Sylva 1976; Vandenberg 1978) have indicated, play is serious business for children and serves an extremely important purpose in the mastery of social and motor skills.

White (1960) used an example of the weaning process to point out that although the libido theory views weaning as a highly traumatic experience, a competence model provides a positive motivation toward being weaned, since it is a step toward effectiveness in one's own life.

Erikson's treatment of the first year pointed out that at birth a child has very crude regulatory processes and is totally dependent on some adult for its survival. The dependence on adults for feeding and other comforts associated with elimination and temperature regulation, among others, may be responded to reliably by the adult, or it may be thwarted by nonresponsiveness. The critical issue of this period is trust versus mistrust. If children's needs are met adequately, gradually they will learn to trust the environment and will become increasingly sanguine about the adult's (typically mother's) disappearance, trusting that she will return when needed. This development of trust involves the rudiments of an understanding of the relationship between various external events and corresponding internal sensations, thereby allowing a predictability about matters of comfort attainment. The development of trusting relationships with the world is twofold: one must learn to trust oneself and one's ability at drive control ("I will not bite the nipple that appears a minute later than I want it") and also learn to trust the order and predictability of the environment. The tendency is for the former to follow the latter such that hostile environments tend to be met by the child with poor impulse control, whereas benign or supportive environments tend to be met with greater trust in one's capacity for self-management.

Not only will lack of trust in one's self-control follow the failure to develop a sense of basic trust, but the kind of withdrawal that is characteristic of impotence becomes a general orientation toward the world. In extreme cases one fails to develop a sense of "I" vis-à-vis "you" in the generic sense. With no predictable interplay between oneself and the environment, one is unable to learn the boundaries between self and environment, which precludes the possibility of an effective accommodation with the environment. As one's intrinsic need for effective interactions is continually thwarted, gradually one may lose touch with the energy of intrinsic motivation.

*The Second and Third Years*

At about the beginning of a child's second year, the primary locale for libidinal excitation shifts from the mouth to the anus. For children from one to three years, the main source of erotic gratification, according to Freud, is through defecation. This act reduces the tension that builds up as the bowels fill and exert pressure on the surrounding region. As with the process of feeding, in which Freudian theory views feeding more as a sexual satisfaction than a satisfaction of the hunger need, so too does the theory see the relief through defecation to be largely sexual satisfaction rather than satisfaction of the need to eliminate. As the supposed focus of sexual excitation, this region of the body, along with its natural function, becomes the battleground for the war between id and society. The process of tiolet training in which a child brings the eliminative function under voluntary control is said by Freud to be the most significant experience of these two years in the child's life and to have a profound effect on all later years.

The process of gaining control over one's bowel movements does have a number of interesting aspects. It is one of the first natural functions that children are forced to bring under control, and it is perhaps the one that the children have greatest potential for controlling as they choose. Parents have no direct control over the children's bowels, whereas they can use their superior strength to stop behaviors like hitting or kicking. Children can withhold feces when they wish and expel them when they wish. And while there may be substantial costs to doing so, the child may pay those costs in order to have some opportunity for self-determination. Thus toilet training is likely to be an important battleground for struggles over autonomy.

In psychoanalytic theory, the nature of the mother's (or significant adult's) attitude toward toilet training is vitally important for the child's resolution of this developmental issue. Mothers who are strict and overly concerned about cleanliness and about their own control over their children's proper behavior tend to cause traumatic experiences that are said to have lasting effects on the children. These effects take one of two forms or a mix of the two. One is a highly compliant and submissive response mode in which the person is extreme in the direction required by the parent. The other is a rebellious response mode in which the person is extreme in the direction opposite to that which is required.

As with the oral period, White criticized the adequacy of the libido model in the anal stage with its exclusive focus on toilet training as the key factor in the development of such characteristics as dominance, submission, self-control, dependence, stubbornness, and the capacity for love, self-esteem, and cooperation. There is little question that this two-year period is an extraordinarily important one and that matters of self-control and self-esteem are profoundly influenced, yet the assertion that the bathroom is the place in which such matters are settled seems to be unreasonably narrow in focus. Feeding, for example, continues to be a matter of prime import, and many struggles for control between parent and child are played out during meals. Further, with increased motor control and mobility, children begin getting into everything. They are awake for a much larger portion of the day, so much of their time goes into exploration and play. At every turn, the question of who is controlling the child's life seems to pop up.

According to White, this period is important for the development of social competence. The acquisition of mobility is itself a major accomplishment in which the control of muscles and limbs seems as important as the control of one's rectal sphincter. The capacity for intentionality in which means and ends can be understood is also emerging at this time, as is speech. All of these factors are extremely important and are deeply significant for what White called one's sense of competence and, I would add, self-determination.

The fact that psychosomatic illness and anxiety reactions are often based in the gastrointestinal tract does suggest that it is an important region in terms of psychic functioning. However, the throat and respiratory system seem equally as often the seat of afflictions in which control and autonomy are the key underlying issues. While anal control is important in the struggle for autonomy, the somatic region of involvement includes far more than just the anus and bowels, and the behaviors that affect children's developing sense of competence and self-determination range far beyond toilet behaviors.

White (1960) pointed out that just as with the weaning phenomenon during the oral phase, the use of a competence model allows a more positive interpretation of various traits that are acquired during the anal phase. He used as an example the trait of orderliness which in psychoanalytic theory is said to be a reaction-formation (overcompensation) for the desire to be disorderly. Yet orderliness, when possessed in moderation, is an adaptive characteristic that allows for effective interactions with the environment and is an element in asthetics. An effectance motivational basis to the acquisition of such traits is more congruent with the idea of a growing, maturing human being.

Erikson's analysis of these years noted that as children gain a primitive understanding of the relationship between external events and internal responses—the basis for the development of a sense of basic trust—they are increasingly oriented toward separation of self from others and toward assertion of autonomy. This orientation results in a conflict between the child and the environment where, during the second and third years, the central issue is autonomy versus shame and doubt. This period is one in which the child's aim is to respond to urges and desires. Children want to eat when they want to eat, eliminate when they want to eliminate, walk when they want to walk, be amused when they want to be amused. The struggle exists since children are often made to do things at the whim of the parents and not allowed to respond to their own motivations. The characterization of the period is one of being made to do what one does not want to do and being made not to do what one wants to do. The key question is, "Who will be in charge of my life?"

In order to face this conflict directly, the child must have achieved some reasonable resolution of the trust conflict. Building on a sense of trust, the child develops a feeling of automony, which is one of the core components of a generalized sense of competence and self-determination. To the extent that an overassertive environment continually forces children to act against the wisdom of their own motivations, they will experience shame and doubt. They will feel exposed, as though their basic human integrity has been violated.

For parents this period is often a difficult one. Children must be allowed sufficient latitude of responding so that they will become self-determining, yet the parents must provide the type of structures and limits that require the children to accomodate to the environment. Children's motives are strong and nondiscriminative at this stage, and the parents must facilitate the discrimination that allows mutual regulation without being rigid in a way that produces shame and doubt in the children. This is no easy feat for parents, and in our culture parents typically err on the side of overcontrol.

Each of us, as an adult, undoubtedly knows of instances in which the stubborn insistence of a two-year-old raises his or her own stubbornness and causes rigid dominance. These child-rearing practices—whether one planned them having decided they are good for the child or one fell into them when stressed even though one planned to be more flexible and responsive—seem to lead to the development of a rather compulsive and controlled mode of interacting with the environment. Gradually the contingencies established by parents become internalized and are an important determinant of behavior.

*The Fourth through Sixth Years*

Around the end of the third year, the child moves into what in the libido model is the most significant developmental period: The phallic stage. The dominant locale for erotic delight shifts from the anus to the genitals, and the child experiences a brief preview of adult sexuality. According to Freudian theory, children of this period are preoccupied with genital stimulation and fascinated with the genitals of others (particularly those of their parents) and with the processes of conception and birth. "Where do babies come from?" is an oft-heard query from children of four or five. This newfound excitability in the genitals is accompanied by a sexual attraction for the parent of the opposite sex, manifested in a desire to replace the same-sex parent as the partner for the other parent. This is the core of the oedipal (for boys) and electra (for girls) complexes.

Boys intensify the love for their mothers in a more directly sexual way with the secret desire to couple. This desire creates a rivalry between the boy and his father, such that the boy's affectionate feelings toward father become more distant and antagonistic. This change occurs with substantial cost to the boy since the father is decidedly larger and more powerful, so the boy comes to fear the father. Given the sexual nature of the rivalry, the boy is particularly fearful that the father will castrate him, thereby removing the basis of the boy's threat. To reduce the threat, the boy develops a strong identification with the father; by becoming one with the father, there is nothing to fear. And there is a side payoff of symbolically gaining the desired possession of mother by having identified with the one who has her.

To a lesser extent, the same identification process works in reverse. Freud explained that all people are bisexual by nature, so during the oedipal phase the boy feels some attraction to dad and thus identifies with mom as a way of winning dad. To some extent, these identifications with parents of both sexes replace the earlier cathexes toward the parents and free the boy to begin the process of finding a suitable mate.

The identification with parents at this point in development is the basis of the development of a superego. Through identification, the boy internalizes a wide range of the parents' admonitions, proscriptions, and beliefs, so the superego develops as an inner representation of the parents. With the prescriptions and proscriptions come sanctions that are used by the superego to control the child. The primary sanction is guilt; when one does as the superego demands, one avoids guilt and may even receive praise from the superego.

The emotional crisis of the oedipal period is said to be the basis for most of an adult's neurotic behavior. By the sixth year, when the boy moves out of this period, the structure of his personality, with its healthy as well as unhealthy elements, is said to have jelled.

For girls in this phase, the focus on genitals and the issue of castration are also prominent, though the dynamics are somewhat different. In the theory, a girl, like a boy, begins with a strong cathexis toward mother. Gradually, however, this weakens as the girl becomes aware that she has no penis and blames this state of affairs on her mother. She has, she believes, been castrated, and her resentment creates distance between her and her mother. At the same time, it is said, she begins to feel attraction for her father, which is mixed with an envy that he has the sexual organ that she has lost. This penis envy is the female counterpart to the castration complex. The oedipal phase is resolved in boys largely because the fear of castration leads to an identification with the father, but the process in females has not been so elegantly formulated by Freud. There is no real motivation for the girl to identify with her mother. Rather, out of a realization that she cannot possess father, she gradually identifies with mother, thereby assuming the fundamentals of a female identity, the beginning of a superego, and the freedom to develop love relationships with other men. As is the case with boys, girls are basically bisexual and therefore have attraction for the mother and identification with the father to regain the lost love of the mother and to gain the penis of the father as a substitute for her lost penis.

White (1960) suggested that there is much more going on for the child during the phallic stage than just a preoccupation with the genitals and the sexual desire for parents. It is a time of profound change in which the child is mastering and achieving in many realms. Children are unendingly curious; they besiege the parents with questions, using their recently mastered language to do so. Children develop a sense of understanding of their relationship to family and friends. It is a time of moving to adult-size beds and sitting at the table with adults. Yet it is also a frustrating time, for as White explained, children will be comparing themselves to adults and will find themselves wanting in every regard—physical characteristics, motor behavior, language use, and so on. While children of this age can be readily seen to be curious about sex, they are similarly curious about a thousand other matters. Thus, sexuality might be seen as one element of the more general struggle to achieve an understanding of oneself vis-à-vis one's surroundings and an effective interplay with those surroundings.

To make his point clearer, White suggested that one imagine a child of four with no genital sensitivity but normal in all other ways. That child would still face a number of emotional and interpersonal crises, would make progress in speech, motor behavior, and cognitive functioning; would make many self-comparisons to adults and experience frustration; and would face most of the problems and feel most of the triumphs of the normal, genitally sensitive children of that age. To be sure, the libidinized genitals add complication to the picture, but they do not form the organizing principal for the varying events of the period.

As with the anal period, White pointed out that Freud, in using the oedipal complex as the central struggle, was using a conflict that, like toilet training, was always won by the parents. Children are doomed to give up the oedipal wish, so as White noted, it is easy to understand, using a Freudian model, how people acquire guilt and shame, but it is hard to understand how they could come through these two battles (if they were so central) having lost both and still acquired a sense of competence and self-determination.

This third phase of development is referred to by Erickson as the struggle between initiation and guilt. Erickson saw this as a period of vigorous unfolding in which the child deals with a crisis of fear and clumsiness that, if resolved, leads to unified activity. Whereas the autonomy phase was a period typified by the child's not doing as the parents want, the initiative phase is typified by the child's doing many things that the parents do not want, sins of commission rather than omission. While Erikson's theorizing was less focused on libidinally based longing for the parent of the opposite sex, he nonetheless characterized the period in terms of the male child's attacking in the phallic-intrusive mode, whereas the female's orientation is incorporative and involves aggressive catching.

Guilt, which follows from thwarted initiation, is said to follow aggressive activities of many sorts, not only sexual ones. Still, Erikson referred to it as the stage of the castration complex in which the child fears harm to the newly eroticized genitals. While Freud used the idea of the castration fear as the motivation for the development of the superego, Erikson suggested that this is the critical period in which the child moves from total attachment to parents toward becoming a parent. This movement, however, results in both parts—the childlike and the adultlike—co-habiting in an often tumultuous fashion. The "infant" part pushes for gratification and growth, while the "parent" part demands self-restraint.

Guilt, the tool of the superego, is often used ruthlessly and without reason. The child's limited cognitive capabilities lead to an internalization of demands and a dispensing of punishments that may be primitive and sadistic. The ways in which the guilt processes defy reason and create rigidities result in fascinating paradoxes. Highly moralistic people, for example, may applaud cruelty and killing when they create an us-them dichotomy, as in wars, where "us" means good and "them" means bad. Guilt often leaves people passive, impotent, or ill, broken by the punishment and fearful of future punishment.

The initiative phase is said to lead to an identification with the same-sex parent, with energy for learning and doing. This oedipal-initiative stage results in both a moral sense that oppresses and a future orientation that directs and energizes movement toward adulthood.

## Middle Childhood: Seven to Twelve

According to Freud, by the time children have finished six years, they are generally through the oedipal phase, having achieved either adequate or inadequate resolution of the first three stages of development and having, according to psychoanalytic theory, the outline of their personalities set for life. The period of pregenital or infantile sexuality with its narcissistic character has passed. And, Freud asserted, the child enters a period in which the libido is held in check by the newly acquired superego, so there is a period lasting for several years until puberty in which there is relative quiescence in the sexual realm.

Since Freud proposed that there was a period of dormancy following the oedipal phase and terminating with the onset of puberty, he gave little attention to this period of development, though many later writers of psychoanalytic theory gave it greater attention (such as Hartmann, Kris, and Loewenstein 1949; Sullivan 1953). As White noted, this is an extremely important time, for the child ventures from the home for the first time and must handle the interpersonal, cognitive, and motor demands of school.

Erikson characterized this period in terms of the conflict between industry and inferiority. He emphasized that this is the period in which the child, in a sexually latent stage, is concerned with becoming productive in preparation for the role of parent. The organ modes, with their immature sexuality, have been mastered, and the children turn their attention to mastery of specific tools and activities. Formal instruction teaches the child fundamentals of achievement in that culture. The feared outcomes from encounters with the technology of a system are feelings of inferiority and inadequacy, and particularly so since attempts at mastery typically involve social interactions; thus the child who fails is open to ridicule from others as well as from self.

## Development of Personality Orientations

A person's general sense of competence and self-determination is formulated in these first four developmental epochs as the child achieves either resolution or nonresolution of the four conflicts. While this sense continues to be modifiable through later experiences, the baseline from which changes proceed is set during these early years.

The importance of the early years in one's adult experience and behavior has been widely debated. Within the behavioristic school, the early years are given very little attention since the focus is on conditioning processes to strengthen desired behaviors. Orthodox psychoanalytic theory considers adult behavior to be determined largely by the events of the first six years. Each of these points of view seems to be extreme. I hold that the first four conflicts represent the foundation in a structure of development, and although the later experiences do much to shape the structure of the person, the foundation on which that structure is built develops during the early experiences and therefore affects the later structure.

In the first year, the child's primary concern is with an investigation of the responsivity of the environment. Out of these early interactions comes a generalized sense of trust or mistrust of oneself and the environment. This is at the core of one's willfulness. Without a reasonable sense of trust in the predictable responsivity of the environment and oneself, there can be no meaningful self-determination.

In the second and third years, the primary concern is separation of self from other and the establishment of self as an autonomous, effective agent.

With a trust in the responsivity of the environment, children begin pushing on the environment to get their own way. The combination of these first two stages represents the crucial period for the development of self-determination. Self-determined behavior necessitates a sense of trust and autonomy.

In the fourth through sixth years, children become more active and coordinated in their initiations. Having found a rudimentary sense of self, independent of the environment, they begin to act on the environment in search of competent interactions. It is a period of trial-and-error learning in which children are testing their effectiveness and competence. Having established a preliminary separateness from adults, children begin to emulate and identify. With their developing linguistic capacity they begin to mediate behavior verbally and govern themselves with thoughts of "I'm good when I do or think X," and "I'm bad when I do or think Y."

From the seventh year to puberty, children are struggling for an accommodation with the social environment. In some ways this period is different from the first three in that children venture from the home and from the exclusive focus on parents into a world of peers and substitute parents. In this period, some of the problems of childhood can be rectified through identification, imitation, peership, and cognitive understanding.

Piaget (1967) suggested that during these years, children attain a level of coherence and noncontradiction in their cognitive functioning and social interacting. In their social relations, the self-centeredness is replaced by the process of reciprocity and cooperation. This capacity for reciprocity can be the basis for at least partial reparation of earlier training and for a more integrated sense of self that is able to regulate one's affective life.

Whereas the first two developmental stages are the critical ones for a sense of self-determination, of trusting autonomy, the second two stages are more critical ones for a sense of competence. Children's concerns are with doing well, with managing effectively in an increasingly complicated world.

*Internal-Causality Orientation*

A child who successfully resolves the self-determination and, subsequently, the competence conflicts will tend to have an internal-causality orientation. As adults these people will tend to be healthiest. They will display a maximum of self-determined and automatized behaviors and a minimum of automatic behaviors; they will have the strongest sense of competence and self-determination.

Intrinsic motivation is integrally involved with the developmental process during the struggles for self-determination and competence. The intrinsic need for competence and self-determination provides the energy that is needed to take on the environment; it provides the energy to work through the conflicts. With adequate resolutions, the motivation remains strong and is a primary energy source for the internal-causality orientation. It will be available to motivate overt behaviors such as play and exploration and covert processes of choice and information selection. With an internal-causality orientation, extrinsically motivated behaviors will tend to be self-determined (chosen) rather than automatic, for the behavioral sequences will be motivated by a combination of intrinsic and extrinsic motivation.

Some writers in the psychoanalytic tradition have acknowledged a source of energy other than libido that is involved in development. Hartmann (1958) suggested that the ego does not develop solely as a function of the war between id and environment, but rather that there is an innate ego capacity, which unfolds in the developmental sequence and is energized by an autonomous ego energy that is independent of the instincts. Hendrick (1943) has also written in a similar vein, suggesting that the human organism has a need for mastery and that gratification accrues from effective ego functioning.

The idea of ego functioning bears similarity to what I have called the will. The ego is the decision maker in psychoanalytic psychology. Hartmann and Hendrick have therefore suggested the importance of intrinsic motivation and will, and White has gone still further in building a competence annex to the psychosexual developmental structure. Yet these writers have failed to deal fully with the idea of self-determination and its relation to intrinsic motivation, will, and development. The intrinsic need for competence and self-determination energizes the developmental sequence, which sets the stage for whatever machinations the instincts may produce. The aim of the intrinsically motivated developmental process is the establishment of an internal-causality orientation and a strong sense of competence and self-determination. These will allow one to encounter the physical and social environment and one's internal needs in a way that facilitates autonomous and effective gratification of needs within the context of the environment.

**Toward Internal Causality**. Internal causality involves deciding how to behave based on a processing of information from internal and external sources and accommodating to constraints from internal and external sources. To develop these capacities, a child must live in a responsive environment where there is a relationship between behavior and outcomes. There is a rather extensive literature on attachment in infants that attests to the importance of a responsive environment for the development of a secure attachment with the primary caregiver, which in turn has been shown to be important for healthy development (Bowlby 1969; Ainsworth 1973; Yarrow, Rubenstein, and Pederson 1975). As Ainsworth (1969) pointed out, a healthy attachment does not depend solely on drive reduction as psychoanalytic theory suggests. Rather intrinsic motivation seems to motivate the infant toward the development of a secure attachment, and responsivity of the parents to the infant's initiations seems to be the critical factor from the environment that allows a secure attachment and a trusting of oneself and the environment. These are necessary ingredients for the development of self-determination.

Having a responsive environment does not mean that all of a child's desires should be fulfilled. Children need to know that their parents are responsive to them, but they also need to learn that they cannot have everything they want. Thus parents should convey that they respect their children and their children's needs, even though they will not satisfy all of the needs. That will set the stage for children's learning that all of their needs and feelings are acceptable and natural but that many behaviors are not. In other words, they must learn to allow awareness of their motives and emotions and to decide how to behave on the basis of those awarenesses and the processing of relevant information.

In child rearing this is often accomplished through limit setting in the context of parental acceptance and responsivity. Limits ought to be set as wide as possible, given the situation, so that children will learn to accommodate to constraints but will also have a maximum of freedom to decide for themselves and to learn through trial and error. As children behave and observe the consequences, they learn, and their intrinsic motivation to learn is maintained or strengthened. Rewards should be used as sources of competence information rather than as controls. Punishments might better be thought of as consequences for transgression of limits. These consequences, like the limits themselves, should be clearly stated before the fact and administered informationally. In other words, as often as possible, children should be given the choice even to cross the limits and pay the consequences. In some cases, children must be controlled; a young child must not be allowed to play in a busy intersection, for example. But when transgressions do not cause threats to the child or to others, the structures should be primarily informational rather than controlling.

When a child crosses a limit, it is important to understand why. There was a reason for the behavior—perhaps some motive was being satisfied or some automatic behavior was being exhibited—and exploring what it was provides an important opportunity for the child to learn and to problem solve. A parent can explore with the child what was involved in the situation and look for alternative ways to get the satisfaction without transgressing the limits. The more the solution is generated by the child, the more the child will be learning to self-determine.

**Self-Determination in Infants**. In the explication of internal causality and self-determination, I have focused on the process of choice. One might ask, therefore, whether babies decide to behave. Does a two-week-old neonate, for example, decide to kick and wiggle in order to feel competent and self-determining? Quite clearly not; yet the behavior is intrinsically motivated and the child may be developing an internal causality orientation. This query focuses attention on the nature of motivational processes as they develop in children. Human beings are survial- and growth-oriented, and they need to do a variety of things to survive and grow. They must, for example, eat. Yet a new baby does not decide to cry in order to get food. The crying simply happens in response to some inner discomfort. The child does not yet have the cognitive capacity to choose in the sense that we typically mean the word or to understand the nature of purposive behavior. As Hunt (1965) pointed out, a child is well into its first year before even a very rudimentary form of purposive behavior is evident, and a child is nearly a year old before it displays the type of intrinsically motivated behavior that involves seeking novelty or challenge.

Gradually through experience a child develops the cognitive structures necessary to mediate motivated behavior with thoughts, decisions, and desires. Thus a newborn simply kicks and wiggles; activity is built into the system as part of the growth and survival of the organism. Increasingly with intrinsic motivation as with drives and emotions, the behaviors become cognitively mediated and take on a structure that could properly be called purposive, decided, or self-determined.

*External-Causality Orientation*

Externally oriented people tend to be competent but not self-determining. Their behavior is governed by an interplay of external cues and non-conscious motives; it is not self-determined. Yet they will often be very effective in using external cues to get desired outcomes. Externals often gain power, status, and money through competent compliance with the external contingencies and cues.

In terms of the developmental phases, they will tend to have inadequate resolution of the self-determination conflicts—trust and autonomy—but they will tend to have more adequate resolution of the competence conflicts—initiation and industry.

Externally oriented people will have learned that there is a relationship between behavior and outcomes—indeed they are characterized by their dependence on these outcomes—but that learning alone does not imply self-determination. An external orientation will result from experiences during the early years in which the parents did not respond to the child's initiations but rather demanded that the child behave in certain ways in order to get rewards. The circumstances of upbringing were controlling rather than informational, so the child learned about the relationship between behavior and outcomes in terms of the outcomes being the cause of the behavior. The child thus learned to be a pawn to the rewards.

In learning to respond primarily to external contingencies, children must also learn to block their own motives and emotions from awareness. Since the environment does not respond to their initiations, they would be in conflict if they allowed awareness of the motives and emotions that would prompt internally caused behavior. The blocking of these motives and emotions from awareness creates the nonconscious motives that interact with external cues to motivate the automatic behavior that characterizes a pure external-causality orientation.

As children, externals' attempts at autonomy typically would have been blocked. When they were autonomous they may have been punished for this behavior. For example, defecation or nondefecation is an arena in which a child can win an autonomy battle, for the child, rather than the parents, has direct control over the muscles and organs that are involved in elimination. Unfortunately when children (who become externals) win such a struggle, they are likely to be punished for doing so. Thus children who live in a primarily controlling environment typically pay dearly for winning an autonomy struggle and eventually learn to comply with the external contingencies, demands, and cues.

Rebellious noncompliance will be displayed by externals at times. This is often mistaken for true self-determination, though it is important to recognize that when the behavior is aimed at defying some external or internalized command, it is in a sense controlled by that command (in the form of a negative relationship) and therefore not self-determined. According to self-determination theory, rebellious noncompliance is automatic behavior that is controlled by the interaction of environmental forces and nonconscious motives, which would have resulted from thwarted attempts at autonomy.

Controlling environments often involve power struggles that end badly for the child. When parents become defensive and behave automatically themselves, they give their children no room to self-determine, and they therefore foster the development of automatic behaving in their children. Parents are stronger than children so parents usually "win" in the struggle, and the results are unfortunate for the child's self-determination and sense of self.

An external-causality orientation evidences a predominance of the operation of the extrinsic motivational subsystem and automatic behavior. There tends to be a paucity of choice, for behaviors tend to follow automatically from external contingencies. Of course, all behaviors that are extrinsically motivated need not be automatic; one can choose among extrinsic motives and among goals to satisfy the chosen motive(s). In such cases, however, there must be some input of intrinsic motivation to the process. Children whose initiations are responded to will develop the general sense of trust and autonomy—the general sense of self-determination—that allows choice to mediate extrinsically motivated behavior. These children, however, will be internals. Externals are people whose initiations were not responded to, so they learned to fit into the mold of contingency-determined behavior. For them there is little choice in the satisfaction of extrinsic needs.

## Impersonal-Causality Orientation

People with an impersonal-causality orientation tend to experience no relationship between their behaviors and the outcomes they receive. They see little use in responding, for responding does no good. They often feel helpless and depressed, and the amotivational subsystem plays a primary role in their lives.

Developmentally they fail to achieve adequate resolution of any of the self-determination or competence conflicts. Impersonals end the first year with a sense of mistrust, for the world did not respond to their needs and discomforts; by the end of the third year they have added to that a sense of shame, which results from thwarted attempts at being autonomous; and in the following years when their initiation attempts are blocked, they acquire a sense of guilt. Within five or six years they are set to react to the world helplessly. Furthermore they were unable during middle childhood to repair the damage of the early years once they ventured from the home to a world of peers and substitute parents.

Ginott (1965) pointed out that much parental talking with children involves criticism and demands. The hidden message that they convey is that the child is incompetent, and the result is an undermining of his or her sense of competence and self-determination. In continual, heavy doses, it will be the basis of an impersonal-causality orientation.

Unlike externals, for whom the environment also tended not to respond to their initiations, impersonals additionally experienced an environment that failed to provide controlling contingencies. Thus impersonals saw no consistent dependence between behavior and outcomes, whether the behavior was caused by the person or the environment. Impersonals tend to be focused inward. Having been unable to establish a workable relationship between themselves and the people and objects of their environment, they retreat to themselves and their own bodies as their only basis for coping with stress. Extreme examples would include autistic children and catatonic adults.

*Shame and Guilt*

Failure to resolve one's struggle for self-determination results in shame. This develops before one has clarified the distinction between self and others, and in fact develops as one fails in one's attempt at achieving that independence. Externals, I hypothesize, having failed to resolve the autonomy struggle, will tend to experience shame rather acutely. Impersonals, on the other hand, will tend to be rocked by guilt and inferiority as well as shame, since they failed to resolve the competence conflicts, as well as the earlier ones.

Adult versions of shame and guilt are seldom distinguished one from the other, yet the difference is very interesting. Shame is a feeling of being exposed, a feeling of other people witnessing one's inner world. The person experiences a conflict between various of his or her natural thoughts, feelings, and desires and what the environment deems appropriate. "They say I am bad to be like this," the person thinks. "I must not let them see this part of me."

Guilt is different; it is a feeling that one is bad for doing something even when one is alone and has no fear of being found out. Guilt develops in the initiative stage when a child turns toward his or her parents to imitate and identify. Their thoughts or statements about the child's goodness and badness become internalized to form what Freud has called the superego, and the child believes these judgments to be true.

Adults might notice the difference phenomenologically by paying attention to aspects of their inner experience. For example, when you have done or wanted something that is socially inappropriate, do you tend to think, "They wouldn't like me (they would think I'm bad) if they knew," or do you tend to think, "I'm bad for doing or wanting that?" When you are alone, with no fears of being found out, are you comfortable with having done or thought what you did or thought? The orientation toward others and the comfort when alone are indicators of shame, the remnants of the earlier autonomy struggle; the self-judgments and discomfort when alone are remnants of the later initiative struggle.

White (1960) has distinguished shame and guilt somewhat differently. He stated that shame is associated with incompetence, with the inability to do something that someone thinks we should do. It means loss of respect. Guilt, on the other hand, said White, follows from having done what one ought not to have done. It involves moral violation. This characterization relates to the difference between sins of omission in the autonomy phase and sins of commission in the initiative stage. And, indeed, shame evolves in the former period and guilt in the latter. To some extent, these differences, which were noted by White, do persist into adulthood, yet adults might feel shame rather than guilt for committing a morally inappropriate act, for the morality is in the eye of the watcher as well as the doer. This would be particularly true in situations where one has not internalized the morals. Similarly, when one fails to do something competently, one would feel guilty if one believes one should have done it well. The other- versus self-mediated distinction between shame and guilt seems to hold up better than White's distinction of incompetence versus moral transgression.

Shame and guilt are generally not so distinct, yet the tendency toward one or the other does exist. Often guilt will be piled on top of shame. For example, someone might have superego admonitions, such as "Don't let others see that part of me." Thus there is a shame basis of fearing what others will think, with an overlay of guilt from thinking I am bad for having been found out. There are many examples of the mingling of shame and guilt. In fact, shame is less frequenty discussed than guilt and is often treated as if it were guilt. The distinction is an important one, however, particularly in terms of its implications for therapy and self-direction.

### Adult Development

I have focused on development prior to puberty, but each of the three theories that I outlined paid some attention to later development. Freud posited an adult genital stage in which one's sexuality is said to be directed toward reproduction and results in genital union with members of the opposite sex. According to psychoanalytic theory, this is not so much a period in which personality develops as it is a period in which the patterns that developed in the early years come into full bloom.

In White's discussion of the adult genital period, the focus was on teenage preparation for the work of adulthood. He examined the development of the kind of ego control that allows one to work well with the environment and with others. He excluded matters of creativity, passion, inspiration, enjoyment of food and sex, and athletics. It became a model of work rather than of a more holistic, competent and self-determining, mode of living.

Erikson's theory traced four distinct phases to the developmental process following puberty. The fifth through seventh tended to have a social focus, concerned with role identity, intimacy, and generativity. Only in the eighth and final phase, ego integrity versus despair, did he return to a lifelong concern with competence and self-determination. At this stage, people take stock of their lives, and for those who have moved successfully through the earlier phases, the struggles come to fruition with a sense of integrity and acceptance of oneself and others for who they are. This ego integrity is similar to what Goldstein (1939) and Maslow (1970) have called self-actualization, that sense of having utilized one's potentials and appreciated one's limitations. While each life is different, each person who experiences ego integrity accepts his or her life as being as it should be and is willing to defend it against all others. With this acceptance and the accompanying identification with all of humanity comes a reconciliation with the prospects of death. Death, too, becomes a transition rather than something to cause dread and panic. A failure to achieve this integrity leaves one fearing death, for one has not come to grips with one's life and cannot be ready to pass from it. The result is despair and regret for who one is and what one has done.

## Innate Differences

In our discussion we have focused on situational factors that tend to facilitate internal-, external-, and impersonal-causality orientations. It is important to note, however, that the environment alone does not create a causality orientation; the person who enters the environment has an effect as well. In the case of early development, the person differences are genetically determined. Newborns have different levels of intrinsic motivation, evidenced, for example, in different levels of persistence and activity.

Intrinsic motivation energizes the struggles for trust, autonomy, initiation, and industry. In a given environment, infants with more intrinsic motivation will fare better in their struggles than will infants with less. Often one sees cases in which several siblings grow up in an impoverished setting and one fares well whereas all the rest do badly; one might become an internal, for example, while the others become impersonals. The one child apparently inherited more intrinsic motivation and stronger capacities.

People play an active role in shaping themselves. For neonates, it is the innate differences that account for the different ways in which they cope with the environment and shape themselves.

I have focused on environmental rather than genetic antecedents of personalities, for it is in the realm of environment that we can make a meaningful impact on the development of self-determination—the development of an internal-causality orientation and a centrally operative intrinsic motivational subsystem.

# 7

# The Dynamics
# of Ill-Being

The theoretical processes through which self-determination and well-being are undermined—in other words, through which one becomes externally or impersonally oriented—tend to have the greatest impact on one's causality orientation (and thus on self-determination and well-being) during one's early developmental stages; however, the same processes continue to operate throughout life. The processes of cognitive evaluation theory are hypothesized, in a short-term analysis, to affect which motivational subsystem is operative and, in a longer-term analysis, to affect one's causality orientation.

At any given time, a person has a measurable causality orientation, and the person exists within an environmental context. The person may be primarily an internal, an external, or an impersonal. The environment may be responsive and informational, it may be controlling, or it may be nonresponsive. If the person is internal, the intrinsic motivational subsystem will tend to be operative; if the person is external, the extrinsic motivational subsystem will tend to be operative; and if the person is impersonal, the amotivational subsystem will tend to be operative.

Similarly if the environment is responsive and informational, the intrinsic motivational subsystem will tend to be operative; if the environment is controlling, the extrinsic motivational subsystem will tend to be operative; and if the environment is nonresponsive or capricious, the amotivational subsystem will tend to be operative.

Environmental factors tend to move one from subsystem to subsystem; cognitive evaluation theory explains how this occurs. Personality orientations tend to keep one in the motivational subsystem that corresponds to the orientation; however, the environmental factors will tend to move one to the subsystem that corresponds to the environmental forces, regardless of the orientation. Thus, I hypothesize that one's orientation makes one resistant to the environmental forces (in other words, makes one interpret the environment to be in accord with one's orientation), but the environmental forces tend gradually to win out and to initiate the motivational subsystem that corresponds to the environmental forces in spite of the resistance caused by the orientation.

The second hypothesis is that when one is exposed to consistent environmental forces for a long period, such that the corresponding motivational subsystem is more or less continually operative, one's causality orientation will shift gradually to accommodate to the environment and the operative subsystem. For example, suppose a woman is an internal at time 1. She moves into a very controlling environment. She will tend to interpret the environment from the internal perspective and engage in chosen, extrinsic behavior (see figures 3-4 and 7-2). However, within a fairly short time, the extrinsic motivational subsystem will become centrally operative (hypothesis 1) and, eventually, if she remains in a highly controlling environment for a long time, her causality orientation will become slightly more external (hypothesis 2). The modifications to one's causality orientation in later life tend to be smaller and slower than in one's early years; adults are less malleable. Thus one's early experiences tend to create a baseline causality orientation, and later experiences can cause deviations from it.

## Cognitive Evaluation Theory

In presenting the propositions of cognitive evaluation theory, I suggested that external factors can affect a person's intrinsic motivation and willfulness by inducing a shift in the perceived locus of causality or in one's perceived competence. When a controlling reward or constraint is present, the person will tend to interpret the behavior as a means to an end (attaining the reward or complying with the constraint); there will tend to be a shift to the person's extrinsic motivational subsystem as centrally operative. The perceived locus of causality would become external. When there is a salient absence of controlling rewards or constraints and there is choice in the situation, there will tend to be a shift to the person's intrinsic motivational subsystem as centrally operative. The perceived locus of causality would become internal.

The impact of competence feedback is slightly more complicated, for competence feedback can occur either within the context of a choice or the context of control and force. Cognitive evaluation theory suggests that when the situation provides positive competence feedback, one will become more intrinsically motivated. However, this necessitates a certain amount of choice, of self-determination. Fisher (1978) found a strong correlation between competence feedback and intrinsic motivation only in situations of personal causation. If there is positive competence feedback in a forced or controlled situation, one will become more extrinsically motivated. One would be a very competent, externally controlled person. Intrinsic motivation (and an internal orientation) necessitates competence and self-determination. The mix of high competence and low self-determination favors extrinsic motivation and an external orientation. For example, the Type-A behavior pattern (Glass 1977), which is an archetype of external causality, is an extremely competent, highly driven external.

On the other hand, negative competence feedback suggests incompetence; it suggests that one cannot achieve desired outcomes, so it tends to move one toward impersonal causality. The two processes of cognitive evaluation theory—change in perceived locus of causality and change in perceived competence—appear respectively as feedback channels 1 and 2 in figure 7-3. They also appear in figure 7-1. The change in perceived locus of causality shifts one from the intrinsic to extrinsic or from the extrinsic to intrinsic motivational subsystems; the change in perceived competence shifts one from the intrinsic to amotivational or from the amotivational to intrinsic subsystems if there is some self-determination; it shifts one from the extrinsic to amotivational or from the amotivational to extrinsic subsystems if there is no self-determination.

While high competence and low self-determination constitute a stable state that reflects the extrinsic motivational subsystem and external causality, low competence and high self-determination does not constitute a stable state. If one is self-determining, one will tend to move toward competence either by mastering the challenge with repeated attempts or by moving to a more optimal challenge. One will move back to the intrinsic cell. If one continues to fail in spite of one's attempts at conquering the challenge, one will come to feel unable to attain desired outcomes. In other words, one will begin to experience an independence of behavior and outcomes, so one will lose one's sense of self-determination and end up in the amotivational cell. Finally, one might deal with repeated failures by giving in to the environment and doing it "their way"; one would move to the extrinsic cell.

Increasingly in recent years, cognitive, information-processing theories have gained centrality in the explanation of behavior (see Mischel 1979). Cognitions are said to be the determinants of behavior and the mediators of change. Cognitive evaluation theory is stated in terms of cognitions or perceptions as being the mediators of changes in people's intrinsic motivation. In fact, changes in perceptions of causality and competence represent the cognitive component of an underlying change in motivational processes. When the environment and personality orientation interact to instigate the intrinsic motivational subsystem, one will perceive internal causality and high competence; when they interact to instigate the extrinsic motivational subsystem, one will perceive external causality and at least some degree of competence; when they interact to instigate the amotivational subsystem, one will perceive incompetence and impersonal causation.

I have consistently stated cognitive evaluation theory in terms of cognitive mediation for two reasons: first, because the organismic theory involves continual processing and interpreting of information, such that processing and evaluation of information from the environment and the person's need structure (often at a preconscious level) precede the instigation of a motivational subsystem; and second, the use of perceptions of

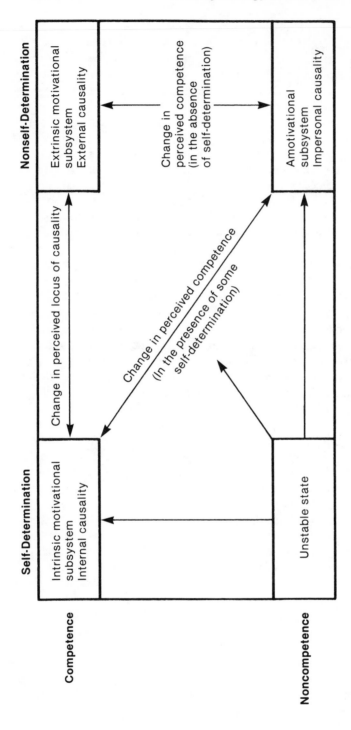

Note: This schematic representation also shows the processes of cognitive evaluation theory as shifts among the subsystems and corresponding causality orientations.

**Figure 7-1.** The Self-Determination and Competence Components of the Motivational Subsystems and Causality Orientations

causality and competence as the causes of changes in intrinsic motivation allows precise statements that facilitate empirical research.

To recapitulate, information from the environment and the person's need structure call one of the motivational subsystems into operation. This operation of a subsystem involves characteristic perceptions of causality and competence. Cognitive evaluation theory is stated in terms of these perceptions because of its utility for the generation of experimentally testable hypotheses. A statement of the theory that is more theoretically precise but that has less empirical utility would be that when external factors affect a person in such a way that one perceives greater competence and more internal causality, one's intrinsic motivational subsystem will have been instigated; when one perceives an external locus of causality, one's extrinsic motivational subsystem will have been instigated; when one perceives incompetence, one's amotivational subsystem will have been instigated.

## Causality Orientations and Well-Being

Human functioning that approximates internal causality represents the model of organismic well-being. The two processes of cognitive evaluation theory—the shift to a perceived external locus of causality and the shift to perceived incompetence—are the dynamics through which people develop personality orientations characterized by external-causality or impersonal-causality, both of which involve a loss of well-being. This may be evidenced as extreme pathological states or as mild states of externality or impersonality.

### External Causality

The so-called change in perceived locus-of-causality process involves the development of instrumentalities between a behavior (or set of behaviors) and an external contingency. The behavior is then under the control of the external contingency in that the contingency has become a necessary prerequisite for the behavior, and the presence of the contingency guarantees the behavior. This process places the extrinsic motivational subsystem in the foreground, involves the development of instrumentalities, and has the cognitive correlate of a change in perceived locus of causality. It is the primary dynamic underlying the development of an external-causality personality orientation.

The change in locus-of-causality process from internal to external involves three psychological consequences: giving up control of one's behavior, in that behavior becomes automatic rather than self-determined; losing awareness of one's organismic needs and of the so-called undesirable emotional responses, both of which will remain nonconscious; and developing a set of substitute needs to replace or supplement the organismic ones.

As people are continually subjected to controlling extrinsic contingencies (typically administered by parents), they gradually develop a personality orientation toward external causality. They become less governed by their own intrinsic motivation and become more a pawn to external contingencies (deCharms 1968). Externals respond to controls and demands that originated in the environment and may have become internalized as "shoulds" or "oughts." Externals will experience shame and fear of repercussions when they do not do what is demanded of them. They tend to do what they should do not by choice, not by processing information, evaluating outcomes, and making decisions, but by behaving automatically.

The idea of internalization of controls and demands that are enforced by the process of shame for externals (and by guilt as well as shame by impersonals) raises an interesting issue. The term *extrinsic* is defined operationally in terms of a reward that is external to the person. If one sees an external reward, the behavior is said to be extrinsically motivated. Often the terms *intrinsic* and *extrinsic* are used interchangeably with *internal* and *external*, and the distinction is based on the presence or absence of a reward that is external to the person.

This general distinction and categorization has great heuristic utility, for it lends itself nicely to empirical research; however, it has a serious drawback when one employs a dynamic, psychological perspective. Dynamically, behavior that is controlled by an internalized contingency with shame or guilt as a sanction is extrinsically motivated. It is also characteristic of external causality. It is external in the sense that it is an introjection of external demands, and the behavior that is governed by shoulds and oughts, by shame and guilt, is automatic rather than self-determined. The person has no choice; the person must do it.

In recent years, many behaviorists have shifted focus from behaviors to cognitive control of them (for example, Bandura 1977b; Michenbaum 1976). They emphasize the internal control of behavior, a point that is to be commended. But by dealing only with internal control, they do not have the mechanism to distinguish between intrinsically motivated behavior—that which one does with interest out of one's effectance needs—and behavior that is internally controlled by introjected admonitions—that which one forces oneself to do because one fears the self-condemning consequences of not doing it. Both are internally controlled, but the motivational mechanisms are quite different; the former is intrinsically motivated, self-determined behavior; the latter is extrinsically motivated, automatic behavior, even though the controlling contingencies have been internalized (see Ryan and Deci 1980 for a further discussion of this point).

Automatic behavior is determined by the interaction of extrinsic cues and nonconscious motives and emotions. The nonconscious motives and emotions have their etiology in conflicts between a person's needs and feelings and the environment's demands. When one is in a controlling environment, one must disattend to much of what one wants and feels in order not to experience conflict and anxiety. If a child's parents, for example, do not respond to the child's autonomous activity, if they reward what they want and punish what they do not want, the child will learn to ignore what he or she wants and feels in order to please his or her parents, to get rewards, and to avoid punishments. For example, if a boy wants to play outside with his friends, but is "made" by his mother to stay inside and practice the piano, gradually he may block awareness of his desire to play outside. The highly controlling rewards and constraints keep him focused on the piano, so he might manage the discomfort of the conflict between his desire to play outside and the controlling rewards by blocking awareness of the desire to be outdoors. Not being allowed to do what he wanted initially will be frustrating and typically cause some type of anger or upset. Yet if the boy is not allowed to experience and express those feelings, they too will need to be pushed out of awareness. Hence the child is left with both motives and emotions that are nonconscious, can be dynamic energizers of automatic behavior, and can produce psychosomatic symptoms.

In discussing Freud's early work, Menninger (1958) stated that an idea (an awareness of a need or an emotion) is painful if it conflicts with a person's values, ideals, or moral standards—that is, the ego or the superego. When this occurs, the ego exerts a counterforce that blocks the idea from awareness. I am suggesting something similar. When control contingencies exist (that may or may not be internalized as shoulds), people block awareness of conflicting needs and emotions; they tend to lose touch with their organismic needs. The process of blocking one's motives and emotions from conscious awareness is tied closely to the matter of self-deception. When one behaves automatically, one must justify the behavior, so one believes that one wants what one is seeking and does not want the things that are being blocked from awareness.

Nisbett and Wilson (1977) reported that often people are not aware of the stimulus that initiated their behavior. They further stated that people often give accounts of their behavior that are inferential rather than perceived. I suggest that these phenomena are characteristic of the external-causality orientation. Externals tend to behave automatically, and they may well be unaware of the external contingency that prompted the behavior. However, they will need to justify their behavior for the sake of some quiescence, so they will tend to provide an inferential account.

The internal-causality orientation is characterized by greater awareness of internal cues, by conscious awareness of motives and emotions, and by choice among motives and among behavioral options. Thus Nisbett and Wilson's hypotheses and findings that behavior is controlled largely by non-conscious processes and that reasons are then offered to justify the behavior are directly applicable to external causality, though not to internal causality.

The third consequence of the development of externality is the gradual replacement of basic needs by substitute needs. People's need structures become modified by an overlay of acquired needs. For example, as people's intrinsic need to be self-determining is thwarted, they may develop an intensely rigid need to control; that would be a substitute need. Similarly it is often suggested that people eat a lot as a substitute for not receiving love. The need to eat becomes stronger as one loses touch with one's need for love. Eating is no longer in one-to-one relationship with the organismic hunger need. Instead the need to eat develops in a way that is separate from organismic hunger and becomes a partial substitute for the organismic love need. The person loses touch with the two organismic needs and substitutes a need for food as a replacement for both. These substitute needs will be the apparent cause of the automatic responding that is actually controlled by the external contingencies and nonconscious motives.

Schachter and Rodin (1974) have reported evidence that obese humans tend to be controlled more by external cues than do nonobese humans. Their data are consistent with my point of view. I would say that obesity is one possible manifestation of an external-causality orientation; the overeating is automatic behavior under the control of external cues and nonconscious motives. The behavior appears to be controlled by external cues because the motivational determinants are nonconscious.

Here we can see a clear example of how people behaving with an external-causality orientation, characterized by automatic responding and an inflexible dominance of the extrinsic motivational subsystem, look deceptively as if they are being self-determining. An overeater can be said to have a need to eat with the conscious experience of that need being the motive. Then the person decides between cake and peanut butter cookies. All elements of self-determined behavior—the motive to eat and the decision about what to eat—seem present. Yet this behavior of eating is automatic. The person does not have control over the fact of eating; it is automatic and controlled by nonconscious motives and emotions. In reflective moments, such people report feeling as if they have no control.

Considering such behaviors to be self-determined and utilizing that framework for analyzing the behaviors may have utility for predictive purposes. Yet one can regain control of the behaviors only through recognizing that they are involved with nonconscious motivational processes and that the apparent causes are actually substitute needs covering up for underlying processes.

There is a small amount of empirical support for the assertion of the development of substitute needs. Gordon (1975) found that people whose basic need for love was not well satisfied developed inordinately strong needs for money. This is an example of developing stronger extrinsic, substitute needs as people fail to satisfy their basic needs. Gordon focused on the love need; I suggest that the same is true for the need for competence and self-determination, as well as other organismic needs.

The process of developing an external-causality orientation and the concomitant establishment of extrinsic substitute needs is evidenced in the so-called mongers—the power-monger and the control-monger, whose needs for power and control are substitutes for some unsatisfied organismic need(s) such as competence and self-determination. The aggressive hoarder is obsessed by the accumulation of wealth as a substitute for unsatisfied love and/or competence needs. Such people tend to give little attention to and derive little satisfaction from the basic needs: competence, self-determination, love, hunger, and so on. Behaviors are not meaningfully related to the organismic needs and tend to be evaluated as good or bad in terms of whether they lead to the satisfaction of the externally based substitute needs.

An interesting case of automatic, substitute behavior is rebellion. Often, though not exclusively, during teenage years, people engage in behaviors that are defiant and rebellious. They do the opposite of what their parents demand. This self-assertion is often at grave costs as is captured in the familiar saying, "Biting off one's nose to spite one's face." Defiant behaviors result when thwarted attempts at autonomy lead one to block awareness of the need to be autonomous or self-determining. The behavior is controlled by the interaction of this nonconscious need and the environmental contingencies, though an interesting aspect of the behavior is that it is negatively rather than positively correlated with the demands. With the blocking from awareness of the need for self-determination, people develop substitute needs. For example, teenagers who break curfew may think they are staying out late because of a need to be with their friends, whereas the primary motivation is the reaction against demands. Here is an instance in which Nisbett and Wilson's (1977) analysis is directly appropriate. The attributed causes are more rationalizations for the behavior that is caused by motives that are blocked from awareness.

*Impersonal Causality*

The second process of cognitive evaluation theory, change in perceived competence, involves a decrease in intrinsic motivation and willfulness when one receives negative information about one's competence and self-determination. (This process is represented as feedback channel 2 in figure 7-3.) One learns that one cannot achieve one's desired outcomes. As Seligman (1975) stated, one learns that there is response-outcome independence. As people continue to receive negative information, they gradually lose their motivation to respond, their rate of learning slows down, and they become emotional and dependent. In short, they lose their willfulness; their sense of competence and self-determination becomes severely undermined, and they gradually give up making active choices. They become helpless (Seligman 1975); their orientation is external control (Rotter 1966); they experience impersonal causality (Heider 1958). Perceived incompetence activates one's amotivational subsystem. Through prolonged experiences of perceived incompetence, particularly in early and middle childhood, one will develop an impersonal-causality orientation.

In its extreme pathological form, severe depression results. When people believe that responding is useless, they become passive, and there is no apparent aggression. Psychoanalytic theory susggests that the aggression has been turned against oneself, that the ego defenses and the superego gain an excess of energy from the id and immobilize the person (Freud 1959b). Whether or not one chooses a psychoanalytic interpretation, the symptoms are quite evident. Depressed people lose the belief in themselves as effective human beings; they lose their appetites for food and sex and their desires to work and to relate to others.

Clearly impersonal-causality people block many of their needs and emotions. Such a string of unsuccessful interactions with the environment necessarily involves much frustration and anger. Yet these emotions are not experienced directly and fully. They are blocked from awareness because helpless people feel as if they do not have the energy to cope with strong feelings and needs. The needs and emotions that are blocked from awareness provide the basis for automatic responding, much of it maladaptive and counterproductive.

There is some evidence that an external locus of control, which is conceptually analogous to an impersonal locus of causality, is associated with various pathological states (see Lefcourt 1976). For example, Feather (1967) found external control (impersonal causality) to be related to debilitating anxiety for male subjects and test anxiety for female subjects. Ray and Katahn (1968) found complementary results, as did Watson (1967), Burnes, Brown, and Keating (1971), and others. Several other researchers have found a relationship between an external locus of control and diagnosed psychosis. Shybut (1968) established a relationship between severity of disturbance and external causality, and Palmer (1971) reported that a sample of psychiatric patients was more external than a sample of non-psychiatric patients. Other researchers have reported similar results (for example, Smith, Pryer, and Distefano 1971; Lottman and DeWolfe 1972), thereby confirming that an external locus of control or an impersonal-causality orientation is associated with various types of malfunctioning.

In its pure form, the amotivational subsystem and the impersonal orientation involve people's not behaving. Catatonic schizophrenia is an extreme case, and the most extreme case is sudden deaths. The automatic responding of a person who feels helpless would result from a mix of the amotivational and extrinsic subsystems, as represented in figures 3-4 and 7-2.

The loss of one's sense of competence and self-determination and the acquisition of the belief in one's helplessness come from experiences of inefficacy. This occurs following repeated failures and feedback from significant evaluators that attests to one's inefficacy. It may also involve traumatic emotional experiences in which one is overcome by some strong emotions and is left helpless. In such cases the onset would be more abrupt, but the dynamic is the same: one learns that one is incompetent and unable to manage one's need satisfaction in the face of an overpowering environment.

The pathology that follows from the development of external causality is a more active one, whereas the pathology that develops from impersonal causality is more passive. However, clinicians sometimes report that people of the more active former sort plunge into depression and despair when some event leads to the awareness that their lives are meaningless after all, that through all this striving they have really missed the important things in life: the satisfaction of their basic needs for effectance, love, and so on. In one such example, a senior executive for a noted corporation lost his eight-year-old daughter in a traffic accident. He realized suddenly and, as he said, too late that he had not even known her. He had been so busy being successful, achieving and acquiring, that he never got to know his daughter, his relationship with his wife was thin and routinized, and he did not even enjoy what he had achieved and acquired.

Both types of pathology, mild and severe, are associated with blocked emotions and motives. When feelings are unpleasant, people tend to keep them out of conscious awareness. As Janis (1967) stated, people attempt to escape from painful emotions, either physically (for example through flight) or psychologically (for example by blocking them from awareness). But these blocked emotions and motives nonetheless remain operative; they are the basis for maladaptive, automatic behaviors and play a role in somatic malfunctions.

Seligman (1975) argued that helplessness is simply a learned style of interacting with the environment and is not a manifestation of repressed anger (Freud 1959b) or nonconscious motives. He used as evidence the fact that in dreams, depressed people often see themselves as helpless and inactive rather than hostile, hostility being what he asserted should appear if depression is caused by repressed anger. However, as Rank (1950) pointed out, the conscious thoughts of the day are often strong enough to appear in dreams, while the deeper impulses are blocked by ethical repressions. In other words, even though one dreams of paralysis, it is not an indication that the psychological basis is not repressed anger (Freud 1959b) or, as I would prefer, nonconscious motives and emotions. Furthermore, depressed (or helpless) people sometimes do experience strong emotions in their dreams or in therapy sessions, and these experiences may be very therapeutic. Seligman is right; helplessness is a belief about oneself in relation to the environment, but it is much more than that; it involves affective and motivational processes, as well as cognition and behavior.

Impersonal causality is based in a belief that behavior and outcomes are independent and leads people to be anxious and self-blaming for their failures. This seems at first to be paradoxical for, one might argue, if they believe in behavior-outcome independence, they ought not accept responsibility for the failures and therefore not feel anxious and worthless. However, the paradox vanishes when one considers the clinical evidence, which suggests that pathological people whom I would categorize as impersonals typically have been raised by parents who are very blaming and whose messages tend to be, "The world will not respond to you, and it is your fault." Their phenomenological experience is one of not being able to have an impact on the world and being responsible for that.

The converse paradox appears for internals. Internals can fail at a task and accept responsibility for the failure while at the same time not blaming themselves. They use the failure as information about how to do better next time. Attribution theorists (such as Valins and Nisbett 1971; Storms and McCaul 1976) have reported evidence indicating that attributing malfunction to external sources eases the felt anxiety and discomfort; I believe that this may be so for externals and impersonals but not necessarily for internals. Internals, who are guided more by intrinsic interest and less by introjected prescriptions, are freer from the self-condemning scripts (the critical superego) that make it necessary to attribute causality for failure to external sources in order to minimize anxiety and depression.

The common element for externals and impersonals is that they lack a sense of self-determination (though externals may deceive themselves in this regard). The lack of self-determination is accompanied by strong internalized scripts that utilize shame and guilt as sanctions. When externals or impersonals fail, accepting responsibility would lead to self-blame, anxiety, and depression. A major difference between externals and impersonals is that externals tend to blame the environment to escape these feelings, whereas impersonals tend to blame themselves and experience the unpleasant consequences.

Internals, with their strong sense of self-determination, are able to accept responsibility for failures (if they are responsible) and not get caught up in self-blame. They accommodate to situations where they cannot succeed and move on to situations where they can.

A similar kind of apparent paradox appears for internals who are more accurate perceivers of controlling contingencies and yet less likely to be controlled by those contingencies (less likely to become externals, less likely to engage in automatic, extrinsic behavior). However, it is precisely the accurate awareness of the contingencies that allows the people to remain internals. With accurate perceptions of the contingencies and with awareness of their own needs (for whatever reinforcements are associated with the contingencies), they can make choices and thus are more able to resist the encroachment of the contingencies. Externals tend to block awareness of their needs so they are more controlled by the nonconscious motives in interaction with the environment. They are more controlled by external cues, but they are less able to perceive accurately the causes of their behavior. On the one hand, they are more attuned to the external cues but, on the other hand, they often need to misperceive the causes of behavior to protect their own egos. The locus of causality is external, but often they deny it; they deceive themselves. It is primarily during their more reflective moments that they are able to admit to their self-deceptions.

Figure 7-2 summarizes the relationships among environments, causality orientations, motivational subsystems, and behaviors. Responsive environments facilitate the operation of the intrinsic subsystem; controlling environments, the extrinsic subsystem; and nonresponsive environments, the amotivational subsystem. Similarly, internals tend to operate from the intrinsic subsystem, externals from the extrinsic; and impersonals from the amotivational. When the intrinsic subsystem is operative, behavior will be self-determined with either intrinsic or extrinsic goals and perhaps with automatized subroutines. When the extrinsic subsystem is exclusively operative, behavior will be automatic; when it joins with the intrinsic, behavior will be chosen extrinsic, and when it joins with the amotivational, behavior will be automatic helpless. The pure form of the amotivational subsystem involves no behavior.

*Causality and Will*

There are two types of willing. The first is one in which the person is in touch with organismic needs and guides the satisfaction of these needs (and the motives that are the representation, in awareness, of the needs) through appropriate goal selection. The process is easy and natural; it requires a minimum of energy. The second type of willing is one in which people "force" themselves to behave against the opposition of some force such as a conflicting need or emotion. They may be acting in accord with one need or emotion in opposition to another (for example, willing themselves to

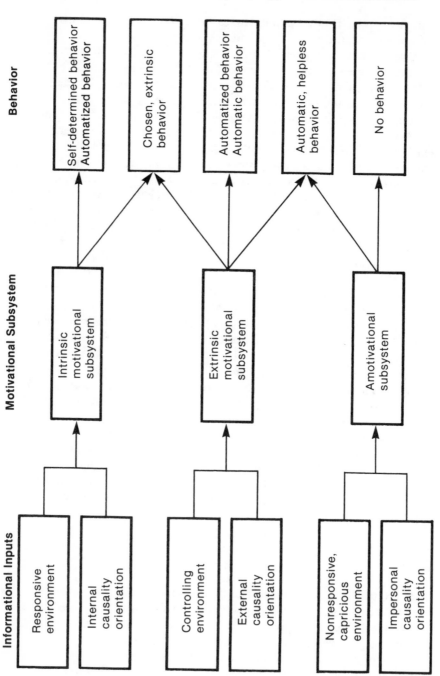

**Figure 7-2.** Relationships among Informational Inputs, Motivational Subsystems, and Types of Behavior

stay awake to read an interesting book when they are very tired); they may be acting in accord with one need or emotion in opposition to an admonition (for example, forcing themselves to express their anger when they believe it is bad to be angry); or they may be acting in accord with an admonition in opposition to a need or emotion (for example, abstaining from extramarital sexual activity because they believe it is wrong).

In internal causality, both types of willing are operative. People will be behaving and creating easily out of their basic needs, and they will also use internal force when necessary. For example, an internal-causality person who fears dark places may force him or herself to explore dark places in order to overcome the fear. In external causality, there will be an abundance of the force-oriented willing, in which people are pushed by internalized scripts and sanctions. The external orientation is characterized by hard-driving behavior against all odds, internal or external. There is, however, a relative absence of the more natural, easy willing in which one allows organismic needs to energize chosen behavior. May (1969b) made a similar point, referring to the two types of will as "will" and "willpower." He stated that willpower involves rationalization and self-deceit, which is, I contend, more evident in externals. Finally, in the impersonal-causality orientation, there appears to be an almost total absence of willing of either sort; the very heart of the matter for helpless or impersonal-causality people is that they seem to have no will.

Some theorists have suggested that the passive, helpless person is actually displaying will of a kind. Rank (1950) called it "negative will"; Perls (1973) referred to it as manipulation. In other words, for helpless people, being withdrawn and passive serves a dual function: it helps to buffer them from the continual feelings of failure, which they expect to follow every attempt to act on the environment effectively—thus it is self-protective; but it is also an aggressive, manipulative stance vis-à-vis the environment—it is passive aggression. The amotivational state, in its pure form, serves primarily the self-protective function. The aggressive manipulative behaviors are automatic and involve a mixture of the amotivational and extrinsic subsystems. An impersonal-causality person may well be both self-protective and aggressive, for although the amotivational subsystem is predominant, the extrinsic subsystem will also feed into an impersonal's behavior.

## The Organismic Framework

In figure 7-3, the central thrust of the schematic model is self-determined behavior. Stimulus inputs from the environment and the person activate the

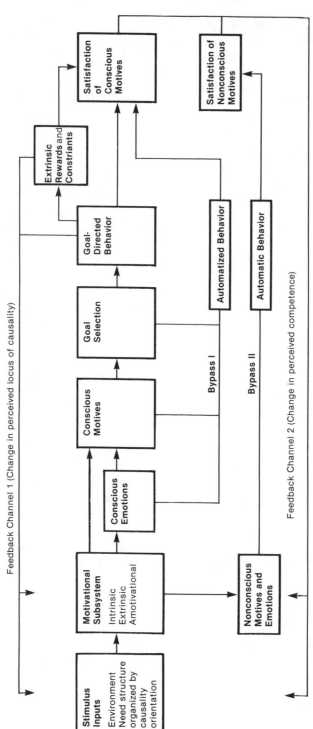

**Figure 7-3.** Self-determined and Automatic Behavior

Note: The central thrust of the model represents self-determined behavior. Stimulus inputs activate a motivational subsystem and enter awareness as conscious motives, which may or may not be mediated by a conscious emotion. Motives lead to goal selection, then goal-directed behavior, and finally satisfaction of the motives, which may or may not be mediated by an extrinsic reward. Feedback channels 1 and 2 represent the process of cognitive evaluation theory. Bypass I represents automatized behavior, and bypass II represents automatic behavior, which is mediated by nonconscious motives and emotions.

intrinsic motivational subsystem and pass into conscious awareness in the form of motives (conscious awarenesses of some future satisfying state). Stimulus inputs from the person come from what I have referred to as the need structure that exists in the memory and physiology of the organism. One's personality or causality orientation is integral to one's need structure; the orientation can be said to organize the need structure. Thus we might interchangeably speak of stimulus inputs form the person as coming from one's need structure or from one's personality (causality) orientation, depending on which concept is more relevant to the point at hand.

Behavior may be self-determined if it is intrinsically motivated (for example, play), and it may also be self-determined if it is extrinsically motivated. In the latter case, overt behavior and covert processes must be distinguished. An internal-causality person may engage in overt, extrinsically motivated behaviors (such as making money) in a self-determined fashion by choosing among motives and behaviors. In this case, the covert processes of choice, information selection, and managing motives would be intrinsically motivated. Thus some intrinsic motivation is necessary for self-determined behavior, though the overt behavior itself may be either intrinsically or extrinsically motivated. These are referred to in figure 7-2 as self-determined behavior and chosen, extrinsic behavior, respectively. An internal-causality person is likely to engage in chosen, extrinsic behavior to satisfy extrinsic needs, whereas external- and impersonal-causality people are likely to engage in automatic behaviors to satisfy these needs.

Conscious motives may form directly from stimulus inputs, or they may evolve from the conscious experience of an emotion. For example, seeing someone who reminds you of a good friend whom you have been out of touch with for a couple of months may lead directly to a motive to communicate with the friend. Or receiving a letter from that friend may make you very excited and happy and that emotional response leads to the motive to communicate with the person.

Once a motive occurs, people select goals that they expect to satisfy the motive. The goal may be simply a set of behaviors, or it may include an extrinsic reward. The motive to communicate with the friend may lead you to decide to telephone. You expect this behavior to satisfy the motive, but if your friend is vacationing on an island without a telephone, the behavior will not produce the desired satisfaction. Hence you choose a new goal: send a wire or letter. This behavior-selection or goal-selection phase is the heart of self-determination; it emphasizes the freedom to behave as one chooses in accord with one's inner thoughts, feelings, and motives. When people are aware of more than one motive at a time, their capacity for self-determination allows them to hold in abeyance any motives that cannot be satisfied at that time.

Internal causality is characterized by this type of self-determined behavior and by the use of programs that allow people to behave with a minimum of attention; that is, they guide automatized behavior. These programs, which are at the service of one's self-determining capacity, are flexible insofar as they are readily reprogrammable when the situation requires it.

Feedback channel 1 in figure 7-3 represents the process of change in perceived locus of causality. This channel passes information about reward and control contingencies and about behavioral instrumentalities back to the need structure (including one's causality orientation) and to the motivational subsystems. It is the process through which people learn what behaviors produce what desired outcomes and through which people either internalize control contingencies or free themselves of control contingencies. An excessive amount of controlling interaction with the environment, particularly in early years during the trust and autonomy struggles, leads to the external-causality orientation that is characteristic, for example, of the Type A behavior pattern (Glass 1977). This movement toward external causality involves a loss of intrinsic motivation, a blocking of many organismic needs and emotions from awareness, the development of externally based substitute needs such as an intense need for control, and the engagement in subsequent automatic behaviors.

Feedback channel 2 represents the change in perceived competence. When this channel carries continual messages of failure, nonsatisfied motives, or thwarted attempts at self-determination, particularly in early years during the trust, autonomy, initiation, and industry struggles, gradually one becomes helpless and develops an orientation toward impersonal causality.

The three personality (causality) orientations develop through the processes of cognitive evaluation, primarily during early years as children pass through the four developmental crises directly related to their sense of competence and self-determination. These orientations are somewhat modifiable throughout life as people have additional experiences of efficacy and inefficacy; however, as people get older, these changes in orientation occur much less easily. Rewards, controls, and feedback will affect people in accord with their interpretation of that information. Some feedback may be clear evidence that the environment is nonresponsive, that the person behaving cannot control the situation, in which case most (perhaps all) people would interpret it that way.

Most feedback, however, is rather ambiguous. Thus, the causality orientation that a person brings to the situation will influence the person's interpretation of information. The meaning of information from feedback channels and stimulus events is a partial function of the orientation of the perceiver. For example, consider three men who receive mildly negative feedback. The first considers it and then incorporates it into his strategy for solving the problem. The second is adamant about overcoming that hurdle;

he is challenged and attempts aggressively to achieve the desired outcome. The third gives up helplessly. Obviously these three responses are characterizations of how people with the three different causality orientations might respond to ambiguous feedback.

The effects of stimuli such as rewards, controls, and feedback depend on their meaning to the person. That meaning is determined partially by the properties of the stimulus and partially by the person's causality orientation. From the above example, one can see that orientations tend to build on themselves; they have spiraling effects. A person who is somewhat helpless (impersonal-causality oriented) will be more likely to interpret stimulus events as being indicative of a nonresponsive environment, thereby strengthening the helplessness.

Wortman and Brehm (1975) have hypothesized about the mediation of the helpless and reactance responses to perceived loss of freedom. I suggest that the individual difference variable of causality orientation (as well as the situation variables that they discussed) mediates people's responses. Further, the Type A behavior pattern described by Glass (1977) is said to be a response to the perceived loss of freedom. I hypothesize that internal-causality people would be motivated to restore their freedom, external-causality people would exhibit the Type A behavior pattern, and impersonal-causality people would act helpless.

*Somatic Illness*

One of the tenets of the organismic theory is that physical and mental health are closely linked. Since the advent of the germ theory of disease, the tendency to split the organism's well-being into psyche and soma has been matter of course. However research (for example, Schmale and Iker 1966; Schulz 1976) points clearly to the interrelationship. Somatic malfunction affects one's psychological experience, just as psychological stress affects one's somatic functioning.

The mechanisms through which a loss of self-determination affects one's physical well-being are only vaguely understood. Glass (1977) has reported that people who respond to uncontrollable environments with the Type-A behavior pattern (externally-causality people) have an increased susceptibility to coronary disease and arteriosclerosis, yet the precise mechanism is not clear. Similarly helpless individuals show increased likelihood for illness and unexpected death; precisely how this occurs is not clear. There are, however, some interesting pieces of evidence and speculation that seem relevant.

Both external and impersonal orientations involve greater blocking from awareness of one's needs and emotions. Izard (1977) has suggested that people's failure to recognize their emotional reactions may result in increased activity in the autonomically innervated organs. Chronic occurrence of such activation can cause somatic weakness or malfunction. Particularly strong emotional reactions will cause stress to the somatic system and may have highly negative effects on the weakened elements of the system. Reich (1949) suggested that unpleasant emotional experiences may result in what he called "character armor," an excessive tightening or rigidity in the musculature that may also make the organism particularly vulnerable at times of high stress and emotionality. In the same way that the collison of an object with a rigid surface will do more damage than a collision with an elastic surface, the strong innervation of organs in a rigid structure will do more damage than will the innervation of organs in an elastic structure.

It also seems to be the case that the external and impersonal orientations result in greater denial of malfunctioning. For example, Weidner and Matthews (1978) reported a laboratory study in which Type-A subjects who were working on an achievement task in an uncontrollable setting were less likely to report physical symptoms such as headaches than were non-Type-A subjects. Greene, Moss, and Goldstein (1974) suggested that Type-A people seem to avoid reporting early symptoms of coronary malfunction so as not to have to miss work while being treated.

Rodin (1978) pointed out that incorrect attributions about illnesses may lead people to avoid seeking medical attention. For example, if people blame themselves for an illness, they are likely to deny the symptoms and delay seeking help. I suggest that helpless, impersonal-causality individuals, being prone toward guilt, are particularly likely to be self-blaming and therefore to fall into this category. Further, helpless people, having given up, tend not to care for themselves, thereby making themselves more susceptible to illness.

I also speculate that some of the same environmental factors that produce the external or impersonal orientations may teach people to be sick. I recently witnessed an interaction between a mother and son in which the boy felt unhappy because he had been ignored. The mother, unwilling or unable to deal with his unhappiness, proclaimed to the rest of us, "Oh, he's not feeling well; he's had an earache," whereupon the boy held his ear, acted as if it hurt, and got a lot of attention. The repetition of such experiences might well lead to his ear hurting as a response to his feeling ignored. Asthma is widely regarded by clinicians to be a response to unhappy childhood events.

It is interesting to speculate that in our culture there is a tendency to blame our bodies for behavior that is not acceptable. For example, overeating and the resulting obesity are generally held in low esteem, and most people recognize that overeating may be a reaction to psychological problems. However, people do not like to admit that on top of the already undesirable overeating, they may have psychological problems since that is also undesirable. On the other hand, physical problems are more acceptable and are considered to be out of people's control, so people may be relieved to find that their overeating is caused by a thyroid malfunction. That way it is more acceptable, and they do not have to take responsibility for it or gain control of it. The interesting point is that the thyroid problem itself is likely to be a result of psychological stress. As we have seen, unrecognized emotional responses may cause generalized arousal that stimulates glandular activity, repeated experience of which can cause malfunction. However, that relationship of psychological stress causing physical malfunctioning, which in turn causes maladaptive behavior such as overeating, is generally ignored. Unfortunately people are giving up the key to gaining control over that automatic, maladaptive behavior of overeating and its resultant obesity by ignoring its relationship to psychological stress.

The attitude of looking to causes over which one has no control and looking for solutions in external agents such as drugs is entirely consistent for externals and impersonals. Thus, for example, an external or impersonal who is having a first interview with a therapist will be looking for the therapist to take responsibility for the problem and provide the solution.

*Maladaptive Styles*

Seligman (1975) likened helplessness to the clinical state of depression, suggesting that when people learn that there is response-outcome independence, they behave in ways that typically have been called depressed. I believe that this is so for many people. Yet depression is not the only style of responding to uncontrollable environments. Why, for example, might one not become impulsive or psychopathic in an environment where there is no relationship between behaviors and outcomes? After all, if behavior and outcomes (punishments) are believed to be unrelated, then there is no reason not to lie, steal, or raise a ruckus. Similarly someone with an external-causality orientation might well display paranoid tendencies (for example, always looking around for the control elements of the situation) or obsessive-compulsive tendencies (for example, continually engaging in ritualistic behaviors and thoughts that evolved to satisfy the control contingencies). There may be variation in people's response to the loss of self-determination. People will acquire either an external or impersonal orientation when they grow up in highly controlling or unresponsive environments. Within these different orientations, people may display different types of behaviors that often have been classified as different neurotic styles (Shapiro 1965).

Much of this discussion has focused on the Type-A behavior pattern for externals and the helpless, depressive response of impersonals. This is primarily because empirical evidence is abundant for these response patterns. However, there may be several response patterns that can be isolated for each causality orientation. An impersonal-causality person may engage in aggressive, automatic behavior when there is a mix of the extrinsic and amotivational subsystems. Thus it might be that an impulsive style, characterized by a belief in response-outcome independence and by automatic behavior, results from a less extreme impersonal-causality orientation that involves a mix of the extrinsic and amotivational subsystems.

The stylistic quality of the maladaptive responding that an externally or impersonally oriented individual may develop is a function of the person's genetic endowment and specific elements in the person's environment. The acquisition is an active process; it is not something that simply happens to the person. Shapiro emphasized the role of genetic factors. He stated that individuals are born with psychological apparatus that differs among individuals and serves to organize and give form to stimulus events. For example, neonates differ in the degree of satiation that produces felt discomfort—in their readiness for sucking, in the directed (versus diffuse) response to experienced tension, and so on. These different capacities perform an organizing function that gives a configural quality to the experience and reduction of drive tension. Thus, for example, one baby may tolerate more tension and (when the threshold is reached) discharge that tension through more directed activity (such as sucking), whereas a second baby may tolerate less tension and discharge it in a much more diffuse way. Then, in turn, these two babies may be responded to very differently since they will be behaving differently and placing different demands on the parents. The ongoing interplay between the initial constitutional equipment and the environment is the basis for the development of styles of interacting, including styles of maladaptive responding.

Shapiro's analysis is very sound, though I also would emphasize that children's adaptation is dependent on the situational context. When faced with thwarted attempts at self-determination, they explore ways of gaining gratification. For example, they may behave in disruptive ways to assert their autonomy, they may charm a grandmother into giving them the freedom that their parents will not permit, or they may act passive if passivity brings a response. The point is that their intrinsic motivation, their need for effective adaptation, leads them to behave in ways that satisfy their organismic needs or at least their developing substitute needs. These emerging styles are acquired because they represent the best adaptation the child can make given one's constitutional structure and the situational influences. The problem is that these behavioral styles become rigid or fixed because of their attachment to the needs and emotions that are being blocked from consciousness during the experiences of thwarted attempts to act effectively and autonomously. These automatic behaviors then become increasingly maladaptive as the situations within which the individual acts require varied responses that the person who is locked into automatic responses cannot produce.

# 8 The Restoration of Well-Being

An internal-causality orientation constitutes the most healthful form of psychological functioning. This orientation is characterized by self-determined behavior and by the use of automatized responding that has been programmed by and is reprogrammable by the will. Internal-causality people are more willful; they have a stronger sense of competence and self-determination. Often they will operate from an intrinsic motivational subsystem, though they will, as the situation warrants it, shift from the intrinsic to the extrinsic motivational subsystem to engage in chosen, extrinsic behavior. An internal person will recognize impersonal causality when it occurs; in other words, they will recognize elements of the situation over which they have no control. They would respond to such situations either by accommodating or by attempting to change the situation rather than by feeling helpless and being passive. In this chapter, we consider the processes through which exernal-causality and impersonal-causality people can become more internal.

## Causality Orientations and the Environment

To a large extent, people will respond to the environment within the context of their causality orientation. When people are in environments that do not match their orientation they tend, initially at least, to interpret the environment in a way that is consistent with their orientations. Thus internals tend to use the structures and contingencies of controlling environments as sources of effectance feedback. They tend to recognize nonresponsive or capricious environments as such and to undertake challenges in areas where there is some chance they can have an impact. Externals tend to view responsive informational environments as sources of control, and if the environments in some way fail to be controlling they tend to become frustrated. Externals tend to react to nonresponsive, capricious environments with an intensified need to force a relationship between behavior and outcome. They are not only controlled by external cues (and nonconscious motives), but out of their lack of self-determination they often have an intense need to control, especially in nonresponsive environments. Behavior-outcome independence is very threatening for externals since their behavior is controlled by outcomes. Finally impersonals tend to see all environments as nonresponsive. They tend to feel ignored by informational environments since the environments are unlikely to provide them with positive feedback or rewards in the absence of goal-directed behavior. Impersonals tend to be upset by controlling environments that seem to be pushing them around. Environments that try to control them exacerbate their own feelings of having no control over the environment.

Since an internal-causality orientation represents the model of well-being, the aim of therapy should be to facilitate self-determination and to develop this orientation. This is not an easy matter, for externals and impersonals tend to interpret their environments in ways that are consistent with their orientations rather than respond to and accommodate to a responsive, informational, therapeutic environment. For instance, externals will want the therapist to solve their problems and change their behaviors; they will resist being supported to solve their own problems and change their own behaviors. Impersonals will remain passive; they see the therapy, like everything else, as being hopeless. Nonetheless orientations are somewhat changeable, and a therapist can work toward those changes. As an aspect of this, the therapist would attempt at least to facilitate some operation of the intrinsic motivational subsystem for externals (even within the context of a rather enduring external orientation) and to facilitate some operation of the intrinsic and extrinsic motivational subsystems (even within the context of a rather enduring impersonal orientation).

One's causality orientation is largely a function of prior experiences of efficacy and inefficacy, particularly during early years when one is dealing with the self-determination and competence conflicts. Certain child-rearing practices foster the development of an internal-causality orientation. In therapy, well-being is restored through movement toward an internal-causality orientation as a result of various therapeutic practices.

Child-rearing and therapy are conceptually similar in many ways, yet there are important differences as well. Whereas in child-rearing a parent must take greater responsibility for decision making for the child, in therapy the decision making must rest to a much greater degree with the client.

The aim of psychotherapy should be the development of internal causality. This necessitates beginning from the client's perspective, working from the client's goals. If, for example, a client states an aim that in essence means strengthening an external orientation, the appropriate place to begin is with an exploration of the selection of that goal. A therapist must neither force the goal of internal causality, for the method of force negates the goal of self-determination, nor accept as an end point the goal of external causality, for that point does not constitute well-being.

There is one type of situation in which the goal of internal causality may be inappropriate. Some clients may be so disturbed that a goal of internal causality is unreachable. In such situations the therapist may provide the kind of support and direction that would solidify an external orientation. Helping a client move from an impersonal to an external orientation is a useful therapeutic outcome, as is returning coherence to the deteriorating experience of a highly disturbed, externally oriented client. In these cases, the manipulation of contingencies by the therapist or the directive participation in problem solving may be appropriate given the aim of creating or solidifying an external orientation that is sufficient to allow the client to function in his or her ongoing environment.

In standard therapy, where the aim is the development of self-determination and internal causality, the most important function of the relationship is to promote the clients' taking responsibility for their own decisions. Therapists may use their expertise to provide clients with information about predictable consequences of various behaviors so the clients may be in a position to make more informed decisions, but the therapist must not usurp the decision making.

## Toward Self-Determination

According to the organismic theory, promoting self-determination means encouraging awareness of internal cues, increasing one's capacity to choose among motives and goals, and reclaiming automatic behaviors through exploration of their nonconscious bases. The heart of the matter is facilitating the operation of the intrinsic motivational subsystem by strengthening people's sense of competence and self-determination. There are five interrelated aspects to the processes of strengthening one's sense of competence and self-determination: awareness, acceptance, choice, expectations, and accommodation.

### *Awareness*

This means allowing nonconscious motives and emotions into consciousness. People learn not to attend to certain needs and certain emotional responses. With the development of an external-causality orientation, one learns that only certain feelings and needs are acceptable and will lead to desired outcomes like approval, avoidance of punishment, and receipt of rewards. Those feelings and needs, which conflict with one's beliefs about what one should feel or want, tend to be kept out of awareness. With the development of an impersonal-causality orientation, people learn that they cannot manage various motives and emotions—the motives and emotions would overwhelm them—so they block awareness of the motives and emotions. Also they have developed the belief that their motives would not be gratified and their feelings not responded to, so there is no use being aware of them.

Awareness involves attending to those motives and emotions that have been denied access to one's conscious experience. Awareness of one's organismic motives and emotions will have implications for one's substitute needs, which developed when one did not gratify the underlying organismic needs. As the basic needs are allowed into awareness and subsequently gratified and as emotions are allowed into awareness and expressed, the substitute needs become secondary. For example, as one becomes more interested in an activity, is more intrinsically motivated to do it, and feels more competent and self-determining in relation to the activity, one might become less rigid and intense in one's needs for control.

Awareness happens when something occurs to the client. This tends to happen through relaxed attending to oneself. A therapist does not tell the client what his or her feelings or needs really are. Instead the therapist might point out ways in which the client is blocking awareness or point out specific behaviors. For example, the therapist might say, "I am struck by the fact that you have made a fist each time you talk about your husband," or "Are you aware that you have made that same point four times in the last few minutes?" These obvious facts are starting points for exploration. The client might attend to what happens as she makes a fist or consider what is being said or hidden through repetition of the point.

*Acceptance*

In the process of facilitating awareness, one must realize that motives and emotions are kept out of awareness because the awareness of them causes discomfort. People acquire the belief that they are bad to want or feel certain things. Thus simple awareness of those parts of themselves will produce anxiety and discomfort if one does not deal also with the evaluations and beliefs that conflict with the motives and emotions. The clients must learn to make a neutral or positive evaluation of the parts of themselves that have been kept nonconscious. The therapist, parent, counselor, or teacher would work toward this acceptance by clarifying the evaluative process and modifying the criteria for self-evaluation.

Beck (1976) pointed out that people typically are involved in an ongoing self-evaluation; they have what he called "automatic thoughts" that are difficult to turn off. These thoughts occur as part of the interpretive process, such that incoming stimuli are examined for implications of one's goodness or badness. For example, when one person asks another, "Are you going to the library?" the second may hear it as, "You should go to the library; you are bad if you do not.'' These so-called automatic thoughts are the key to what I am calling acceptance, for they help to keep motives and emotions out of awareness. The process of acceptance involves attending to these evaluative thoughts and reorienting the evaluative process so awareness is enhanced. In the process of enhancing acceptance and awareness, one begins to see that the evaluations often are based on irrational, inappropriate assumptions and that one need not believe the ingrained messages.

## Choice

The essence of self-determination is making choices among motives and goals. As people have various experiences of efficacy and inefficacy, they develop a belief about their own capcaity to choose. They may, for example, believe that their capacity is slight and that the forces of their motives, emotions, and the environment are too strong for them to manage. Thus they would maintain automatic responding rather than develop self-determination. As awareness and acceptance increase, as more of one's motives and emotions become conscious, one must acquire the belief that they are manageable. If one has become aware of intense anger and the inclination to be violent or destructive, one needs to believe that one can manage the anger without doing the violence; in other words, one needs to believe that one has the capacity to manage motives and make rational decisions about behaviors—to be self-determining—even when the affect and motivation is quite intense. A therapist must be working to modify people's capacity for choice and beliefs about their capacity for choice. This element of the restoration of self-determination is evident in such folk wisdom rules-of-thumb as "Count to ten before doing anything when you are angry.'' A therapist can work with both attitudes and techniques for managing behavior in the presence of strong forces.

This process of choosing is closely related to acceptance. As Beck suggested, one's response to a stimulus is in part a function of one's evaluation of the stimulus and of oneself. If people interpret a stimulus as meaning that they are in some way bad—inadequate, nonefficacious, inappropriately affective—they are likely to have a strong reaction to their negative self-evaluation, which in turn would be more difficult to control. However, if their interpretation of the stimulus does not include the implicit negative self-evaluation, their reactions are likely to be less intense and less difficult to self-determine.

## Expectations

Behavioral choices are based on people's expectations about the relationship between behaviors and the satisfaction of motives. These expectations are learned and may become quite discrepant from reality. Thus, in the therapeutic process, one must be cognizant of the client's beliefs about behavior-satisfaction relationships. Even when people gain an increased sense of awareness and self-determination, they may behave in somewhat maladaptive ways if they are operating with an incorrect set of expectations.

Consider an example of a young woman who is afraid of men. Suppose her fears arose in early experiences with her parents and she had been blocking awareness and responding automatically in her recent interactions with men. As a result of these and other factors, she has had a series of punishing experiences that have created for her a set of expectations of what can be done or gained in relating to a man. While a therapeutic experience may help her with an understanding of her fears and with an increased sense of confidence and self-determination, she may continue to have unsatisfactory interactions with men if some of her behavior-outcome expectations are not modified.

*Accommodation*

The final aspects of the therapeutic process that facilitate self-determination and internal causality involve learning to discriminate what aspects of the environment are changeable and what are not. It is simply a fact that there is behavior-outcome independence for some people (perhaps all people) in some situations. When that is so, those are not good situations for those people to act upon. No one can move the Empire State building by hand; it is silly to try. Someone who sets that as a goal will be unendingly frustrated. It makes more sense to recognize that the task cannot be done and to undertake a different one.

I am not suggesting that people should do only easy things. Indeed intrinsically motivated behavior involves dealing with challenges by seeking and conquering them. Yet these challenges must be optimal for the person at that time, and people, particularly those who are working therapeutically to build their sense of competence and self-determination, will need to deal with situations that are responsive to their initiations, challenges that are optimal for them at that time.

The process of accommodation was well illustrated in an anecdote reported by Matthiessen (1978). In the Dolpo region of the Tibetan Himalayas, at Tsakang—a house of solitude—lives an elderly Buddhist tulku, a high holy man. The tulku is badly crippled and since the only access to Tsakang requires several days of walking through high, snow-covered mountain passes, the tulku must live out his life in simplicity at Tsakang, where he has been for years, often with but one or two other inhabitants. When asked how he felt about living in that isolation for the rest of his life, he replied that it was wonderful and he loved it there, especially because he had no choice. Through his acceptance of the situation, he was "free" to make the most of it; he could be self-determining. If he were forever bemoaning his fate (and behaving automatically), he would not be "free" to live a satisfying life within the constraints. The accommodation to what cannot be changed provides the opportunity for self-determination. The failure to accommodate keeps one locked into the automatic responding of the external or impersonal orientation.

In the Western world there seems to be much greater emphasis on changing the environment, controlling it and controlling others, whereas in the Eastern world there seems to be greater emphasis on accommodation. Self-determination involves both actively effecting change and accommodating to what is not appropriately changed; the therapeutic process should give attention to both processes.

In doing therapy, the five considerations—awareness, acceptance, choice, expectations, and accommodation—are important in helping a client become more self-determining. At times, one of these aspects will be the focus of attention; at other times, others will. An overall therapeutic endeavor requires some attention to each, and the appropriate mix of attention to the various elements will depend on the particular client.

To a large extent, four of the five aspects (all except awareness) are a matter of modifying cognitions. Yet the process is not wholly a cognitive one, for the nonconscious emotion that is involved in all automatic behavior will need to be dealt with in order for the cognitive work to be effective. For example, a therapist who is working to modify a cognition related to acceptance or expectations may find the client resistant to accepting what is a clear and logical solution to a problem or what is a reasonable way to view some interaction. This resistance is a definite indication that there are some nonconscious motives and emotions that need to be allowed into awareness before the cognitions will change. The resistance to solving the problem means that something else is going on at that moment. The apparent problem is not really foreground; there is something else involved that is motivational and emotional in nature. For example, the client may be fighting with the therapist. Before the presenting problem can be solved, attention must be focused on this other matter.

## Therapy and the Organismic Framework

Let us consider the therapeutic process in terms of the organismic model of behavior that appeared as figure 7-3. The aim of therapy being to increase self-determination means that more behavior would be chosen by the person;

in other words, behavior would follow the main path through the model. Additionally the person would make use of automatized responding (bypass I) as part of the overall process of being self-determining.

The main function of the therapeutic endeavor is to bring automatic behaviors (as represented by bypass II) back into the realm of self-determination. This involves awareness (allowing motives and emotions into consciousness), acceptance (giving up the negative evaluations that block motivations and emotions), choice (strengthening one's will by learning that one can manage one's motives and emotions and choosing behaviors to satisfy the conscious motives), expectations (modifying one's beliefs about the behavior-reward and behavior-satisfaction relationships), and accommodation (learning what outcomes cannot be attained, that is, what behavior-reward and behavior-satisfaction relationships do not exist). These aspects of the therapeutic process give attention to each element of the organismic model that is an aspect of self-determined behavior. The summation of effects is the strengthening of people's intrinsic motivational subsystem. It will include increasing people's sense of competence and self-determination, decreasing their automatic responding, and moving them toward a more internal-causality orientation.

*Cognitive Evaluation Theory and*
*Causality Orientations*

People's causality orientations tend to lead them to seek environments that are consistent with their orientations and to interpret environments as being more consistent with their orientation than they are. Nonetheless, when people are in environments that are inconsistent, in time they will begin to respond to the difference. In therapy, the therapist affects the client's behaviors and internal states by creating a certain kind of environment to which the client will respond. Ideally the therapist would provide a responsive, informational environment conducive to intrinsic motivation and internal causality. Truly responsive, informational environments are ones in which the therapist supports the client's initiations and uses rewards and structures to convey competence information to the client. In therapy, one would typically emphasize the positive information, though at times the negative information is important as well to facilitate appropriate accommodation.

Responsive, informational environments affect people's behavior and internal states through the operation of the processes of cognitive evaluation theory. The processes work as feedback channels to let people see that they can have choice, that there can be an internal locus of causality, and that they can be competent and efficacious. Elsewhere (Ryan and Deci

1980) we have reviewed evidence demonstrating that changes that occur in therapy seem to persist following termination of treatment only when they have affected people's perceptions of causality and competence. The enhancement of intrinsic motivation seems to be the key to maintenance and transfer of therapeutic change.

Intrinsic motivation and internal causality necessitate perceptions of both competence and self-determination (see figure 7-1). Thus for an external to become an internal, the focus will be on promoting self-determination; the person must learn to attend to internal, organismic cues and act on the environment rather than be a pawn to the environment (in conjunction, of course, with nonconscious motives and emotions). For an impersonal to become an internal, there must be a focus on both competence and self-determination. To be competent, one must see a relationship between behaviors and outcomes and behave in a way that yields the outcomes. This can be accomplished from either an internal or an external orientation. An external sees the connections and responds to external forces; an internal sees the connections and acts on the environment to satisfy organismic needs. The point is that becoming competent by learning about the dependence between behaviors and outcomes and learning to do the appropriate behaviors well does not ensure intrinsic motivation and internal causality. Competence can move one toward extrinsic motivation and external causality from amotivation and impersonal causality, but without self-determination one cannot move to intrinsic motivation and internal causality.

Seligman (1975) has suggested that depressed patients should be placed in situations where contingencies exist between behavior and outcomes. Clearly this is important, but it is not enough to achieve internal causality. A controlling environment that makes demands and dispenses rewards for compliance involves a behavior-outcome dependence but fosters an external rather than internal orientation. Being more active and having an external orientation is preferable to the severe depression of impersonal-causality clients and therefore is a useful first step in treatment. However, it is important to move beyond the use of controlling rewards (and the resulting external causality) to internal causality.

The one exception to this assertion is when people are sufficiently disturbed that intrinsic motivation and internal causality are unrealistic goals. When working with such people, one might aim for a relatively effective working of the extrinsic subsystem and external orientation. In such cases, manipulation of contingencies and directive interventions would be appropriate to establish the perception of competence, without true self-determination.

In most cases, I would advocate working toward internal causality. Thus when it is necessary to use controlling communications (directives) or controlling rewards as a first step with impersonal, amotivational clients, the directives and rewards should be used as sparingly as possible; they should be decreased when appropriate and withdrawn as soon as possible. They should be used to convey positive information about the person's efficacy—information that the person is worthy and competent and can achieve desired outcomes. The decreasing reliance on controlling communications and rewards allows for increasing self-determination. In short, a treatment approach should convey to patients or clients that they can be willful and achieve desired outcomes. Since empirical evidence indicates that people who believe they are self-determining behave as if they were (Steiner 1970), the belief in one's capacity to choose should strengthen the capacity. The therapist's job would be to align him or herself with the person's capacity for self-determination so as to oppose the messages of incompetence, whether they are coming from a hostile environment or the so-called condemning superego.

The strengthening of one's intrinsic motivation and internal causality will lead to the person's interpreting stimulus inputs as sources of information rather than as controllers of behavior. In particular, the client in treatment will need to move from experiencing the therapist as a controller of behavior (one who knows what is best, and whose comments are interpreted as "shoulds" to be accepted or rebelled against) to experiencing the therapist as a source of information that may be useful in making decisions. When external events move from control to information, the person will be more involved with the process of deciding. Deciding will be intrinsically rewarding in and of itself.

## Doing Therapy

In doing therapy one should work toward greater self-determination and internal causality in the client by attending to awareness, acceptance, choice, expectations, and accommodation. There may be an exception to this general aim—for example, in working with a relatively distressed person, on a short-term basis, in a relatively deprived area, in which case it may be best to use a particular behavioral technique that could create some rapid change. It is unlikely that the change will last unless the therapist has access to a whole system, such as the client's family or work place, and can change some structural components of the system to perpetuate the change; however, for the client to have had some relief from distress is better than having none, and the experience may have some small feedback effect, which will slightly enhance the person's feelings of worth. Unless the nature of the circumstances specifically prevents working with the client's internal cognitive, emotional, and motivational processes, I contend that that is the most effective and meaningful approach.

The first principle in doing therapy is that one must recognize that all behaviors make sense and can be understood in motivational terms. However, there are two important considerations in this understanding: first, that behaviors are based on information as it is interpreted by the behaver, and, second, that the motive may be nonconscious so that the behaviors are automatic and inflexible. If a behavior appears not to make sense to a therapist, the therapist is lacking relevant information. Perhaps the client is lying or withholding important elements of the story. More often, however, the relevant information is out of the client's awareness. When the information is not in conscious awareness, the client can gain access to it. Beck (1976) contended that all of the relevant information exists in the person's consciousness, but I think he was wrong. It is precisely that assumption that limits the effectiveness of cognitive therapy, for it leads therapists to ignore the importance of promoting awareness.

To illustrate, when working with a depressed client, it is possible for the client to understand that his or her passivity is a response to feeling helpless, that it is an attempt to manipulate people, and that it is not working effectively as a means of getting gratification. Still the client may continue to be passive. The client fully understands; all of the apparently relevant cognitions are foreground for the client, yet the behavior persists. This is to be expected, for if the client does not become aware of the blocked motives and emotions that are motivating this automatic, passive behavior, the behavior will continue.

Maier (1949) made a similar point in discussing frustration responses. People who are behaving emotionally (expressing frustration) cannot be reasoned with in the same way as when they are rationally problem solving. In such situations there are nonconscious elements that are centrally important and are not responsive to information unless they come into conscious awareness.

The second principle of this approach states that the most important function of the therapist is to convey a sense of personal worth. Rogers (1951) spoke of this as providing unconditional positive regard. The therapist must hear the client fully and convey that interest to the client. This is a somewhat complicated process, with a variety of ramifications. Accepting clients and affirming their personal worth does not mean praising them for various behaviors, for praise, like any other reward, has a controlling as well as an informational aspect and can create instrumentalities and dependencies. The client who is praised by a therapist will begin to engage in behaviors that will yield praise. If this occurs, the process of therapy will be somewhat undermined, for it will be facilitating external causality.

A therapist also will need to frustrate the client's attempts at neurotic manipulation of the therapist. For example, if a client pleads, "I can't do it; please, you'll have to do it for me," a therapist would not (except in rare circumstances) yield to such a statement. The therapist must both convey acceptance of the person and not give in to the manipulation attempt. The therapist, however, must understand that there is a reason for the pleading. Thus it is necessary to work toward an understanding of what is at stake for the client—in other words, what nonconscious motives and emotions underlie the behavior—and to encourage the client to learn different, more effective behaviors for satisfying the same needs. Sometimes the amount of fear that is associated with giving up the maladaptive behavior is very great. In this case the therapist must not push the client to stop the maladaptive behavior; rather the therapist should provide the setting in which the client can choose to stop the behavior.

An example of a circumstance in which yielding to a client's plea is appropriate would be when the therapist believes that not yielding would result in the client's doing physical injury to him or herself or to someone else. The more severely disturbed the client, the more it will be necessary for the therapist to take care of the client, to accept responsibility for the client's behavior, particularly during early phases of treatment.

Third, it is important to emphasize that all feelings and desires are acceptable though all behaviors are not. This point relates to conveying a sense of personal worth, but it gets precisely to the matter of people's blocking awareness of the motives and emotions that are often considered unacceptable. When the therapist accepts all motives and emotions, the client will be motivated to explore and accept those that have been kept nonconscious. Clients may need to learn that it is appropriate to have various angry or sexual feelings, even the so-called bad ones; that these feelings do not make the person bad; that recognizing the feelings allows one to stop the automatic, maladaptive behaviors that were associated with them; and that the feelings can be managed (that is, the person can choose acceptable ways of satisfying the motives or expressing the emotions). It is acceptable to feel intense hate and to think thoughts like, "I'd like to smash him in the face," but it is generally not acceptable to smash him in the face. Thus one learns to express the anger in more appropriate ways, such as verbal interchange or smashing a "dummy." As the emotions are less often blocked, their intensity will tend to lessen, and they will be easier to manage.

Fourth, and finally, therapists must be careful not to confuse their own needs with the well-being of the client. People do therapy to satisfy their own needs—for feelings of effectance, for money, for status, and so on—and in specific moments they act out of their own motives and emotions. For example, when a client does not respond as expected, a therapist may get angry. Therapists must recognize the anger as their own response and neither hold the client responsible for it nor punish the client for instigating it. Therapists must monitor their own behavior carefully so as to distinguish between their own expressive reactions and behaviors that are chosen for their therapeutic value. This, of course, requires that the therapists be particularly aware of their own emotions and motives.

The therapist also should avoid power struggles. Seldom is there therapeutic value in fighting with clients. Therapists ought not give in to attacks by the client, yet neither ought they counterattack. Therapists should see the behavior as an attack and deal with it as such rather than getting caught up in it. Similarly therapists should not threaten clients; they simply provide information.

People develop external or impersonal orientations because they live in controlling or nonresponsive environments. These environments exist because the significant others, such as parents, teachers, or therapists, themselves are behaving automatically. For example, out of their own distress, their own external and impersonal orientations, parents and teachers behave automatically and either control or act inconsistently toward the children and pupils. To provide a responsive, informational environment, the significant others must remain self-determining. Thus therapists must be continually checking their own behavior to ensure that they are being self-determining, responsive, and informational.

This does not mean that therapists have no rights. They are, of course, at liberty to insist that a client not break their office furniture; yet they would not make threats, they would simply indicate that it is not acceptable and that they will not work with clients who do it. No expressions of therapists' anger, no assertions of supremacy are necessary or useful; therapists simply state the limits and the consequences of transgression and then hold to the limits and the consequences. Setting limits, allowing maximum freedom within the limits, and being informational rather than controlling about transgressions is as important for therapists who are working toward the enhancement of intrinsic motivation and internal causality as it is for parents who are attempting to rear intrinsically motivated, self-determining children.

Resistance by a client to the therapist's suggestions or interpretations is frequent in therapy. Rank (1950) pointed out that in one sense resistances are good signs, for they are expressions of the client's will. Therapists should not see these resistances as bad and convey that evaluation to the client, for this interpretation will perpetuate the maladaptive self-evaluative process of the client. Resistances should be considered in terms of their functions and their costs to the clients.

In summary, the therapeutic process is one of enhancing people's awareness and acceptance of their own emotions and motives in conjunction with enhancing their capacity to self-determine behaviors, to manage the motives and emotions and select behaviors. Rigidly held ideas and self-imposed requirements restrict people's freedom. They diminish responsivity to new situations and often cause people to block the awareness of conflicting motivations and emotions. They often lead people to self-flagellation when they fail to meet the standards, and they block effective problem solving. These inflexible ideas are a component of the external- and impersonal-causality orientations. In therapy, the therapist helps the client explore these fixed ideas, the "shoulds" and "musts," so the client can decide whether to hold on to them or to ease the ideas and allow greater freedom. One learns to allow internal forces such as anxiety and to manage them effectively rather than fight them. The acceptance of feelings such as anxiety interrupts the negative spiral in which such feelings build on themselves. If one is about to give a speech and feels anxious, one might say to oneself, "So, I'm anxious now; it's OK." A more common and less effective response is, "Oh my God, I'm nervous, what if I forget what I'm supposed to say?" This response has a synergistic effect, for each thought creates a symptom (weak knees or sweaty palms perhaps), and each symptom creates another fearful thought. Thus in therapy, one simply allows awareness of the motives and emotions and selects behaviors to satisfy some motives while holding others in abeyance. The acceptance, or allowing awareness, is necessary to bring the motives and emotions under the control of the will; otherwise they energize automatic behavior, which is generally counterproductive for the person.

**Therapeutic Approaches**

I shall now consider three treatment approaches—behavioristic, psychoanalytic, and Gestalt—from the point of view of the organismic theory. I will not attempt to assess the effectiveness of the approaches but rather will consider the ways in which their expressed aims and procedures relate to the organismic model and to the therapeutic aims of an intrinsic motivation, self-determination view of behavior and therapy.

*Behavior Therapy*

Wolpe (1964, 1969) stated that from a behavioristic perspective, neuroses are persisting, maladaptive, conditioned habits. The aim of behavioristic therapy (or conditioning therapy) is to decondition the target habits—in other words, to change the behavior with conditioning principles. In its most basic form, there are two general approaches in behavioristic therapy. The first recognizes that much maladaptive behavior involves anxiety; thus the approach, often called desensitization, is intended to decondition anxiety responses. The second applies the principles of operant conditioning (Skinner 1938) to strengthen desired behaviors.

Considering the first approach, Wolpe has described the principle of reciprocal inhibition in which people are placed in the presence of an anxiety-eliciting stimulus while an anxiety-inhibiting response is reinforced. Thus, it is believed, the stimulus-anxiety association will be weakened. The client would be exposed to the relevant anxiety-provoking stimulus, such as the sight of a raised fist, often beginning with a mild version of the stimulus. The client is induced to relax and/or engage in some particular asserting behavior such as saying, "Put down that fist." Through repeated experiences, adaptive responses become associated with the stimuli that formerly elicited maladaptive responses.

In the second, closely related approach, specific behaviors are isolated, which, it is believed, will alleviate the client's suffering, and those behaviors are conditioned using reinforcement procedures. For example, Bachrach (1964) described a woman with anorexia nervosa for whom eating behavior was conditioned. First, it was determined what things were reinforcing for the client: music, visits, reading, and television. The client was then deprived of all these by being placed in a barren room. All of her desired activities were made contingent upon a certain amount of food ingestion. There was no attempt to understand the reasons for her noneating; she was simply reinforced for eating. According to Bachrach, after a year of such conditioning, she had made considerable gains and was continuing to do so.

The conditioning approach to psychotherapy developed out of a mechanistic conception of the person and works to change specific behaviors by giving attention to reward contingencies in the treatment setting and the client's natural setting. This is done with but a minimum of attention paid to affect, motivation, catharsis, or psychodynamics in general. In terms of the organismic model of motivation, the focus of behavioristic therapy is on the behavior and extrinsic rewards. With the behavioristic assumption that behavior is caused by conditioning histories and reinforcement contingencies, there is no heed given to the detrimental effects of extrinsic rewards outlined by cognitive evaluation theory. Assuming simply that rewards strengthen the rate of responding, applied behavioral systems such as behavior therapy tend to rely on use of extrinsic rewards to change observable, overt behaviors.

The behavioristic approach utilizes extrinsic rather than intrinsic motivational principles and is consistent with external rather than internal causality. It advocates the blocking from awareness of those emotions and motives that are not congruent with external control, and it can foster the development of substitute needs. As such it may increase the occurrence of automatic responding.

Directive, controlling procedures can be useful in certain situations, particularly with extremely disturbed clients over a short time span. But it is important to recognize that the result of such treatments will be external causality rather than internal causality, so the procedures should be used only when the development of external causality is one's aim. Behavioristic procedures can improve one's competence but they will not enhance one's self-determination. May (1969b) asserted that the function of behavior therapy is the establishment of habit patterns and thus is not really psychotherapy.

**Recent Developments.** During the 1970s, the nature of behavior therapy has changed considerably (see, for example, Bandura 1977a; Kanfer 1975; Mahoney and Thoreson 1974) and moved toward an emphasis on mediating cognitive variables. As Kanfer has pointed out, extrinsic reinforcements administered by a therapist are not readily applicable to many kinds of behaviors, such as thoughts, self-evaluations, and overt behaviors that are done in privacy or in inaccessible settings. Further, clients must ultimately assume responsibility for their own behavior if changes are to persist. Thus Kanfer outlined a behavioral system for self-management, which consists of three steps: self-monitoring, self-evaluation, and self-reinforcement. Self-monitoring involves the observation of one's behavior and the environmental circumstances in which it occurs. One is directed to observe one's current situation and to note one's expectations. One then engages in phase two, self-evaluation. With the expectations serving as a standard of comparison, one determines the discrepancy between the standard and one's current state. Finally, having noted the discrepancy, one creates a self-reinforcement contingency to bring out the behavior that will match the standard. Kanfer described two types of self-reinforcement: material and verbal. He suggested that one should decide to give oneself a little present such as a new shirt or a coffee break, or a verbal-symbolic reward of self-praise for completing the behavior that allows one to meet the standard.

Let us now consider Kanfer's system as it relates to the earlier, pure form of behavior therapy and also as it relates to the organismic theory of behavior. Although the system purports to be an operant one and retains many behavioral terms, it has deviated substantially from the earlier conditioning model. It no longer focuses on only specific, overt behaviors but has been extended to include even internal verbalizations. Kanfer also used certain terms that imply that the person's internal processes are determinative of behavior. For example, he spoke of the person's accepting responsibility for behavior change.

In the third phase of the self-management system, Kanfer stated that the client administers self-reinforcements. What was left unsaid is that someone must decide what behaviors the client will undertake and what reinforcements will be self-administered for the chosen behaviors. If these two critical decisions are made by the therapist, I believe that the process will be undermined; if the behaviors and self-reinforcements are chosen by the client, the system would have a much greater likelihood of promoting self-determination.

This system has moved somewhat toward the organismic theory, particularly when the behaviors and self-reinforcements are chosen by the client. It is immediately apparent that the structure of the self-management system is very similar to Miller, Galanter, and Pribram's (1960) TOTE feedback loop, which I suggested was the basis for directing one's self-determined behavior. Kanfer described the process in behavioristic terms, but the process cannot be meaningfully understood without the use of the concepts of information processing and decision making.

Kanfer's behavioristic orientation perhaps is most evident in his focus of self-reinforcement, those material or verbal rewards that follow the behavior. His system, however, is based on the idea of wanting reinforcements and doing behaviors to get them. This is a sharp contrast to operant theory in which behaviors are said to be determined by past reinforcements rather than desired, future reinforcements. The idea of desired reinforcements bears relationship to the cognitive expectancy theories (such as Atkinson 1964; Vroom 1964) in which it is asserted that people behave in an attempt to achieve positively valent outcomes.

There are also several important differences between Kanfer's system and the organismic model. Kanfer focused on behaviors and reinforcements (emphasizing that with his terminology) and in so doing failed to attend specifically to needs, motives, and emotions. He spoke of reinforcements, but as is true of behaviorism in general, he failed to address the question of why outcomes are reinforcing. The answer, quite simply, is that they satisfy motives that are based in the needs of the organism. Thus Kanfer failed to explicate underlying motivational processes.

Second, Kanfer did not focus on behavioral decision making (the operation of will), so he failed to recognize that decision making is at the heart of self-determined behavior.

Third, in ignoring motivational variables, Kanfer failed to acknowledge that the intrinsic need for competence and self-determination is a powerful motivator, so the feeling of competence and self-determination is a powerful reinforcer. In fact, the focus on material reinforcements runs the risk of promoting extrinsic motivation and external causality rather than intrinsic motivation and internal causality. If the client sees the little presents as the cause of the behavior, the client will not really be developing self-determination. Even the use of specific self-praise such as, "You are a good person for doing that," runs a risk of fostering what, in a dynamic psychological sense, is external causality. Introjected "shoulds" and "oughts" that are characteristic of external and impersonal causality are accompanied by self-praise and self-incriminations. These are tools of what psychoanalytic theory calls the superego. Self-determination involves choice rather than automatic behavior that complies with internalized, controlling contingencies; it involves control by the ego, not the superego.

Finally, Kanfer implied that most behavior is of the types that I have called automatized and automatic, whereas I assert that more behavior is self-determined, particularly for internal-causality people. There is an implicit difference here in metatheory. I assume that most behaviors are initially voluntary, with many of them becoming automatized or automatic. Kanfer's metatheory is more mechanistic and conditioning oriented, although his outline of self-management, with its implicit assumptions about cognitions being causative, is actually inconsistent with the metatheory of behaviorism.

Bandura (1977a) proposed a theory of behavioral change that also focused on mediating cognitive variables. He asserted hat cognitions about one's efficacy are the central elements that determine behavioral change. If people expect that they can successfully execute the behavior that is required to produce a particular outcome, they will engage in the behavior. But if they know that a certain behavior will produce the outcome and do not believe they can successfully complete the behavior, they will not begin it. Self-efficacy, then, is a belief that one's own behavior will produce outcomes; it is close to Seligman's notion of expectation of response-outcome dependence.

I think the use of the term *self-efficacy* is important. Although self-efficacy is defined as an expectation (thus, merely a cognition), it must necessarily derive from one's feelings of efficacy—in other words, from intrinsic satisfaction. While Bandura steadfastly eschewed the use of the concepts of need and feelings in the name of operationalism, it is difficult to understand why the perception of oneself as effective would be reinforcing and would encourage one to behave if one did not need to feel effective. The importance of intrinsic motivation—the need to feel competent and self-determining—is integral to Bandura's theory if the theory is to be complete and meaningful. There has been a tendency for people who apply Bandura's theory to focus on skills acquisition in therapy settings. This is unfortunate for it does not deal with the motivational and emotional considerations that are involved in the maladaptation. Competence without self-determination leads to an external rather than an internal orientation. Without focusing on blocked motives and emotions, and on choice, as well as on requisite skills, the therapeutic process will not create self-determination and internal causality.

Bandura, like Kanfer, avoided discussion of needs, motives, emotions, and satisfaction, and he failed to address directly the decision making that is necessary for the theory to operate effectively. Bandura specifically asserted that concepts such as needs are not useful for psychological theorizing, yet I suggest that ignoring these important concepts makes the theory rather hollow.

Bandura's idea of efficacy expectations resembles my use of the term *sense of competence and self-determination*; however, Bandura used the term more narrowly as expectations about a particular behavior, while I have used it in a generalized sense. A general sense of competence and self-determination is the cumulative effect of feelings of competence and self-determination in relation to specific activities. One's general sense of efficacy will be one of the things that gives one a positive expectation of efficacy in relation to a partiuclar behavior. With a strong general sense of efficacy, one will be willing to experiment with a specific behavior even if one's efficacy expectation for that particular behavior is not high. Bandura's theory is to be commended for placing importance on the idea of efficacy. It is also a parsimonious and readily operationalized theory. It fails, however, to give a full account of behavior and behavioral change since it ignores the important motivational and emotional determinants of behavior. Self-efficacy may be defined as a cognition or expectation, but it is based in motivational and emotional processes and cannot be fully understood without reference to those processes.

**Cognitive Therapy**. The recent trend in behavior therapy has been toward an emphasis on cognitive variables as mediators of behavior and behavior change. Beck (1976) has introduced an approach to therapy, called cognitive therapy, which exemplifies most clearly the reorientation from reward contingencies to cognitive mediation. Beck did not consider cognitive therapy to be a behavior therapy, though it is an extrapolation of the emerging cognitive orientation in behavior therapy. He suggested that the effectiveness of behavior therapy derives from changes in attitudes and cognitions.

In cognitive therapy, which bears much similarity to Ellis's (1962) rational emotive therapy, it is asserted that maladaptive behaviors result from the client's erroneous assumptions and beliefs, which cause distortions of reality. All behavior is assumed to follow directly from the client's cognitions. The problem is that the client has learned false information or has derived inappropriate generalizations from atypical experiences. In cognitive therapy, the aim of the therapeutic process is to isolate and modify the client's incorrect cognitions and to have the client develop new cognitive structures for interpreting experience.

Beck was particularly concerned with what he called automatic thoughts, ongoing evaluative thoughts that provide the basis for interpretation of stimuli and of which the client may be only dimly aware. For example, you ask an acquaintance to lunch and find that she is busy and cannot go. You interpret the response as a rejection, your automatic evaluation concludes that you are unlikeable, so you end up depressed and angry at your acquaintance. The example may seem farfetched, since being busy is a good reason for not going. But interpretations such as this one are quite common and illustrate Beck's point well. In cognitive therapy, the aim would be to work toward interpreting the person's response simply as an indication that she is busy rather than drawing inferences about your personal worth. Further, even if it were actually a rejection, even if the person did not want to be with you, you should not conclude personal unworth but rather should attempt to understand why the person responded that way. Perhaps she has too many personal commitments and is reluctant to get involved with still more. Or perhaps you have displayed some behaviors she did not like, in which case you could evaluate whether you wish to change those behaviors. This example shows that the core assumption of cognitive therapy is that it is a person's interpretation of stimulus events rather than the events themselves that causally precede behavior and lead to maladaptation.

In terms of the organismic theory of behavior and its five components of the therapeutic process (awareness, acceptance, choice, expectations, and accommodation), cognitive therapy deals with the last four. These four are all cognitive in nature—they involve learning, unlearning, and relearning—and would therefore be used by a flexible cognitive therapist. The main point of difference is the awareness component. Beck asserted that the elements that are responsible for a person's emotional upset or behavioral maladaptation are in conscious awareness. I think he is wrong on that point. Those elements are accessible to conscious awareness, but often the person is blocking them from awareness. And it is this interruption of the awareness process that is at the heart of automatic, maladaptive behavior.

Reconsider your asking the acquaintance to lunch. We saw that the difficulty stemmed from your interpretation of the response as a rejection and an indication of personal unworth. This interpretation may or may not have been consciously made. However, the important point is that in automatic behavior, the client persists in making these interpretations and responding accordingly, even when they are made in conscious awareness and even when the client recognizes them as inappropriate. The interpretations are made for reasons; the reasons are based in emotional and motivational processes that have been blocked from awareness; and the interpretations (and resultant responses) will persist until those blocked processes are allowed into conscious awareness.

Cognitive therapy often will produce positive results. When it does, one of two things has occurred. Either an automatized (as opposed to an automatic) behavior has been changed (for example, the person may learn some relevant information quite easily that allows a reprogramming), or an automatic behavior has been changed because the relevant information—the blocked emotion or motive—came into awareness (perhaps inadvertently, if the therapist did not realize it was necessary) to allow the necessary adjustments. Clients who understand their automatic thoughts and learn that their interpretations are inappropriate will continue to respond maladaptively if they do not allow the blocked emotions and motivations into conscious awareness.

*Psychoanalytic Therapy*

The process of therapy in the psychoanalytic vein involves an understanding of the interaction of three personality systems: the id, the ego, and the superego. The id is the person's genetic endowment and is composed primarily of one's instincts or drives. In terms of the organismic model (see figure 3-5), the id would be said to exist in the physiology of the need structure, which is one of the sources of stimulus inputs. According to psychoanalytic theory, the id is the initial source of all energy. Gradually as the child interacts with the environment (particularly parents), the ego develops as a mediator between the instinctual demands of the id and the demands of the world. Finally, the superego emerges as the home of internalized parental admonitions. It too, like the id, makes demands upon the person and is uninterested in reason. It simply aims to keep the person in line, largely as a messenger of the parental demands. The superego is the seat of internalized reward contingencies, not in the reasonable sense of "I can get X by doing Y" but rather in a mechanistic sense of "I must do X." It is the home of the shoulds and oughts. The ego, therefore, has the job of managing the forces of the id and the superego.

In the organismic model, the superego would reside in the need structure and would be influential in the operation of the extrinsic and impersonal subsystems. Externals and impersonals behave in automatic ways that in psychoanalytic theory would be said to be caused by the superego. When the superego is the determinant of behavior, there is no choice; one does what one must. The superego works to block awareness of organismic needs, which in psychoanalytic theory are of just two types, the life instincts and the death instincts—sex and aggression.

In psychoanalytic theory, maladaptiveness is said to occur when the ego is too weak to manage the demands of the id, the superego, and the environment in such a way as to guide adaptive behavior. Thus the purpose of psychotherapy is to strengthen the ego. As Freud (1969) stated, the ego becomes weakened by internal conflicts so the therapist must go to its aid. In terms of our model, the ego is focused primarily at the point of decision making. Strengthening the ego means strengthening one's capacity to choose adaptive behaviors and to treat the id and superego as sources of information rather than as controllers of behavior; to become less dominated by conflicts between organismic needs and blockages to awareness of those needs, to be more able to will.

In psychoanalytic therapy, the therapist steadfastly attempts to engage the ego of the client and in an ego-to-ego communication makes interpretations that help to bring unconscious material into consciousness (Mac-Kinnon and Michels 1971). It is assumed that by strengthening the ego, the ego in turn will go freely to the demands of the id (to the need structure).

In psychoanalytic therapy, treatment is centered around the transferential relationship between client and therapist. The therapists, who play a relatively passive role, allow the clients to transfer onto them the feelings, desires, and conflicts they have with their parents. Psychological problems are believed to have developed in the first few years of life during one's progression through the first three stages of psychosexual development (oral, anal, phallic). Since problems are said to be based in sexually oriented conflicts with parents, the transferential relationship with the therapist leads the client to uncover the roots of these problems, for the client begins to experience the same feelings and issues in relation to the therapist.

Therapy is done in one of two ways: long-term, intensive psychoanalysis or shorter-term, psychoanalytically oriented therapy. In psychoanalysis, clients, through the transferential relationship, are supposed to relive their psychosexual development in a way that allows resolution of the oral, anal, and phallic conflicts, thereby restructuring the personality. In psychoanalytic therapy, the aims are more modest. The therapist works to engage and strengthen the client's so-called observing ego by relating only to the ego and by clarifying projections, introjections, and other processes that interfere with the functioning of the observing ego.

There are both similarities and differences between psychoanalytic theory and the organismic framework. The ego bears much similarity to the will, so ego-determined behavior is what I have called self-determined behavior. The primary difference between the ego and the will is that the ego is said to be a derivative of the id and is said to get its energy by draining it from the id. I have proposed that the will has a primary energy source—intrinsic motivation—which is available for growth, development, and willing from the time of birth. I proposed, in fact, that intrinsic motivation motivates the child to proceed through the self-determination and competence struggles (the oral, anal, and phallic conflicts, plus the period of latency). Later writers in the psychoanalytic tradition (Hartmann 1958; White 1960) recognized the difficulty caused by the hypothesis that the ego is wholly derivative and called for the use of the concept of independent ego energy.

The unconscious of psychoanalytic theory differs somewhat from my use of the term *nonconscious*. I assert that needs exist in the need structure and come readily into awareness to motivate self-determined behavior unless they are blocked by internalized contingencies that develop through the operation of cognitive evaluation theory. In psychoanalytic theory, motivation is said to reside in the unconscious id, and most of one's behavior is said to be unconsciously motivated. The libidinal and aggressive forces are unconscious, with only a portion of their manifestations breaking into consciousness. Anxiety is experienced when these manifestations come close to consciousness.

The matter of nonconscious activity points to a rather fundamental difference in the assumptions of psychoanalytic theory versus the organismic theory. Psychoanalytic theory holds a darker view of the person in which unpleasant and destructive forces of great magnitude exist in the unconscious. Self-determination theory as described in the organismic theory holds that one's organismic needs are not in and of themselves unpleasant or destructive and that they are more easily accessible to consciousness. One's needs proceed naturally to consciousness when they are salient unless one learns that they are unacceptable and therefore develops barriers that keep them out of awareness. With a lowered sense of competence and self-determination, one is unable to manage motives, particularly ones that are considered unacceptable, so they are blocked from awareness and motivate automatic behavior.

The awareness component of therapy involves the client's learning to recognize the motives and emotions and learning not to block them from awareness. Allowing awareness of motives and emotions that have been blocked typically will bring into awareness the past experiences that led to the motives' and emotions' being blocked. These may, for example, be experiences of being punished or frightened. Stimulus events that produced strong emotional reactions that were blocked from awareness may remain in memory and influence one's interpretation of subsequent stimulus events. For example, the person, described in chapter 3, who fears department stores will need to "relive" the experience of being accosted in order to be freed of the fear. By developing an image of or fantasizing about the situation while consciously experiencing the fear, anger, and whatever other affect was involved, the person will learn that those emotions are manageable, that they can be accepted and acted upon by one's will. It is not necessary to relive one's psychosexual development in order to resolve this problem fully; on the other hand, simply being conditioned to go into the department store is not adequate to resolve the problem. One must come to grips with the emotions and motivations that were involved in the incident and are now blocked from awareness; otherwise they will persist in memory and will affect one's interpretation of subsequent events.

Wachtel (1977) asserted that the psychoanalytic and behavioral modes of psychotherapy are much more compatible than is generally recognized and that an integration of the two would be a valuable step for the practice of psychiatry and clinical psychology. The essence of his proposed integration is based on the premise that psychoanalytic theory has revolutionized understanding of psychopathology but that its passive treatment approach has failed to produce desired behavior change in an efficient way; whereas behavior therapy, espousing a somewhat superficial and inadequate theory of psychopathology, has nonetheless developed active interventions that seem to have utility for affecting maladaptive behaviors. Psychoanalytic theory, he stated, has contributed more to the understanding of latent meanings and unconscious motivations than to the causal explanation of behavior. Behaviorism has contributed a causal focus that has led to prescriptions for change that do not require a restructuring of the personality.

Wachtel might, for example, acknowledge that anorexia nervosa has its roots in oral conflicts, such as fear of oral impregnation, yet he would suggest that the client's eating behavior has much to do with interpersonal events in later life that have perpetuated the neurosis. An understanding of these interpersonal events, he would suggest, provides the basis for active intervention and is more useful in bringing about change in behavior than is an uncovering of the oral conflicts.

My own analysis, which has evolved from the organismic model, has some commonalities with Wachtel's, as well as some differences. First, both formulations recognize the part played by dynamic factors in psychopathology. It is acknowledged that maladaptive behaviors have their roots in childhood experiences, though the organismic model subscribes to a competence-self-determination-interpersonal analysis of the developmental process rather than a libidinally based psychoanalytic analysis. Later experiences are recognized by both Wachtel's and my theories as affecting, perpetuating, and in some cases causing maladaptive behavior, for it is recognized that interactions with the environment continually affect people's motivation, beliefs, expectations, and emotions, which in turn affect their behavior.

Wachtel acknowledged unconscious motives. He did not specifically link nonconscious emotions and motives to maladaptive (automatic) behavior as I have done, though, of course, in strict Freudian theory, the unconscious is linked directly to maladaptive behavior.

Both Wachtel and I emphasized the importance of active involvement on the part of the therapist, for like Sullivan (1954) we believe that the therapist has a vantage point and a set of learnings that may provide greater clarity and better judgment about what would be useful than the client has. This is, of course, a very tricky matter, for it is important that this be done in a way that enhances rather than undermines the client's self-determination. The therapist must work as a source of information rather than a controller of behavior. The active therapist will be concerned not specifically with inducing behaviors but with creating the antecedents that allow the client to choose behaviors. The therapist should work with awareness, acceptance, choice, expectations, and accommodations.

*Humanistic (Gestalt) Therapy*

In recent years, a new school of psychology, humanistic psychology, has begun to gain some recognition. Referred to as third-force psychology, this approach has had its greatest impact in the so-called human potential movement, outside of academic and traditional therapeutic settings. Maslow (1954, 1962) has generally been credited as the founder of this approach to psychology, though Rogers (1951) has contributed greatly to its prominence, and its roots can be readily traced to the work of Goldstein (1939) and Rank (1950) among others.

This approach is characterized by a more existential, less deterministic view of the human being and focuses on the idea of self-actualization (Goldstein 1939; Maslow 1954), of utilizing one's potential. People are believed to be motivated toward growth and development and will achieve self-actualization in a setting that permits it. This approach also emphasizes experience, or phenomenology, seeing it as the fundamental human quality.

The approach began somewhat iconoclastically, theorizing in vague ways, and paying but the slightest attention to empirical research. Only in the past few years have some of the ideas of humanistic psychology begun to receive attention in academic circles, where people have become concerned with more sophisticated theorizing and experimentation from a humanistic perspective.

As with behavior therapy, there are many types of humanistic therapy, and it is somewhat difficult to characterize the field. Nonetheless, I shall discuss Gestalt therapy—in its relatively pure form as outlined by Perls and his associates (Perls, Hefferline, and Goodman 1951; Perls 1973)—as representative of the humanistic approach.

The expressed aim of Gestalt therapy is the enhancement of awareness. This means gaining an increased connection with one's organismic needs and emotions. It also means gaining an experiential understanding of the ways in which one blocks awareness of motives and emotions. Perls favored a short-term, intensive workshop format for the practice of Gestalt therapy, and particularly in that format the emphasis was on awareness, often with concomitant cathartic experiences. The assumption was that behavioral decision making (or willing) would follow in course from the awareness. This is the opposite assumption from that of psychoanalytic therapy, which focused on the strengthening of the ego (or will) and assumed that awareness would follow.

Perls (1978) emphasized that awareness is not so much a matter of dealing with the content of censored material, which he asserted was the psychoanalytic interpretation of awareness, but rather a matter of recognizing the processes one uses to block emotions and motivations from consciousness.

One learns how one interrupts the ongoing process of perceiving one's needs and feelings and acting on them.

Perls placed much emphasis on nonverbal communication, suggesting that the clues to one's needs and feelings and to how one blocks awareness of those can be found in expressive movements of the body—posture, tightness of muscles, facial expressions, and so on. Verbalizations, he stated, are under the direct control of one's thought processes and therefore are subject to the distortions and rationalizations that one has learned. Often, said Perls, one thinks what one "should" think and therefore distorts or interrupts awareness so as to keep it in line with what one should think, feel, or want. The expressive movements are less subject to these distortions and therefore give clearer indication of what is happening for the person. Thus, in Gestalt therapy the client's attention is often focused on material from somatic awareness (a process developed in the practice of sensory awareness; see Brooks 1974) or with material from dreams (as was also done by Freud), since these types of data are said to be relatively free from cognitive distortions.

In Gestalt therapy, one utilizes a need-oriented, homeostatic view of the person and assumes that what the organism needs will be readily apparent unless one blocks that awareness. It further assumes that one is motivated to complete gestalts—in other words, to complete any situation—and suggests that maladaptive behavior results from unfinished business in past situations. Gestalts that have not been completed are said to remain in memory and to impair one's current interaction with the environment. Completed gestalts, on the other hand, will become assimilated into the organism and will not create interruptions to the ongoing process. Thus therapy in the gestalt mode can be conceptualized as a process of completing old gestalts that are interfering with current functioning. In the department store example, if every department store is "experienced" in essence as the one department store associated with the traumatic episode, then the incomplete gestalt (not having fully experienced the affect and assimilated the event) will continue to influence one's experience of the present (for example, making all department stores equivalent to that one).

The idea of awareness that was emphasized by Gestalt therapy is extremely important, for it takes one to the motives and emotions that underlie maladaptive behaviors, and it can allow one to stop interfering with perceptions of emotions and motives. However, I believe Gestalt therapy has tended to go too far with awareness in its assertion that awareness is the primary aim of therapy. One needs a strong sense of competence and self-determination to remain aware. If a client is forced to be aware of painful material without having a strong sense of competence and self-determination, the client will be faced with a barrage of feelings and desires that will cause great conflict and strife. While increasing awareness, a therapist must be working with the client toward an acceptance of the thoughts, feelings, and motives that come into awareness; toward a realization that these forces can be managed and adaptive behaviors can be chosen; and toward an understanding of which situations will be responsive and to which one must accommodate.

People block their awareness of needs and emotions to avoid the pain that results when something in their cognitive structure conflicts with the awareness. Thus, to encourage awareness without simultaneously dealing with elements of the cognitive structure may do more of a disservice than a service. I would assert that those Gestalt therapists who are effective are working with cognitive reorganization, as well as focusing on increasing awareness.

# Part III
# Overview and Integration

# 9 Summary and Comment

This book outlines a framework for the analysis of motivated behavior. The framework evolved as a mix of induction and deduction. Parts of this system are quite specifically articulated; other parts are quite vague. Some elements have substantial empirical support, while others are highly speculative. The speculative elements are, however, consistent with and extrapolations of elements that have been firmly established by empirical procedures. As such they constitute questions and hypotheses for future research.

Much of twentieth-century psychology has utilized a metatheory that Chein (1972) referred to as robotism. The human being has been seen as a passive mechanism that is responsive to and determined by forces in the environment or in the person's unconscious. Recently there has been an increasing focus on cognitive processes as mediators of behavior. I have suggested that the cognitive models have tended also to view the person as a passive processor of information and that they have ignored deeper motivational and affective processes (Ryan and Deci, 1979). Thus I proposed the use of a metatheory that emphasizes the active nature of the human organism; that allows for cognitive, affective, and motivational processes as mediators of behavior; that recognizes the human capacity for choosing how to behave; and that acknowledges the limitations to that capacity. While being active and having choice, the person's capacity to choose often loses out to the strength of environmental and nonconscious forces. Thus the proposed metatheory focuses on the interplay of freedom and boundedness in human behavior.

## Types of Behavior

Work by various researchers has pointed to the inadequacy of the conditioning models of human behavior, thereby highlighting the need for a framework of motivated behavior that affords the possibilities for self-determination while accepting that many behaviors are conditioned or automated. Sperry's (1969) work has provided a plausible account of consciousness and of the interaction of physiology and consciousness that provides support for the idea of mental events being causal mediators of behavior.

The current framework for the study of behavior asserts that there are two general classes of motivated behaviors: those that are self-determined or chosen (in other words, those that are mediated by conscious motives and decisions), and those that are not chosen (in other words, those that appear to have been conditioned). Self-determined behaviors are under the control of the will. This does not imply freedom from causation; it means simply that humans have the capacity to choose and that the capacity operates in lawful and ordered ways; it seeks gratification of human needs.

Many behaviors, however, are not chosen; they occur with little or no conscious attention. This capacity for nonchosen behaving is very important for it frees one's will and attention for other matters. It is useful, for example, to be able to type without deciding to put one's left ring finger on the *s* and one's right middle finger on the *i*. However, the other blade of this double-edged sword is the fact that some habitual responses are rigid and inflexible. They resist change and restrict one's freedom.

There are two types of nonchosen behaviors that are distinguished operationally in terms of their resistance to change. Some behaviors can be reprogrammed readily by the will to meet the demands of new situations; these behaviors I have called automatized. Others cannot be readily reprogrammed; they seem to persist in spite of people's attempts at changing them. These I referred to as automatic. Dynamically, automatized and automatic behaviors can be distinguished by the fact that automatic behaviors are motivated by nonconscious motives and emotions. Automatic behaviors resist change until the nonconscious motivations are allowed into conscious awareness. At that time the behaviors are, like automatized behaviors, available to be reprogrammed.

**Motivation and Will**

Previous theories of will have assumed that the energy for the operation of will was derived from the basic drives such as hunger, thirst, and sex. I asserted, however, that the energy for willing, the energy for the very process of deciding, is a basic, innate motivational propensity. It is intrinsic motivation, the human need to be competent and self-determining. This source of motivation is similar to what Hartmann (1958) called independent ego energy and White (1959) called effectance motivation. Intrinsic motivation provides the energy for the various functions of the will. It underlies the process of deciding whether one is choosing behaviors to satisfy physiological drives or intrinsic and affective needs; it provides the energy to oppose the force of drives and to control the forces of emotions; and it allows the will to hold in abeyance motives that for one reason or another cannot be satisfied at that time.

Overt behaviors such as walking, singing, or lifting cement blocks may be either intrinsically or extrinsically motivated. These are distinguished operationally by whether they are performed for an extrinsic reward or constraint. Dynamically they are distinguished in terms of the underlying needs. Extrinsic motivation is based in physiological drives and the so-called derivative, substitute needs. Intrinsic motivation is based in the need for competence and self-determination and the specific needs that differentiate out of the basic need (see Deci 1975, chapter 3).

Overt behaviors that are either intrinsically motivated or extrinsically motivated can be self-determined. In self-determined behavior, there will be covert processes of choice, information search, and holding motives in abeyance. These covert processes are intrinsically motivated; the process of willing is intrinsically motivated. Thus self-determined behavior necessitates some intrinsic motivation, whether the overt behavior is itself in the service of intrinsic or extrinsic needs. In the absence of any intrinsic motivation, the extrinsically motivated behavior will be automatic.

With the introduction of intrinsic motivation and the hypothesis that it motivates the functions of the will, the current theory of motivation deviates from most prior theories in two fundamentally important ways: it asserts that all behaviors are not based in physiological drives, and it recognizes that humans have the capacity to choose behaviors, that all behaviors are not caused by associative bonds. Much recent work in psychology is consistent with one or both of these fundamental principles.

The importance of self-determination as a motivational propensity has been verified empirically in a variety of studies that have shown that the opportunity to be self-determining is intrinsically motivating and denial of the opportunity to be self-determining undermines people's motivation, learning, and general sense of organismic well-being. Indeed in extreme cases, anecdotal and survey data suggest that the stress of losing the opportunity to be self-determining may cause severe somatic malfunctions and even death.

## Motivational Subsystems

Human behavior is said to be motivated by three motivational subsystems: intrinsic, extrinsic, and amotivatonal. A motivational subsystem is a set of attitudes, beliefs about self and others, affective experiences, and programs for behavior, all of them organized by motivational processes. The concept of subsystems was introduced to accomplish two things. First, it addresses the frequently discussed cross-situation consistency problem. Psychologists have long debated whether behavior is consistent across various situations (the person-trait point of view) or is a function of the situation and therefore differs from situation to situation (the behavioristic point of view). The resolution of the debate follows the realization that both are true: the motivational subsystem concept allows for an integration of the two sides of the debate. There will be consistency among behaviors that are motivated by a given subsystem, and there will be differences between that set of behaviors and those that are motivated by a different subsystem. A given subsystem will be called into play by an interaction of environmental forces (the situation) and one's causality orientation (a personal trait).

The second function served by the motivational subsystem concept is that it accounts for the internal consistency that exists among variables such as attitudes, emotions, and motives. For example, Deci, Nezlek, and Sheinman (in press) found that children in autonomy-oriented classrooms had both higher intrinsic motivation and higher self-esteem than did children in control-oriented classrooms. There was consistency between motivation and beliefs about self.

When the intrinsic motivational subsystem is centrally operative, behavior will be self-determined. Emotions and motives will form in conscious awareness, and behavior will be chosen in expectation of satisfying the motives. When the extrinsic motivational subsystem is centrally operative, behavior will be automatic. The nature of extrinsic motivation, based in the physiological drives, is such that it operates mechanistically unless the intrinsic motivational subsystem is also instigated to manage the extrinsic motives and make choices. Thus when the intrinsic and extrinsic motivational subsystems work jointly (as opposed to one or the other operating exclusively), there will be chosen, extrinsic behavior; the overt, extrinsically motivated behavior will be self-determined. When the amotivational subsystem is centrally operative, there will be a minimum of behavior. The subsystem is such that people feel helpless and hopeless, they have critical attitudes toward themselves, and they do not behave because they see no use in behaving. More typically, there will be a joint operation of the amotivational and extrinsic subsystems in which people feel helpless, but they also engage in automatic (often aggressive) behavior. Passive aggressive or manipulative behaviors frequently would be evidenced when the extrinsic and amotivational subsystems are jointly operative.

**Personality Orientations**

I described three personality orientations that are characterized in terms of people's beliefs about the nature of causality: internal causality, external causality, and impersonal causality.

The internal-causality orientation encompases a belief in the relationship between behavior and outcomes and an understanding of oneself as the initiator of behavior. One's awareness of one's needs is the cause of behavior, and outcomes are the effect of behavior. With an internal-causality orientation, one's intrinsic motivational subsystem will be centrally operative. At times it will operate independently to motivate intrinsic behavior, and at times it will operate in conjunction with the extrinsic subsystem to motivate chosen, extrinsic behavior. Thus both intrinsically and extrinsically motivated behavior will tend to be self-determined, and the person will shift flexibly between the intrinsic and extrinsic subsystems. Internals will also recognize elements of a situation that are not controllable and will accommodate to them.

An external-causality orientation also involves a belief in reward-outcome dependence, though the outcomes, rather than the person's awareness of needs, appear to be the cause of the behavior. The extrinsic motivational subsystem tends to dominate the person, and behavior tends to be automatic. There is less flexibility in behavior and in the shift among subsystems. One's motives and emotions tend not to be allowed into awareness and therefore become the motivational basis of the automatic behavior. Many substitute needs are in evidence. These people tend to display what Glass (1977) called the Type A behavior pattern.

An impersonal-causality orientation is based on a belief in response-outcome independence. These people are ones to whom Seligman (1975) referred as helpless and Rotter (1966) referred to as external controls. They are characterized by the centrality of the amotivational subsystem and a relative absence of behavior. The behaviors they do display tend to be automatic.

I have used the term *willfulness* to refer to the extent that one utilizes one's capacity to will. This, of course, differs from person to person, and for any given person, it differs with time and situation. Still it represents a general personality characteristic. One's willfulness depends on one's general sense of competence and self-determination; therefore as experiences of efficacy and inefficacy affect one's sense of competence and self-determination, the person's capacity to will is similarly affected. The internal-causality person has a high level of willfulness, the external-causality person has a moderate level of willfulness, and the impersonal-causality person has a low level of willfulness.

## Environments and Cognitive Evaluation Theory

Environments (or elements of the environment) are categorized into three types. Some are responsive and informational; they tend to respond to the person's initiations, and the structures of the environment provide information about the person's competence and self-determination. Others do not respond to the person's initiations but demand various behaviors from the person. The structures tend to be very controlling. Still others are not responsive to the person's initiations and tend to be capricious in their delivery of outcomes. Contingencies are unclear and cannot be mastered by the person.

Responsive, informational environments foster intrinsic motivation, internal causality, and self-determined behavior. Controlling environments foster extrinsic motivation, external causality, and automatic behavior. Nonresponsive, capricious environments foster amotivation, impersonal causality, and nonbehavior.

Environments affect people's motivation, orientation, and subsequent behavior through the operation of the processes described by cognitive evaluation theory. When salient elements of the environment are controlling, they lead to a perceived external locus of causality, a strengthening of one's extrinsic motivation, and a weakening of one's intrinsic motivation. When salient elements of the environment are noncontrolling and allow choice, they lead to a perceived internal locus of causality and a strengthening of one's intrinsic motivation. Thus the control-noncontrol elements of the environment produce shifts from the intrinsic to extrinsic or extrinsic to intrinsic motivational subsystems that are described by a change in perceived locus of causality from internal to external or external to internal.

When salient elements of the environment convey information that one is competent, it will strengthen one's intrinsic motivation if it is within the context of some choice, and it will strengthen one's extrinsic motivation if it is in the context of force and demand. When salient elements of the environment convey information that one is incompetent, it will leave one helpless and amotivational.

Cognitive evaluation theory asserts that environmental factors such as rewards and communication have both control and informational aspects. The relative salience of the two aspects, coupled with their meaning (control versus choice, positive versus negative information), determines the effects of the environmental factors on the person's motivation, causality orientation, and behavior.

## The Person and the Environment

The environment affects people, but it is their subjective experience of the environment rather than the objective environment itself that affects them. People interpret or evaluate the environment as informational, controlling, or nonresponsive, and these evaluations are caused by an interaction of the person's causality orientation and the objective elements of the environment.

Internal-causality people tend to interpret the environment informationally. They see controlling and nonresponsive elements, yet they tend to use all of the elements as information that is relevant for their self-determination. External-causality people tend to see the environment as controlling even when it is responsive and informational. When it is nonresponsive, they become anxious and experience a heightened need for a control relationship. Finally impersonal-causality people tend to see all environments as nonresponsive and hopeless.

People's evaluation of the environment will depend on their orientation, the objective environment, and the relative strength of the two. For example, very strong internals will tend to interpret weakly controlling environments as informational (the orientation will be most influential); however, weakly internal people will tend to interpret strongly controlling environments as controlling (the environment will be most influential).

We are left with the facts that people's evaluations of the environment affect their motivational subsystems and their causality orientation. Additionally their causality orientation affects their evaluation of environments. It is an ongoing interactive process between the person and the environment that affects their behavior and the adjustment of their internal states. Thus to make accurate predictions about behavior and internal states, one must utilize the person's orientation at that time and the characteristics of the environment at that time. The predictive process is somewhat easier than it may sound, however, for one's causality orientation is relatively stable. Changes in causality orientation occur relatively slowly. Thus the orientation acts like a resistance to the infringement of environmental forces that are inconsistent with it; however, in spite of the resistance, the strength of the environmental forces can affect the person first by initiating the motivational subsystem that parallels the environmental characteristics (intrinsic for informational, extrinsic for controlling, amotivational for nonresponsive). Over a prolonged period, the environment can affect not only the motivational subsystem but also the causality orientation (internal for informational, external for controlling, impersonal for nonresponsive).

In sum, the theory asserts the following. (1) People are born with unique levels of intrinsic motivation. (2) They pass through the self-determination (trust and autonomy) and competence (initiation and industry) conflicts, and the nature of the environment affects the resolution of the conflicts and the development of a causality orientation. Responsive, informational environments facilitate the adequate resolution of the conflicts and the development of internal causality; controlling environments thwart the resolution of the self-determination conflicts, allow resolution of the competence conflicts, and promote the development of external causality; nonresponsive environments undermine the resolution of all the conflicts and promote impersonal causality. (3) Higher levels of innate intrinsic motivation allow children to be more resistant to the impact of controlling and nonresponsive environments, so as to be more willful, to have better resolution of the conflicts, and to become more internal. (4) By the end of middle childhood and the onset of puberty, a person has a baseline causality orientation that affects his or her evaluations of the environment and the operation of the motivational subsystems. There is a tendency to interpret the environment in line with one's orientation, though environments will impinge upon the person, first to initiate the operation of the subsystem that corresponds to the environment and then, perhaps, to modify one's orientation. These later modifications tend to occur slowly and to be relatively small in magnitude.

Not only does one's causality orientation affect the way people perceive the world, but it also affects the way one operates in the world. People who are internals tend to be responsive and informational toward others; people who are externals tend to be controlling of others; people who are impersonals tend to be nonresponsive and inconsistent toward others. Thus, for example, parents, teachers, managers, and therapists out of their own orientations create environments that either facilitate or undermine the intrinsic motivation and internal causality of their children, students, subordinates, and clients. When influential people behave automatically, they tend to foster extrinsic or amotivation and external or impersonal causality for the people who are in those environments. Finally, I suggest that all people tend toward the controlling and inconsistent use of extrinsic rewards and external structures as they become more anxious and feel less self-determining in a particular situation. The elements of the person, the environment, and the person-environment interaction appear in Table 9.1.

## The Current Framework and Others

In outlining this system for the study of motivated behavior, I have attempted to afford credibility to previous systems and to provide a means for integrating what I consider to be the more important elements of each.

Behavioral psychology has made many important contributions. It has emphasized the human tendency to become controlled by various forces in the environment; it has theorized in a way that facilitates empirical research and has provided many tools for that research; it has explored and outlined the determinants and consequences of conditioning. It has erred, however, in utilizing a metatheory of robotism, which suggests that all behaviors are conditioned. Its theorizing has been rather superficial, and it has failed to consider the causal importance and richness of the person variables: motivation, emotion, and cognition. The most important contribution has been the detailing of conditioning processes, for when considered in the

**Table 9-1**
**Concepts in the Organismic Framework**

|  | Internality Concepts | Externality Concepts | Impersonality Concepts |
|---|---|---|---|
| Environment | Responsive and informational | Controlling and demanding | Nonresponsive and capricious |
| Personality orientation | Internal causality | External causality | Impersonal causality |
| Motivational subsystem | Intrinsic | Extrinsic | Amotivational |
| Willfulness | High | Medium | Low |
| Predominant type of behavior | Self-determined | Automatic | Nonbehavior |
| Control of behavior | Conscious motives, will, and environmental possibilities | External cues and nonconscious motives | Nonbehavior controlled by noncontingency |
| Cognitive evaluation | Internal-causality and high competence | External-causality and high competence | Impersonal causality and low competence |
| Affective experience | Self-determination and competence | Urgency, competence, and stress | Incompetence, helplessness |

light of our freedom-boundedness metatheory, it allows one to understand the ways in which behaviors become automatized or automatic, and it points to the vulnerability of self-determination.

Humanistic psychology has also made many important contributions. It has highlighted possibilities for choice and growth; it has explored much of the richness of human consciousness; it has brought the important interrelationship between psyche and soma into focus; and it has stressed growth motivation and self-actualization. It has failed to acknowledge the force of environmental and situational variables and has treated conditioning processes as a villain when they are considered at all. Typically it has used definitions and concepts that are vague and nonoperational; its theorizing has been imprecise; and it has ignored empirical research. The most important contribution has been the emphasis on human experience—conscious awareness—and the possibilities for choice and self-responsibility as determinants of behavior. This has influenced my description of the self-determined behaviors.

Psychoanalytic psychology has also contributed much. It was the system that made us aware of the importance of psychodynamic influences on behavior; it detailed the development of personality during early years as one passes through various conflicts; it verified that nonconscious processes are important motivational forces; and it utilized concepts such as repression and defense to show how people block aspects of their psychic activity from conscious awareness. It has erred by overstating the role of drives, particularly the sexual drive, in motivation and development. Only Hartmann (1958) acknowledged an independent ego energy, which is analogous to what I have called intrinsic motivation. Further, it emphasized the unconscious motivational processes in a way that slighted the importance of choice and conscious motivational processes. Like humanistic psychology, its theorizing has downplayed the impact of environmental forces, and it has failed to generate experimental investigations. It is empirical in that the theory, particularly early psychoanalytic theory, evolved from systematic observations of psychiatric patients, but there has been a minimum of experimental or survey procedures in the verification of concepts. The most important contributions have been the study of nonconscious processes and the ways that people defend against recognition of their motivations and emotions and the ways that nonconscious processes and counterforces affect development. These elements have been incorporated into the current theoretical system in the description of automatic behaviors; motives and emotions that are blocked from awareness form the motivational basis of automatic behavior. Further, psychoanalytic psychology influenced my description of the development of causality orientations during early and middle childhood.

In this theoretical system I have attempted to provide a framework that allows exploration of human consciousness and human potentials while recognizing the limits to self-determined responding—the susceptibility to control by environmental forces and the strength of internal drive forces. Further, I have attempted to formulate the system in a way that is conducive to research.

Many elements of the system have received substantial empirical verification. Cognitive evaluation theory has been supported by much research (see Deci and Ryan 1980); the importance of self-determination for organismic well-being has been clearly verified; the distinction between personal (internal and external) causality (internal locus of control) and impersonal causality (an external locus of control) has been studied by Rotter's (1966) locus-of-control scale (see Lefcourt 1976), though the internal-causality and external-causality orientations have not been empirically contrasted; expectancy theories have been found useful for the prediction of behavior; several processes of the human emotions have been researched (see Izard 1977); and the conditioning processes have been investigated in thousands of studies.

On the other hand, many aspects have not been explored and the particular ways that I have integrated the researched elements need empirical scrutiny. I have offered many hypotheses and speculations that I hope will be the basis for future research endeavors.

## Values in Society and Psychology

Whenever people coexist there is some need for integration and accommodation because individuals' needs will often conflict. The more complex the coexistence and the more people who are involved, the more important is the integration and accommodation.

The idea of integration and accommodation is often understood in terms of control—controlling people to behave in certain specifiable ways. The idea of control is a central value in society and psychology. In organizations of all sorts, there are hierarchies and policies that are based on control principles, often aimed toward profit and power. In psychology, control of behavior has been used as the main criterion for understanding. With the value that has been placed on control, behavioral psychology—with its emphasis on environmental control and its perfecting of the conditioning processes that are aimed at the control of specific behaviors—has fit societal concerns and has therefore received much recognition.

Much has been learned from the behavioristic perspective and a knowledge of the conditioning procedures is invaluable, but I place great value on individual choice, on the opportunity for intrinsic motivation, self-determination, and internal causality. It seems clear that there are human possibilities for integration and accommodation that are different from the control-oriented procedures of conditioning. With the use of rewards, information rather than control could, for example, be emphasized so that internal self-control rather than environmental control would be encouraged. This may be difficult at times, for there are a variety of pressures that exist on all members of all organizations. These pressures make the leaders more external and impersonal, and they cause them to use rewards controllingly, so that the followers, in turn, become more external and impersonal.

Nevertheless an understanding of the interplay between self-determined behaviors and internal causality on the one hand and automatic or automatized behaviors and external or impersonal causalities on the other hand provides the basis for a system of psychology that can offer prescriptions for personal choice when it is appropriate and for external control when it is appropriate. But the external control would be used only to the extent that it is necessary. Limits are necessary, but they should be as wide as possible and allow freedom within those limits.

In various applied areas, theorists and practitioners have experimented with ideas related to self-determination. In organizational psychology, for example, McGregor (1960) has outlined what he called theory Y management, based on the notions of encouraging individual choice and promoting self-actualization. Likert (1967) reported research indicating that the individual, participatory approach can be more effective than the authoritarian approach in private enterprise organizations. Bruner (1962) has similarly called for educational environments that encourage exploration and self-determination rather than conditioning or controlling particular behavioral responses.

In chapter 8 I applied the current theoretical framework to the area of therapy. There I emphasized that the overriding aim of therapy should be self-determination and internal causality—the central thrust of the organismic theory of motivation—yet I also suggested that control procedures may be more appropriate in some situations.

The ideas of internal causality and self-determination are often understood as permissiveness—for example, "Let the kid do whatever he or she wants." Such is not the meaning of internal causality or self-determination, however. Internal causality involves making choices, deciding for oneself, and being self-determining, but it also includes the ideas of responsibility and accommodation. To be self-determining, one must accommodate to some aspects of the environment and choose within the limits of those accommodations.

Organizations that encourage self-determination will also encourage some accommodation. People learn to weigh the possibilities, benefits, and costs of their actions, for their own good and for the good of the human race and its societies. This can come about when people accept structures and work to change them rather than acting defiantly free of them. The structures should be informational rather than controlling and should encourage individual choices that take account of the common good. I think the major research task that faces us is to explore ways of creating such structures. Perhaps the theoretical framework presented in this book can provide an understanding of motivated behavior that could guide such an exploration.

# References

Abelson, R.P. "Script Processing in Attitude Formation and Decision Making." In J.S. Carroll and J.W. Payne, eds., *Cognition and Social Behavior*. Hillsdale, N.J.: Erlbaum, 1976.

Abelson, R.P.; Aronson, E.; McGuire, W.J.; Newcomb, T.M.; Rosenberg, M.; and Tannenbaum, P.H., eds., *Theories of Cognitive Consistency: A Sourcebook*. Chicago: Rand-McNally, 1968.

Ainsworth, M.D.S. "Object Relations, Dependency, and Attachment: A Theoretical Review of the Infant-Mother Relationship." *Child Development* 40 (1969):969-1025.

_____ . "The Development of Infant-Mother Attachment." In B. Caldwell and H. Ricciuti, eds., *Review of Child Development Research*, vol. 3. Chicago: University of Chicago Press, 1973.

Arnold, M.B. *Emotion and Personality*. Vol. 1: *Psychological Aspects*. New York: Columbia University Press, 1960.

Aronson, E. "The Theory of Cognitive Dissonance: A Current Perspective." In L. Berkowitz, ed., *Advances in Experimental Social Psychology*, 4:1-34. New York: Academic Press, 1969.

Atkinson, J.W. *An Introduction to Motivation*. Princeton, N.J.: Van Nostrand, 1964.

_____ . "The Mainspring of Achievement Oriented Activity." In J.W. Atkinson and J.O. Raynor, eds., *Motivation and Achievement*, pp. 13-42. Washington, D.C.: Winston, 1974.

Averill, J.R. "Personal Control over Aversive Stimuli and Its Relationship to Stress." *Psychological Bulletin* 80 (1973):286-303.

Bach, S., and Klein, G.S. "The Effects of Prolonged Subliminal Exposure of Words." Paper presented at the American Psychological Association, New York, 1957. Abstract appears in *American Psychologist* 12 (1957):397.

Bachrach, A.J. "Some Applications of Operant Conditioning to Behavior Therapy." In J. Wolpe, A. Salter, and L.J. Reyna, eds., *The Conditioning Therapies*. New York: Holt, Rinehart & Winston, 1964.

Bandura, A. "Self-Efficacy: Toward a Unifying Theory of Behavioral Change." *Psychological Review* 84 (1977):191-215.

_____ . *Social Learning Theory*. Englewood Cliffs, N.J.: Prentice-Hall, 1977b.

Beck, A.T. *Cognitive Therapy and the Emotional Disorders*. New York: International Universities Press, 1976.

Berlyne, D.E. "Exploration and Curiosity." *Science* 153 (1966):25-33.

Bowlby, J. *Attachment and Loss*. Vol. 1: *Attachment*. New York: Basic Books, 1969.

219

Brehm, J.W. *A Theory of Psychological Reactance.* New York: Academic Press, 1966.

———. *Responses to Loss of Freedom: A Theory of Psychological Reactance.* Morristown, N.J.: General Learning Press, 1972.

Breland, K., and Breland, M. "The Misbehavior of Organisms." *American Psychologist* 16 (1961):681-684.

Broadbent, D. *Perception and Communication.* Oxford: Pergamon Press, 1958.

Brooks, C.v.W. *Sensory Awareness: The Rediscovery of Experiencing.* New York: Viking, 1974.

Brown, I., and Inouye, D.K. "Learned Helplessness Through Modeling: The Role of Perceived Similarity in Competence." *Journal of Personality and Social Psychology* 36 (1978):900-908.

Bruner, J.S. *On Knowing: Essays for the Left Hand.* Cambridge: Harvard University Press, 1962.

Bruner, J.S.; Jolly, A.; and Sylva, K., eds., *Play.* New York: Basic Books, 1976.

Burnes, K.; Brown, W.A.; and Keating, G.W. "Dimensions of Control: Correlations between MMPI and I-E Scores." *Journal of Consulting and Clinical Psychology* 36 (1971):301.

Butler, R.Z. "Discrimination Learning by Rhesus Monkeys to Visual Exploration Motivation." *Journal of Comparative and Physiological Psychology* 46 (1953):95-98.

Chein, I. *The Science of Behavior and the Image of Man.* New York: Basic Books, 1972.

Csikszentmihalyi, M. *Beyond Boredom and Anxiety.* San Francisco: Jossey-Bass, 1975.

Darwin, C. *The Expressions of the Emotions in Man and Animal.* London: John Murray, 1872.

deCharms, R. *Personal Causation: The Internal Affective Determinants of Behavior.* New York: Academic Press, 1968.

Deci, E.L. *Intrinsic Motivation.* New York: Plenum, 1975.

Deci, E.L.; Cascio, W.F.; and Krusell, J. "Cognitive Evaluation Theory and Some Comments on the Calder, Staw Critique." *Journal of Personality and Social Psychology* 31 (1975):81-85.

Deci, E.L.; Nezlek, J.; and Sheinman, L. "Characteristics of the Rewarder and Intrinsic Motivation of the Rewardee." *Journal of Personality and Social Psychology.* In press.

Deci, E.L., and Ryan, R.M. "The Empirical Exploration of Intrinsic Motivational Processes." In L. Berkowitz, ed., *Advances in Experimental Social Psychology*, vol. 13:39-80. New York: Academic Press, 1980.

Dember, W.N., and Earl, R.W. "Analysis of Exploratory, Manipulatory and Curiosity Behaviors." *Psychological Review* 64 (1957):91-96.

DeVellis, R.F.; DeVellis, B.M.; and McCauley, C. "Vicarious Acquisition of Learned Helplessness." *Journal of Personality and Social Psychology* 36 (1978):894-899.

Dixon, F. *Subliminal Perception: The Nature of a Controversy.* London: McGraw-Hill, 1971.

Dollard, J.; Doob, L.W.; Miller, N.E.; and Sears, R.R. *Frustration and Aggression.* New Haven: Yale University Press, 1939.

Duffy, E. *Activation and Behavior.* New York: Wiley, 1962.

Ellis, A. *Reason and Emotion in Psychotherapy.* New York: Lyle Stuart, 1962.

Engel, G.L. "Sudden and Rapid Death during Psychological Stress: Folklore or Folkwisdom?" *Annals of Internal Medicine* 74 (1971):771-782.

Enzle, M.E., and Ross, J. "Increasing and Decreasing Intrinsic Interest with Contingent Rewards: A Test of Cognitive Evaluation Theory." *Journal of Experimental Social Psychology* 14 (1978):588-597.

Erikson, E.H. *Childhood and Society.* New York: Norton, 1950.

Feather, N.T. "Some Personality Correlates of External Control." *Australian Journal of Psychology* 19 (1967):253-260.

Ferrari, N.A. "Institutionalization and Attitude Change in an Aged Population: A Field Study in Dissonance Theory." Ph.D. dissertation, Western Reserve University, 1962.

Festinger, L. *A Theory of Cognitive Dissonance.* Evanston, Ill.: Row, Peterson, 1957.

Fisher, C.D. "The Effects of Personal Control, Competence, and Extrinsic Reward Systems on Intrinsic Motivation." *Organizational Behavior and Human Performance* 21 (1978):273-288.

Frankl, V.E. *Man's Search for Meaning.* Boston: Beacon Press, 1959.

Freud, S. *Collected Papers.* London: Hogarth, 1924.

———. *The Interpretation of Dreams.* 1900. New York: Basic Books, 1955.

———. "Repression." 1915. In *Collected Papers*, vol. 4. New York: Basic Books, 1959a.

———. "Mourning and Melancholia." 1917. In *Collected Papers*, vol. 4. New York: Basic Books, 1959b.

———. *The Ego and the Id.* 1923. New York: Norton, 1962.

———. *An Outline of Psycho-analysis.* Rev. ed. New York: Norton, 1969.

Garcia, J., and Koelling, R.A. "Relation of Cue to Consequence in Avoidance Learning." *Psychonomic Science* 4 (1966):123-124.

Ginott, H.G. *Between Parent and Child.* New York: Macmillan, 1965.

Glass, D.C. *Behavior Patterns, Stress and Coronary Disease.* Hillsdale, N.J.: Erlbaum, 1977.

Glass, D.C., and Singer, J.E. *Urban Stress: Experiments on Noise and Social Stressors.* New York: Academic Press, 1972.

Goldstein, K. *The Organism*. New York: American Book Co., 1939.

Gordon, R.M. "The Effects of Interpersonal and Economic Resources upon Value and the Quality of Life." Ph.D. dissertation, Temple University, 1975.

Greene, W.A.; Moss, A.J.; and Goldstein, S. "Delay, Denial and Death in Coronary Heart Disease." In R.S. Eliot, ed., *Stress and the Heart*. New York: Futura, 1974.

Hammock, T., and Brehm, J.W. "The Attractiveness of Choice Alternatives When Freedom to Choose is Eliminated by a Social Agent." *Journal of Personality* 34 (1966):546-554.

Harlow, H.F. "Motivation as a Factor in the Acquisition of New Responses." *Nebraska Symposium on Motivation* 1 (1953):24-49.

Harré, R., and Secord, P.F. *The Explanation of Social Behavior*. Oxford: Basil Blackwell, 1972.

Hartmann, H. *Ego Psychology and the Problem of Adaptation*. New York: International Universities Press, 1958.

Hartmann, H.; Kris, E.; and Loewenstein, R. "Notes on the Theory of Aggression." *Psychoanalytic Study of the Child* 3 (1949):9-36.

Hebb, D.O. "Drives and the C.N.S. (Conceptual Nervous System)." *Psychological Review* 62 (1955):243-254.

Heider, F. *The Psychology of Interpersonal Relations*. New York: Wiley, 1958.

Hendrick, I. "Work and the Pleasure Principle." *Psychoanalytic Quarterly* 12 (1943):311-329.

Hilgard, E.R. "A Neodissociation Interpretation of Pain Reduction in Hypnosis." *American Psychologist* 28 (1973):396-411.

_____. *Divided Consciousness*. New York: Wiley, 1977.

Hiroto, D.S. "Locus of Control and Learned Helplessness." *Journal of Experimental Psychology* 102 (1974):187-193.

Horney, K. *New Ways in Psychoanalysis*. New York: Norton, 1939.

Hull, C.L. *Principles of Behavior: An Introduction to Behavior Theory*. New York: Appleton-Century-Crofts, 1943.

Hunt, J. McV. "Intrinsic Motivation and Its Role in Psychological Development." *Nebraska Symposium on Motivation* 13 (1965):189-282.

Immergluck, L. "Determinism-Freedom in Contemporary Psychology." *American Psychologist* 19 (1964):270-281.

Isaac, W. "Evidence for a Sensory Drive in Monkeys." *Psychological Reports* 11 (1962):175-181.

Izard, C.E. *Human Emotions*. New York: Plenum, 1977.

James, W. "What Is Emotion?" *Mind* 9 (1884):188-205.

_____. *The Principles of Psychology*. Vol. 2. New York: Holt, 1890.

Janis, I.L. "Effects of Fear Arousal on Attitude Change: Recent Developments in Theory and Experimental Research." In L. Berkowitz, (ed.), *Advances in Experimental Social Psychology*, 3:166-224. New York: Academic Press, 1967.

Jenkins, C.D.; Rosenman, R.H.; and Friedman, M. "Development of an Objective Psychological Test for the Determination of the Coronary Prone Behavior Pattern in Employed Men." *Journal of Chronic Diseases* 20 (1967):371-379.

Kagan, J. "Motives and Development." *Journal of Personality and Social Psychology* 22 (1972):51-66.

_____ . "The Baby's Elastic Mind." *Human Nature* (January 1978): 66-73.

Kanfer, F.H. "Self-Management Methods." In F.H. Kanfer and A.P. Goldstein, eds., *Helping People Change: A Textbook of Methods*. New York: Pergamon, 1975.

Kelly, G.A. *The Psychology of Personal Constructs*. New York: Norton, 1955.

Knight, R. "Determinism, Freedom, and Psychotherapy." *Psychiatry* 9 (1946):251-262.

Koehler, W. *Gestalt Psychology*. New York: Mentor Books, 1947.

Lange, C. *The Emotions*. Translated by I.A. Haupt and edited by K. Dunlap. 1885. Baltimore: Williams & Wilkins, 1922.

Langer, E.J. "The Illusion of Control." *Journal of Personality and Social Psychology* 32 (1975):311-328.

_____ . "Rethinking the Role of Thought in Social Interaction." In J.H. Harvey, W.J. Ickes, and R.F. Kidd, eds., *New Directions in Attribution Research*, vol. 2. Hillsdale, N.J.: Erlbaum, 1978.

Langer, E.J., and Benevento, A. "Self-Induced Dependence." *Journal of Personality and Social Psychology* 36 (1978):886-893.

Langer, E.J.; Blank, A.; and Chanowitz, B. "Minimal Information Processing." Unpublished manuscript, City University of New York, 1976.

Langer, E.J.; Janis, I.L.; and Wolfer, J.A. "Reduction of Psychological Stress in Surgical Patients." *Journal of Experimental Social Psychology* 11 (1975):155-165.

Langer, E.J., and Rodin, J. "The Effects of Choice and Enhanced Personal Responsibility for the Aged: A Field Experiment in an Institutional Setting." *Journal of Personality and Social Psychology* 34 (1976):191-198.

Langer, E., and Saegert, S. "Crowding and Cognitive Control." *Journal of Personality and Social Psychology* 35 (1977):175-182.

Lazarus, R.S. "Emotions and Adaptation: Conceptual and Empirical Relations." *Nebraska Symposium on Motivation* 16 (1968):195-266.

_____ . "Cognitive and Coping Processes in Emotion." In B. Weiner, ed. *Cognitive Views of Human Motivation*, pp. 21-32. New York. Academic Press, 1974.

Lazarus, R.S.; Averill, J.R.; and Opton, E.M. "Towards a Cognitive Theory of Emotion." In M.B. Arnold, ed., *Feelings and Emotions.* New York: Academic Press, 1970.

Leeper, R.W. "A Motivational Theory of Emotion to Replace 'Emotion as Disorganized Response.'" *Psychological Review* 55 (1948):5-21.

Lefcourt, H.M. "The Function of the Illusions of Control and Freedom." *American Psychologist* 28 (1973):417-425.

―――. *Locus of Control: Current Trends in Theory and Research.* Hillsdale, N.J.: Erlbaum, 1976.

Lepper, M.R.; Greene, D.; and Nisbett, R.E. "Undermining Children's Intrinsic Interest with Extrinsic Rewards: A Test of the 'Overjustification' Hypothesis." *Journal of Personality and Social Psychology* 28 (1973):129-137.

Lewin, K. *The Conceptual Representation and Measurement of Psychological Forces.* Durham, N.C.: Duke University Press, 1938.

―――. "Intention, Will, and Need." In D. Rapaport, ed., *Organization and Pathology of Thought*, pp. 95-153. New York: Columbia University Press, 1951.

Lewis, P., and Blanchard, E.B. "Perception of Choice and Locus of Control." *Psychological Reports* 28 (1971):67-70.

Likert, R. *The Human Organization.* New York: McGraw-Hill, 1967.

Lindsley, D.B. "Psychophysiology and Motivation." *Nebraska Symposium on Motivation* 5 (1957):44-105.

Locke, E.A. "Toward a Theory of Task Motivation and Incentives." *Organizational Behavior and Human Performance* 3 (1968):157-189.

Lottman, T.J., and DeWolfe, A.S. "Internal versus External Control in Reactive and Process Schizophrenia." *Journal of Consulting and Clinical Psychology* 39 (1972):344.

Luchins, A.S. "Mechanization in Problem Solving: The Effect of Einstellung." *Psychological Monographs* 54 (1942).

McClelland, D.C. *The Achieving Society.* Princeton, N.J.: Van Nostrand, 1961.

McClelland, D.C.; Atkinson, J.W.; Clark, R.W.; and Lowell, E.L. *The Achievement Motive.* New York: Appleton-Century-Crofts, 1953.

McGraw, K.O. "The Detrimental Effects of Reward on Performance: A Literature Review and a Prediction Model." In M.R. Lepper and D. Greene, eds., *The Hidden Costs of Reward*, pp. 33-60. Hillsdale, N.J.: Erlbaum, 1978.

McGraw, K.O., and McCullers, J.C. "Evidence of a Detrimental Effect of Extrinsic Incentives on Breaking a Mental Set." *Journal of Experimental Social Psychology* 15 (1979):285-294.

McGregor, D. *The Human Side of Enterprise.* New York: Academic Press, 1960.

MacKinnon, R.A., and Michels, R. *The Psychiatric Interview in Clinical Practice*. Philadelphia: Saunders, 1971.

Mahoney, M.J., and Thoreson, C.E. *Self-Control: Power to the Person*. Monterey, Calif.: Brooks-Cole, 1974.

Maier, N.R.F. *Frustration: The Study of Behavior without a Goal*. New York: McGraw-Hill, 1949.

——— . "Frustration Theory: Restatement and Extension." *Psychological Review* 63 (1956):370-388.

Mandler, G. *Mind and Emotion*. New York: Wiley, 1975.

Maslow, A.H. *Motivation and Personality*. New York: Harper, 1954.

——— . *Toward a Psychology of Being*. Princeton, N.J.: Van Nostrand, 1962.

——— . *Motivation and Personality*. 2d ed. New York: Harper, 1970.

Matthiessen, P. *The Snow Leopard*. New York: Viking, 1978.

May, R. *Psychology and the Human Dilemma*. New York: Van Nostrand, Rineholt, 1967.

——— . "William James' Humanism and the Problems of Will." In R. MacLeod, ed., *William James: Unfinished Business*. Washington, D.C.: American Psychological Association, 1969a.

——— . *Love and Will*. New York: Norton, 1969b.

Menninger, K. *Theory of Psychoanalytic Technique*. New York: Harper and Row, 1958.

Michenbaum, D. "Toward a Cognitive Theory of Self-Control." In G.E. Schwartz and D. Shapiro, eds., *Consciousness and Self-Regulation*, 1:223-260. New York: Plenum, 1976.

Miller, G.A.; Galanter, E.; and Pribram, K.H. *Plans and the Structure of Behavior*. New York: Holt, 1960.

Mischel, W. "On the Interface of Cognition and Personality: Beyond the Person-Situation Debate." *American Psychologist*, 34 (1979):740-754.

Montgomery, K.C. "The Role of Exploratory Drive in Learning." *Journal of Comparative and Physiological Psychology* 47 (1954):60-64.

Monty, R.A., and Perlmuter, L.C. "Persistance of the Effects of Choice on Paired Associate Learning." *Memory and Cognition* 3 (1975):183-187.

Nisbett, R.E., and Bellows, N. "Verbal Reports about Causal Influences on Social Judgment: Private Access versus Public Theory." *Journal of Personality and Social Psychology* 35 (1977):613-624.

Nisbett, R.E., and Valins, S. *Perceiving the Causes of One's Own Behavior*. New York: General Learning Press, 1971.

Nisbett, R.E., and Wilson, T.D. "Telling More Than We Can Know: Verbal Reports on Mental Processes." *Psychological Review* 84 (1977):231-259.

Palmer, R.D. "Parental Perception and Perceived Locus of Control in Psychopathology." *Journal of Personality* 3 (1971):420-431.

Pavlov, I.P. *Conditioned Reflexes*. New York: Dover, 1927.

Peak, H. "Attitude and Motivation." *Nebraska Symposium on Motivation* 3 (1955):149-189.

Pennebaker, J.W.; Burnam, M.A.; Schaeffer, M.A.; and Harper, D.C. "Lack of Control as a Determinant of Perceived Physical Symptoms." *Journal of Personality and Social Psychology* 35 (1977):167-174.

Perlmuter, L.C., and Monty, R.A. "Effect of Choice of Stimulus on Paired Associate Learning." *Journal of Experimental Psychology* 99 (1973):120-123.

_____ . "The Importance of Perceived Control: Fact or Fantasy?" *American Scientist* 65 (1977):759-765.

Perlmuter, L.C.; Monty, R.A.; and Cross, P.M. "Choice as a Disrupter of Performance in Paired-Associate Learning." *Journal of Experimental Psychology* 102 (1974):170-172.

Perls, F.S. *The Gestalt Approach and Eyewitness to Therapy*. Ben Lomond, Calif.: Science and Behavior Books, 1973.

_____ . "Psychiatry in a New Key, Part 2." *Gestalt Journal* 1 (1978):48-67.

Perls, F.S.; Hefferline, R.; and Goodman, P. *Gestalt Therapy*. New York: Dell, 1951.

Piaget, J. *The Origins of Intelligence in Children*. New York: International Universities Press, 1952.

_____ . *Six Psychological Studies*. Edited by D. Elkind. New York: Vintage, 1967.

Polanyi, M. *Personal Knowledge*. Chicago: University of Chicago Press, 1958.

Rank, O. *Will Therapy and Truth and Reality*. 1929. New York: Knopf, 1950.

Rapaport, D. "On the Psychoanalytic Theory of Motivation." *Nebraska Symposium on Motivation* 8 (1960):173-247.

_____ . *Emotions and Memory*. 5th ed. New York: International Universities Press, 1971.

Ray, W.J., and Katahn, M. "Relation of Anxiety to Locus of Control." *Psychological Reports* 23 (1968):1196.

Reich, W. *Character Analysis*. New York: Farrar, Straus & Giroux, 1949.

Rickers-Ovsiankina, M. "Die Wiederanfrahme unterbrochenes handlungen." *Psychologische Furschung* 11 (1928):302-375.

Rodin, J. "Somatopsychics and Attribution." *Personality and Social Psychology Bulletin* 4 (1978):531-540.

Rodin, J., and Langer, E.J. "Long-term Effects of a Control-Relevant Intervention with the Institutionalized Aged." *Journal of Personality and Social Psychology* 35 (1977):897-902.

Rodin, J.; Solomon, S.K.; and Metcalf, J. "Role of Control in Mediating Perceptions of Density." *Journal of Personality and Social Psychology* 36 (1978):988-999.

Rogers, C. *Client Centered Therapy*. Boston: Houghton Mifflin, 1951.

Rotter, J.B. "Generalized Expectancies for Internal versus External Control of Reinforcement." *Psychological Monographs* 80 (1966):1-28.

Ryan, R.M., and Deci, E.L. "Motivational Elements in Information Processing Theories of Attention." *Motivation and Emotion*. 1979.

_____. "On the Importance of Intrinsic Motivation for Maintenance and Transfer of Treatment Gains in Psychotherapy." Unpublished manuscript, University of Rochester, 1980.

Sartre, J.P. *Existentialism and Human Emotion*. New York: Wisdom Library, 1957.

Schachter, S. "The Interaction of Cognitive and Physiological Determinants of Emotional States." In C.D. Spielberger, ed., *Anxiety and Behavior*, pp. 193-224. New York: Academic Press, 1966.

Schachter, S., and Rodin, J. *Obese Humans and Rats*. Hillsdale, N.J.: Erlbaum, 1974.

Schachter, S., and Singer, J.E. "Cognitive, Social, and Physiological Determinants of Emotional States." *Psychological Review* 69 (1962): 379-399.

Schmale, A., and Iker, H. "The Psychological Setting of Uterine Cervical Cancer." *Annals of the New York Academy of Science* 125 (1966): 807-813.

Schneider, W., and Shiffrin, R.M. "Controlled and Automatic Processing: I. Detection, Search, and Attention." *Psychological Review* 84 (1977): 1-66.

Schulz, R. "The Effects of Control and Predictability on the Psychological and Physical Well-Being of the Institutionalized Aged." *Journal of Personality and Social Psychology* 33 (1976):563-573.

Schulz, R., and Hanusa, B.H. "Long-Term Effects of Control and Predictability-Enhancing Interventions: Findings and Ethical Issues." *Journal of Personality and Social Psychology* 36 (1978):1194-1201.

Seligman, M.E.P. *Helplessness: On Depression, Development, and Death*. San Francisco: Freeman, 1975.

Shaffer, L.F. *The Psychology of Adjustment*. Boston: Houghton Mifflin, 1936.

Shallice, T. 'The Dominant Action System: An Information Processing Approach to Consciousness." In K.S. Pope and J.L. Singer, eds., *The Stream of Consciousness*, pp. 117-157. New York: Plenum, 1978.

Shapiro, D. *Neurotic Styles*. New York: Basic Books, 1965.

Sherrod, D.R.; Hage, J.N.; Halpern, P.L.; and Moore, B.S. "Effects of Personal Causation and Perceived Control on Responses to an Aversive Environment: The More Control, the Better." *Journal of Experimental Social Psychology* 13 (1977):14-27.

Shervin, H., and Dickman, S. "The Psychological Unconscious: A Necessary Assumption for All Psychological Theory?" *American Psychologist* 35 (1980):421-434.

Shiffrin, R.M., and Schneider, W. "Controlled and Automatic Human Information Processing: II. Perceptual Learning, Automatic Attending, and a General Theory." *Psychological Review* 84 (1977):127-190.

Shybut, J. "Time Perspective, Internal versus External Control and Severity of Psychological Disturbances." *Journal of Clinical Psychology* 24 (1968):312-315.

Simon, H.A. "Motivational and Emotional Controls of Cognition." *Psychological Review* 74 (1967):29-39.

Skinner, B.F. *The Behavior of Organisms: An Experimental Analysis.* New York: Appleton, 1938.

———. *Science and Human Behavior.* New York: Macmillan, 1953.

———. *Beyond Freedom and Dignity.* New York: Knopf, 1971.

———. *About Behaviorism.* New York: Knopf, 1974.

Smith, C.E.; Pryer, M.W.; and Distefano, M.K. "Internal-External Control and Severity of Emotional Impairment among Psychiatric Patients." *Journal of Clinical Psychology* 27 (1971):449-450.

Smith, E.R., and Miller, F.D. "Limits on Perception of Cognitive Processes: A Reply to Nisbett and Wilson." *Psychological Review* 85 (1978):355-362.

Sperry, R.W. "Mind, Brain, and Humanistic Values." In J.R. Platt, ed., *New Views of the Nature of Man*, pp. 71-92. Chicago: University of Chicago Press, 1965.

———. "A Modified Concept of Consciousness." *Psychological Review* 76 (1969):532-536.

———. "Changing Conceptions of Consciousness and Free Will." *Perspectives in Biology and Medicine* 20 (1976):9-19.

Steiner, I.D. "Perceived Freedom." In L. Berkowitz, ed., *Advances in Experimental Social Psychology*, 5:187-248. New York: Academic Press, 1970.

Storms, M.D., and McCaul, K.D. "Attributional Processes and Emotional Exacerbation of Dysfunctional Behavior." In J.H. Harvey, W.J. Ickes, and R.F. Kidd, eds., *New Directions in Attribution Research*, 1:143-164. Hillsdale, N.J.: Erlbaum, 1976.

Stotland, E., and Blumenthal, A.L. "The Reduction of Anxiety as a Result of the Expectation of Making a Choice." *Canadian Journal of Psychology* 18 (1964):139-145.

Sullivan, H.S. *The Interpersonal Theory of Psychiatry.* New York: Norton, 1953.

———. *The Psychiatric Interview.* New York: Norton, 1954.

Suzuki, S. *Zen Mind, Beginner's Mind.* New York: Walker/Weatherhill, 1970.

Swann, W.B., and Pittman, T.S. "Initiating Play Activity of Children: The Moderating Influence of Verbal Cues on Intrinsic Motivation." *Child Development* 48 (1977):1128-1132.

Thorndike, E.L. *The Psychology of Learning*. New York: Teachers College, Columbia University, 1913.

Tolmon, E.C. *Purposive Behavior in Animals and Men*. New York: Century, 1932.

Tomkins, S.S. *Affect, Imagery, Consciousness*. Vol. 1: *The Positive Affects*. New York: Springer, 1962.

_____ . *Affect, Imagery, Consciousness*. Vol. 2: *The Negative Affects*. New York: Springer, 1963.

_____ . "Affect and the Psychology of Knowledge." In S.S. Tomkins and C.E. Izard, eds., *Affect, Cognition, and Personality*, pp. 72-97. New York: Springer, 1965.

_____ . "Free-Will and the Degrees of Freedom Problem." In R.B. MacLeod, ed., *William James: Unfinished Business*, pp. 103-106. Washington, D.C.: American Psychological Association, 1969.

Treisman, A. "Selective Attention in Man." *British Medical Bulletin* 20 (1964):12-16.

Valins, S., and Nisbett, R.E. *Attribution Processes in the Development and Treatment of Emotional Disorders*. New York: General Learning Press, 1971.

Vandenberg, B. "Play and Development from an Ethological Perspective." *American Psychologist* 33 (1978):724-738.

Vroom, V.H. *Work and Motivation*. New York: Wiley, 1964.

Wachtel, P.L. *Psychoanalysis and Behavior Therapy*. New York: Basic Books, 1977.

Watson, D. "Relationship between Locus of Control and Anxiety." *Journal of Personality and Social Psychology* 6 (1967):91-92.

Watson, J.B. "Psychology as the Behaviorist Views It." *Psychological Review* 20 (1913):158-177.

_____ . "A Schematic Representation of Emotions." *Psychological Review* 26 (1919):165-196.

Webb, W.B. "A Motivational Theory of Emotions. . . ." *Psychological Review* 55 (1948):329-335.

Weidner, G., and Matthews, K.A. "Reported Physical Symptoms Elicited by Unpredictable Events and the Type A Coronary-Prone Behavior Pattern." *Journal of Personality and Social Psychology* 36 (1978):1213-1220.

Weiner, B. *Theories of Motivation: From Mechanism to Cognition*. Chicago: Markham, 1972.

White, R.W. "Motivation Reconsidered: The Concept of Competence." *Psychological Review* 66 (1959):297-333.

_____ . "Competence and the Psychosexual Stages of Development." *Nebraska Symposium on Motivation* 8 (1960):97-140.

_____ . *Ego and Reality in Psychoanalytic Theory*. Psychological Issues Series, Monograph 11. New York: International Universities Press, 1963.

Wolpe, J. "The Comparative Clinical Status of Conditioning Therapies and Psychoanalysis." In J. Wolpe, A. Salter, and L.J. Reyna, eds., *The Conditioning Therapies*. New York: Holt, Rinehart & Winston, 1964.

———. *The Practice of Behavior Therapy*. New York: Pergamon, 1969.

Woodworth, R.S. *Dynamic Psychology*. New York: Columbia University Press, 1918.

———. *Psychology*, 4th ed. New York: Holt, 1940.

Wortman, C.B., and Brehm, J.W. "Responses to Uncontrollable Outcomes: An Integration of Reactance Theory and the Learned Helplessness Model." In L. Berkowitz, ed., *Advances in Experimental Social Psychology*, 8:277-336. New York: Academic Press, 1975.

Yarrow, L.J.; Rubenstein, J.L.; and Pederson, F.A. *Infant and Environment: Early Cognitive and Motivational Development*. New York: Halsted, 1975.

Yerkes, R.M., and Dodson, J.D. "The Relation of Strength of Stimulus to Rapidity of Habit-Formation." *Journal of Comparative and Neurological Psychology* 18 (1908):459-482.

Young, P.T. *Emotion in Man and Animal: Its Nature and Relation to Attitude and Motive*. New York: Wiley, 1943.

———. *Motivation and Emotion*. New York: Wiley, 1961.

Zajonc, R.B. "Feeling and Thinking: Preferences Need No Inferences." *American Psychologist* 35 (1980):151-175.

Zeigarnik, B. "Das behalten erledigter und unerledigter handlungen." *Psychologische Furschung 9*, (1927):1-85.

Zuckerman, M.; Porac, J.; Lathin, D.; Smith, R.; and Deci, E.L. "On the Importance of Self-Determination for Intrinsically Motivated Behavior." *Personality and Social Psychology Bulletin* 4 (1978):443-446.

# Indexes

# Author Index

Abelson, R.P., 42, 59, 219
Ainsworth, M.D.S., 144, 219
Arnold, M., 76-78, 81, 98, 99, 219, 224
Aronson, E., 42, 118, 219
Atkinson, J.W., 21, 32, 47, 53, 193, 219, 224
Averill, J.R., 98, 112, 114, 219, 224

Bach, S., 12, 219
Bachrach, A.J., 191, 219
Bandura, A., 43, 48, 158, 192, 194-195, 219
Beck, A., 78-79, 180-181, 187, 195-196, 219
Bellows, N., 58, 225
Benevento, A., 121, 223
Berkowitz, L., 219, 220, 230
Berlyne, D.E. 32, 33, 219
Blanchard, E.B., 116, 224
Blank, A., 57, 223
Blumenthal, A.L., 108, 228
Bowlby, J., 144, 219
Brehm, J.W., 116-118, 171, 220, 222, 230
Breland, K., 10, 220
Breland, M., 10, 220
Broadbent, D., 80, 220
Brooks, C.W., 202, 220
Brown, I., 121, 220
Brown, W.A., 162, 220
Bruner, J.S., 106, 135, 218, 220
Burnam, M.A., 106, 226
Burnes, K., 162, 220
Butler, R.Z., 35, 220

Caldwell, B., 219
Carroll, J.S., 219
Cascio, W.F., 39, 220
Chanowitz, B., 57, 223
Chein, I., 207, 220
Clark, R.W., 32, 224
Cross, P.M., 110, 118, 226
Csikszentmihalyi, M., 58, 125, 220

Darwin, C., 75, 220
deCharms, R., 33, 36, 69, 123, 158, 220
Deci, E.L., 20, 33-36, 39-45, 49, 50, 89, 105, 118, 123-124, 159, 184, 207, 209, 210, 216, 220, 227, 230
Dember, W.N., 32, 220
DeVellis, B.M., 121, 221
DeVellis, R.F., 121, 221
DeWolfe, A.S., 163, 224
Dickman, S., 11, 69, 84, 227
Distefano, M.K., 163, 228
Dixon, F., 11, 86, 221
Dodson, J.D., 54, 88, 230
Dollard, J., 93, 221
Doob, L.W., 93, 221
Duffy, E., 79, 221
Dunlap, K., 223

Earl, R.W., 32, 220
Eliot, R.S., 222
Elkind, D., 226
Ellis, A., 195, 221
Engel, G.L., 110, 221
Enzle, M.E., 40, 221
Erikson, E.H., 11, 132-133, 135, 137, 140-142, 150, 221

Feather, N.T., 162, 221
Ferrari, N.A., 111, 221
Festinger, L., 33, 221
Fisher, C.D., 37, 129, 154, 221
Frankl, V.E., 110, 221
Friedman, M., 126, 223
Freud, S., 11, 14, 31, 84, 89, 95, 131-134, 136, 139-141, 149-150, 162-164, 197, 202, 221

Galanter, E., 50, 193, 225
Garcia, J., 10, 221
Ginott, H., 148, 221
Glass, D.C., 106, 111, 119-120, 126, 154, 170-171, 211, 221
Goldstein, A.P., 223

Goldstein, K., 150, 201, 222
Goldstein, S., 172, 222
Goodman, P., 201, 226
Gordon, R.M., 161, 222
Greene, D., 35, 224
Greene, W.A., 172, 222

Hage J.N., 106, 227
Halpern, P.L., 106, 227
Hammock, T., 116, 222
Hanusa, B.H., 109, 118, 227
Harlow, H.F., 32, 222
Harper, D.C., 106, 226
Harré, R., 3, 222
Hartmann, H. 32, 142, 144, 198, 208, 216, 222
Harvey, J.H., 223, 228
Haupt, I.A., 223
Hebb, D.O., 32, 222
Hefferline, R., 201, 226
Heider, F., 36, 42, 47, 69, 123-124, 162, 222
Hendrick, I., 144, 222
Hilgard, E.R., 12, 62, 222
Hiroto, D.S., 107, 119, 122, 222
Horney, K., 11, 222
Hull, C.L. 31, 47, 222
Hunt, J. McV., 32-34, 50, 134, 146, 222

Ickes, W.J., 223, 228
Iker, H., 111, 171, 227
Immergluck, L., 12, 222
Inouye, D.K., 121, 220
Isaac, W., 32, 222
Izard, C.E., 48, 76, 87, 98-101, 171, 216, 222, 229

James, W., 19-22, 24-27, 73-77, 85, 95, 100, 222
Janis, I.L., 114, 163, 222, 223
Jenkins, C.D., 126, 223
Jolly, A., 135, 220

Kagan, J., 20, 33, 51, 131, 223
Kanfer, F.H., 192-194, 223
Katahn, M., 162, 226

Keating, G.W., 162, 220
Kelly, G.A., 114, 223
Kidd, R.F., 223, 228
Klein, G.S., 12, 219
Koehler, W., 49, 50, 223
Koelling, R.A., 10, 221
Kris, E., 142, 222
Krusell, J., 39, 220

Lange, C., 73, 223
Langer, E.J., 57, 48, 107, 109-110, 114, 120, 121, 223, 226
Lathin, D., 36, 45, 105, 118, 230
Lazarus, R.S., 76, 98-99, 223, 224
Leeper, R.W., 81-83, 94, 95, 224
Lefcourt, H.M., 13, 110, 122, 162, 216, 224
Lepper, M.R., 35, 224
Lewin, K., 21-28, 47, 50, 53, 224
Lewis, P., 116, 224
Likert, R., 217, 224
Lindsley, D.B., 79, 224
Locke, E.A., 54, 224
Loewenstein, R., 142, 222
Lottman, T.J., 163, 224
Lowell, E.L., 32, 224
Luchins, A.S., 120, 224

McCaul, K.D., 164, 228
McCauley, C., 121, 221
McClelland, D.C., 32, 34, 224
McCullers, J.C., 120, 224
McGraw, K.O., 40, 54, 120, 224
McGregor, D., 106, 217, 224
McGuire, W.J., 42, 219
MacKinnon, R.A., 198, 225
MacLeod, R., 225, 229
Mahoney, M.J., 192, 225
Maier, N.R.F., 80, 94, 95, 187, 225
Mandler, G., 59, 74, 79, 80, 93, 225
Maslow, A.H., 14, 150, 201, 225
Matthews, K.A., 172, 229
Matthiessen, P., 182, 225
May, R., 28, 125, 129, 167, 192, 225
Menninger, K., 159, 225
Metcalf, J., 106, 113, 226
Michels, R., 198, 225

Michenbaum, D., 158, 225
Miller, F.D., 58, 228
Miller, G.A., 50, 193, 225
Miller, N.E., 93, 221
Mischel, W., 43, 155, 225
Montgomery, K.C., 32, 225
Monty, R.A., 106, 110, 118, 225, 226
Morre, B.S., 106, 227
Moss, A.J., 172, 222
Newcomb, T.M., 42, 219
Nezlek, J., 40, 41, 43, 210, 220
Nisbett, R.E., 12, 35, 58, 80, 159,
    161, 164, 224, 225

Opton, E.M., 98, 224

Palmer, R.D., 162, 225
Pavlov, I.P., 76, 226
Payne, J.W., 219
Peak, H., 47, 226
Pederson, F.A., 144, 230
Pennebaker, J.W., 106, 226
Perlmuter, L.C., 106, 110, 118, 225,
    226
Perls, F.S., 31, 74, 125, 167, 201-202,
    226
Piaget, J., 24, 25, 27, 33, 50, 62, 143,
    226
Pittman, T.S., 106, 118, 228
Platt, J.R., 228
Polanyi, M., 80, 125, 226
Pope, K.S., 227
Porac, J., 36, 45, 105, 118, 230
Pribram, K.H., 50, 193, 225
Pryer, M.W., 163, 228

Rank, O., 164, 167, 189, 201, 226
Rapaport, D., 31, 85, 224, 226
Ray, W.J., 162, 226
Raynor, J., 219
Reich, W., 172, 226
Reyna, L.J., 219, 230
Ricciuti, H., 219
Rickers-Ovsiankina, M., 22, 23, 226
Rodin, J., 106, 109-110, 113, 160,
    172, 223, 226, 227
Rogers, C., 78, 187, 201, 227

Rosenberg, M., 42, 219
Rosenman, R.H., 126, 223
Ross, J., 40, 221
Rotter, J.B., 117, 122-124, 162, 211,
    216, 227
Rubenstein, J.L., 144, 230
Ryan, R.M., 35, 36, 44, 49, 159, 184,
    207, 216, 220, 227

Saegert, S., 107, 114, 223
Salter, A., 219, 230
Sartre, J.P., 4, 227
Schachter, S., 76, 79-81, 96, 160, 227
Schaeffer, M.A., 106, 226
Schmale, A., 111, 171, 227
Schneider, W., 57, 227, 228
Schulz, R., 108-110, 118, 171, 227
Schwartz, G.E., 225
Sears, R.R., 93, 221
Secord, P.F., 3, 222
Seligman, M., 107-108, 111, 113, 116,
    119, 123-124, 128, 162-164, 173,
    185, 194, 211, 227
Shaffer, L.F., 82, 227
Shallice, T., 12, 227
Shapiro, D., 173-174, 225, 227
Sheinman, L., 40, 41, 43, 210, 220
Sherrod, D.R., 106, 227
Shevrin, H., 11, 69, 84, 227
Shiffrin, R.M., 57, 227, 228
Shybut, J., 162, 228
Simon, H.A., 56, 82, 228
Singer, J.E., 79, 106, 221, 227
Singer, J.L., 227
Skinner, B.F., 7-10, 12, 14, 47, 59,
    190, 228
Smith, C.E., 163, 228
Smith, E.R., 58, 228
Smith, R., 36, 45, 105, 118, 230
Solomon, S.K., 106, 113, 226
Sperry, R.W., 5, 8, 9, 207, 228
Spielberger, C.D., 227
Steiner, I.D., 117, 186, 228
Storms, M.D., 164, 228
Stotland, E., 108, 228
Sullivan, H.S., 142, 200, 228
Suzuki, S., 114, 228

Swann, W.B., 106, 118, 228
Sylva, K., 135, 220

Tannenbaum, P.H., 42, 219
Thoreson, C.E., 192, 225
Throndike, E.L., 59, 229
Tolmon, E.C., 47, 229
Tomkin, S.S., 5, 76, 98-99, 131, 229
Treisman, A., 80, 229

Valins, S., 80, 164, 225, 229
Vandenberg, B., 135, 229
Vroom, V.H., 21, 47, 53, 95, 193, 229

Wachtel, P., 199-200, 229
Watson, D., 162, 229
Watson, J.B., 7, 82, 229
Webb, W.B., 83, 229

Weidner, G., 172, 229
Weiner, B., 48, 223, 229
White, R.W., 29, 32-34, 132-137, 140,
    142, 144, 149-150, 198, 208, 229
Wilson, T.D., 12, 58, 159, 161, 225
Wolfer, J.A., 114, 223
Wolpe, J., 75, 190-191, 219, 230
Woodworth, R.S., 34, 82, 230
Wortman, C.B., 116-118, 172, 230

Yarrow, L.J., 144, 230
Yerkes, R.M., 54, 88, 230
Young, P.T., 81-83, 87, 91, 101, 230

Zajonc, R., 74, 79, 80, 230
Zeigarnik, B., 22, 23, 230
Zuckerman, M., 36, 45, 105, 118, 230

# Subject Index

Acceptance, 180-181
Accommodation, 182-183; and challenge, 182
Adult development, 150-151
Anal stage. *See* Development, anal stage
Attachment, 144-145
Automated behavior, 16-17, 56-65; and self-determination, 62-65
Automtic behavior, 56-65, 91-93, 120, 147, 158-160, 208; and psychotherapy, 184
Automatic thoughts, 180-181, 195
Automatized behavior, 56-65, 91-93, 208
Autonomy-shame, 137-138
Awareness, 179-180, 188, 201-203; of organismic needs, 158-160, 202-203; of potential satisfaction, 51-52

Behavior therapy, 190-195; and psychoanalytic therapy, 199-200
Behaviorism, 214-215; and mentalism, 7-10

Causality. *See* External causality; Internal causality; Locus of causality; Perceived locus of causality; Personal causality
Causality orientations, 124-129, 142-149, 170, 177-179, 210-211; and behavior, 214; and cognitive evaluation theory, 184-186; development of, 142-149, 213; external, 126-127, 146-148, 157-161, 189-190, 211, 213; and external stimuli, 177-179; and ill-being, 157-165; impersonal, 128, 148, 161-165, 189-190, 211, 213; internal, 125-126, 143-145, 177, 210-211, 213-214; and maladaptive styles, 173-175; and psychotherapy, 184-186; and well-being, 157

Choice, 5, 106, 108, 181, 207; illusion of, 118-119; in psychotherapy, 181
Cognition, and motivation, 43-44, 155-157
Cognitive behaviorism, 192-195
Cognitive control, 158-159
Cognitive evaluation theory, 35-40, 69-71, 153-165, 170, 184-186, 211-212, 216; and causality orientations, 184-186; and motivational subsystems, 42-43, 153-157
Cognitive therapy, 195-197
Conditioning, in psychotherapy, 190-191
Consciousness, 8-9; and physiology, 8-9, 207
Control, 106-110; inner, 114-115; lack of, 107-112, 173; and self-determination, 112-114

Depression, 163-164, 185
Development, 131-151; adult, 150-151; anal stage, 135-137; of causality orientations, 142-149; competence theory of, 132-142; oral stage, 134-135; phallic stage, 138-141; psychoanalytic theory of, 132-142
Differential emotions theory, 99-101

Ego, in psychoanalytic therapy, 197-198
Ego integrity, 150-151
Emotion, 73-101; arousal and cognition, 79-81; and behavior, 90-93; blocked, 188; and bodily change, 73-75; cognitive mediation, 76-81; defined, 85-89; and frustrated goals, 93-96; hedonicity of, 87-88; intensity of, 87 and motivation, 89-90; and motivational subsystems, 96-97; and nonconscious processes, 91, 101; perturbation, 81-84, 88; and reflective judgment, 77, 80, 86-87,

96; reflex theory, 74-77; repression of, 84-85; self theories, 78-79
Energy, independent ego, 198, 208, 216; and will, 25-26
Environments, and causality orientations, 177-179; and cognitive evaluaiton theory, 211-212; controlling and demanding, 146-148, 158, 165-166, 189, 212; nonresponsive, 148, 165-166, 189, 212; responsive, 143-145, 165-166, 212
Expectations, 181-182
External causality, 123-124, 126-127, 146-148, 157-161, 189-190
External cues, and obesity, 160
Extrinsic motivation, and psychotherapy, 191-192
Extrinsic rewards, controlling aspect, 38-39; informational aspect, 38-39

Freewill, 3-5

Gestalt therapy, 201-203
Goal selection, 53
Guilt, 139-140, 149-150

Helplessness, 107-108, 111-112, 119, 123-124, 162, 187, 211; and reactance, 116-117
Humanistic psychology, 215
Hypnosis, 12

Identification, 139-140
Ill-being, dynamics of, 153-175
Illusion of freedom, 12-13, 117-119
Impersonal causality, 123-124, 128, 161-165, 189-190
Independent ego energy, 198, 208, 216
Industry-inferiority, 142
Iniation-guilt, 140-141
Innate differences, 151
Intention, 21-24
Internal causality, 123-126, 143-145, 177; as goal for psychotherapy, 178-179, 185-186; and well-being, 177-178

Internalization, 158-159
Intrinsic motivation, 26, 30-45; and choice, 105-106; and decision making, 56; development of, 34; and extrinsic rewards, 35-40; innate differences, 151; and psychotherapy, 185-186; and self-efficacy, 194; and self-reinforcement, 193; and will, 44-45, 208-209. See also Motivational subsystems, intrinsic
Introjects, 193

Learned helplessness. See Helplessness
Libido, 132-142
Limit setting, 145
Locus of causality, and helplessness, 123-124; and locus of control, 123-124. See also Perceived locus of causality
Locus of control, 122-124, 162-163, 211; and helplessness, 123-124; and locus of causality, 123-124

Maladaptive styles, 173-175
Mentalism, 7-12
Middle childhood, 141-142
Motivation, and cognition, 43-44, 155-157, 183; cognitive theories of, 20-21, 47-49; and emotion, 89-90; and psychotherapy, 187; and will, 25-29, 44-45. See also Intrinsic motivation; Organismic theory
Motivational subsystems, 40-43, 65-69, 96-97, 119-120, 209-210; amotivational, 41, 67, 210; and cognitive evaluation theory, 42-43, 154-157; and emotion, 96-97; extrinsic, 41, 66, 210; intrinsic, 41, 65-66, 210
Motives, acceptance of, 189; conscious, 51-52; and needs, 52; and will, 68-69

Needs, and motives, 52; organismic, 158-159; substitute, 158, 160-161
Neurotic styles, 173

Nonconscious processes, 11-12, 84-85, 91, 101, 159, 188, 200; and the unconscious, 198-199

Oedipal period, 138-140
Oral stage. *See* Development, oral stage
Organismic theory of motivation, 47-71, 167-171, 215; and causality orientations, 167-171; and cognitive evaluation theory, 69-71; and emotions, 73-101; and psychoanalytic therapy, 198-200; self-determined behavior, 49-56, 167-170; and therapy, 183-184

Perceived competence, 36-37, 71, 154, 156, 170
Perceived locus of causality, 36, 67, 69, 154, 156-157, 170. *See also* Locus of causality
Person-environmental interaction, 13-15, 212-214
Personal causality, 123-124
Personal worth, 187
Personality development, 132-151
Phallic stage. *See* Development, phallic stage
Power struggles, in psychotherapy, 189
Psychoanalytic theory, 215-216
Psychoanalytic therapy, 197-200; and behavior therapy, 199-200
Psychosexual development, 132-142
Psychotherapy, 177-203; approaches to, 190-203; and automatic behavior, 184; and causality orientations, 184-186; Gestalt, 201-203; goals for, 178-179, 185-186; humanistic, 201-203; and the organismic theory of motivation, 183-184; the process of, 186-190; psychoanalytic, 197-200

Quasi-need theory, 21-24

Rational emotive therapy, 195
Reactance, 115-117, 171

Rebellious noncompliance, 147, 161
Repression, 84-85
Resistance, in psychotherapy, 189
Rewards. *See* Extrinsic rewards

Self-actualization, 150-151
Self-blame, 164-165
Self-deception, 28-29, 118-120, 127, 164
Self-determination, and automated behavior, 62-65; biased perceptions of, 120-121; and choice, 5, 106; and competence, 128-129, 155-157; and control, 112-114; defined, 5, 26-27; and development, 131-151; and free will, 3-5, 26-27; and health, 108-110, 171-173; and individual differences, 121-124; in infants, 145-146; and intrinsic motivation, 105-106; loss of, 105-129; and psychotherapy, 179-183, 185-186; in society, 217-218; and will, 3-5
Self-determined behavior, 49-56, 90-91, 208
Self-efficacy, 194
Self-evaluation, 180-181
Self-management, 192-195
Self-reinforcement, 193
Shame, 137-138, 149-150, 158
Skill acquisition, in therapy, 194
Somatic illness, 171-173
Stimulus-response theories, 9-10
Subliminal perception, 11-12, 86
Sudden death, 110-111

Therapy. *See* Psychotherapy
TOTE, 50-51, 52-54, 63, 193
Transference, 198
Trust-mistrust, 135
Type-A behavior pattern, 126, 154, 170-173, 211

Unconscious, 198-199

Values, 217-218

Will, 3-5, 19-30, 54, 68-69, 165, 167;
  defined, 26; and ego, 198; and intrinsic motivation, 44-45, 208-209;
  and morality, 24-25; and

psychoanalytic therapy, 198;
  theories of, 19-26
Wilfulness, 29-30, 67-68, 129, 161-162,
  211
Willpower, 27-28, 167

# About the Author

**Edward L. Deci,** a professor of psychology at the University of Rochester, is an internationally known expert in the field of human motivation. His book *Intrinsic Motivation* (1975) has been highly praised and widely cited; it was recently translated into Japanese. He is coauthor or coeditor of four other books, and has published research articles and original contributions in numerous professional journals and edited collections. His works have been translated into several languages, including German, French, and Italian.

Dr. Deci was graduated from Hamilton College, did graduate work at the Universities of London and Pennsylvania, received the Ph.D. from Carnegie-Mellon University, and was an interdisciplinary postdoctoral fellow at Stanford University. He has lectured at more than three dozen colleges and universities and has consulted for a variety of organizations throughout the United States, Canada, and Japan. He is a Fellow of the American Psychological Association and a member of several other professional organizations. Dr. Deci has served as an ad hoc reviewer for twenty professional journals as well as for many publishing houses and granting agencies. He also has a private practice in psychotherapy.